THE ROSE OF
SHAKESPEARE'S SONNETS

An Exercise in Literary Detection

❧

THE ROSE OF SHAKESPEARE'S SONNETS

An Exercise in Literary Detection

BY

EVERT SPRINCHORN

The Printer's Press

POUGHKEEPSIE · 2008

Adrienne Hytier

IN MEMORIAM

FIRST EDITION

ISBN 978-0-615-23759-6

Scorn not the Sonnet; Critic, you have frowned,
Mindless of its just honours; with this key
Shakespeare unlocked his heart.

– Wordsworth

ACKNOWLEDGMENTS

This book would not have appeared in its present form – or perhaps would not have appeared at all – without the encouragement of William Appleton, Eric Bentley, and Joan Hartman. They read the first, much shorter version, saw its strengths, and also saw where it could be improved. Heeding their advice, I added sections on King James's court and changing attitudes towards homosexuality.

I also want to thank the late Eric Sams for correcting some factual errors and Lynn Bartlett for sprucing up my prose in the opening chapters.

—E.S.

CONTENTS

[7]

ILLUSTRATIONS

PREFACE

To ANYONE who likes literary puzzles Shakespeare's sonnets are a treasure-trove of challenges and delights. The mystery that the ordinary reader is most likely to have heard about concerns the identity of the young man to whom Shakespeare addressed the majority of the sonnets. Who was this young man who inspired some of best-known love poems in the English language? Oscar Wilde called it "the greatest mystery of modern literature," before attempting to solve it. And, perhaps equally mysterious, why did Shakespeare promise this young man immortality but not name him?

There are many other enigmas, equally challenging. What, for instance, is the plan behind the sonnets? They are in a numbered sequence, which strongly suggests that Shakespeare wanted them to be read in a certain order to be properly understood. Yet there is little or no agreement as to what Shakespeare had in mind, and from the moment they were first re-issued, editors and commentators, arguing that the poet was not responsible, have tried to impose their own interpretations on them by re-arranging them. All to no avail.

Another mystery is why Shakespeare published these confessional poems in which he often portrays himself in an unflattering light. He presents himself as well past his prime and abjectly in love with someone considerably younger. Why did he not confine their circulation to his friends, who would copy them and pass them on, as happened with some of the sonnets Shakespeare composed in the 1590s? Most of the early commentators said there was no mystery here. They believed that the 1609 Quarto was printed without Shakespeare's permission. But the evidence for that has been whittled away in recent years by diligent scholars. Writing in

1997, Katherine Duncan-Jones declared, "Contrary to what most previous editors have maintained, there is every reason to believe that the 1609 Quarto publication of *Sonnets* was authorized by Shakespeare himself." Powerful support for this position lies in Shakespeare's "repeated deployment of the theme of immortalization through verse."[1]

There are riddles of another sort, puzzles not inherent in the sonnets but created by scholars. Although they have usually dated the sonnets to the 1595-1603 period, the collected sonnets were not published until 1609. Why would Shakespeare wait until then? The whole matter of dating the sonnets calls for re-examination.

So does the question of the poet's relationship to the young man, usually assumed by the commentators to be that of poet and patron. But why would Shakespeare harshly criticize, even insult in very personal terms, his nameless, purported benefactor, as he surely does in several of the sonnets? In sonnet 95, the physical attractiveness of the young man, conventionally known as the Fair Youth, is seen as a cover for unmentioned vices.

> Oh what a mansion have those vices got,
> Which for their habitation chose out thee,
> Where beauties vaile doth cover every blot,
> And all things turnes to faire, that eies can see!

The annals of patronage offer nothing like it. Oscar Wilde took note and proposed that the young man was no nobleman and no patron, but a boy actor in Shakespeare's company. This relationship of employer and servant would allow for the poet's severe reproaches. And the poet does indeed call the young man a boy, as in sonnet 126. But as so often in these sonnets, the usual explanations only create more mysteries. If the young man is a boy actor, why is he addressed as someone far above the poet in social rank?

To read the sonnets with an inquiring mind is like coming upon a cache of fascinating letters, made more intriguing by the lack of dates and reference points. Many of the hoped for signposts are missing, since these poems contain only one side of an exchange. Although the sonnets to the young man must have received some sort of reply, the answers don't survive. Also, there are many allusions, obscure to us, that would have been clear intimations for those who first hurried to buy copies of *Shake-speares Sonnets*.

There is no reason to believe that Shakespeare set out to create a congeries of mysteries. The confessional nature of the poems suggests just the opposite. A great many of the sonnets are difficult to understand because of the complexity of thought behind them, not because the poet wanted to be obscure. Shakespeare knew he was creating a lasting monument in words because he knew he was expanding the possibilities of the sonnet form. One only has to compare Shakespeare's sonnets with those of any other poet of his era to sense that boundaries are being crossed, that the poet is knowingly going where no one had gone before. It is this sense of something new and profound, both in thought and technique, that makes the sonnets unique and astonishing as only the greatest art is. "Shakespeare discovered a newly complex system of expression, unprecedented in the Renaissance lyric," says Helen Vendler in her pioneering analytical study of the sonnets, *The Art of Shakespeare's Sonnets*, which demonstrates with great precision just how complex they are.[2] But, as Vendler makes clear, Shakespeare did not enhance the sonnet form to display his technical skill; he transformed the sonnet because of what he wanted to express emotionally, what he wanted to say philosophically. What may seem like willful obscurity in many of the sonnets is in fact density of meaning, meaning on several levels simultaneously, and together expressing a conflict of emotions or ideas. Vendler's analysis of the poet's technique reveals that within the strict form of the sonnet Shakespeare developed a method of orchestrating sounds, giving each sonnet its own tonality, to reinforce its literal meaning. One only has to read the sonnets aloud to appreciate how true that is.

Some light is being shed on these mysteries because of a resurgence of interest in the sonnets. In the case of Shakespeare's tragedies and comedies, not much has been added to our knowledge and understanding of them in the last fifty years. The sonnets, on the other hand, are being rediscovered, re-examined, and re-evaluated. Several new editions, all with rich and informative commentaries, have been published in the last thirty years. Still, Helen Vendler could assert not so long ago that the sonnets "represent the largest tract of unexamined Shakespearean lines left open to scrutiny."[3] New investigative work has challenged some of the old assumptions. Stylometric studies, involving statistics and the occurrence of rare words, have re-opened the whole question of the dating of the sonnets, with the possibility that some of the sonnets may have been composed, or rewritten, as late as 1607 –1608. This re-dating affects the interpretation of individual sonnets, especially those that clearly allude to events of the time. It also affects the search for the young man. Most of the efforts to identify him assume that the sonnets addressed to him were composed before 1603.

The other major change in the study of the sonnets is a growing acceptance of the homoeroticism of the long sequence devoted to the young man. The fear that Shakespeare may have been gay drove many Bardolaters to shun the obvious. However, this protected area could not escape being invaded by gay studies, and the recent critical editions of the sonnets devote considerable space to the subject.[4] Duncan-Jones in her 1997 edition confronted their "compromising or 'disgraceful' elements" and for the first time contextualized them "within the powerfully 'homosocial' world of James I's court."[5]

There is a thread that ties all these mysteries together, mysteries that are like the corridors of a labyrinth at whose center lies the monster gay sex. The present study begins by asking how gay was life in the court of James and finds that the sexual permissiveness of the royal court may help to explain why Shakespeare's collected sonnets were published in 1609, years after some of them were written. There are many more allusions to manly love in the poems, plays, and letters of the Jacobean period than in the pre-1603 era. They allow us to peek through slightly ajar doors into private chambers and to overhear rumors and gossip of a kind that went unrecorded in the 1590s. What they tell us about homosexuality at the time the sonnets were published is not the frank avowal of gay sex that one as a scholar might have hoped for. In fact, they are just

as perplexing as the sonnets, just as contradictory – apparently –
in their attitudes. However, by bringing the two together, James's
court and Shakespeare's sonnets, we can come to see better how
the gay men of the time saw themselves. Exploring that homosocial world compels one to notice how different the gay scene of
2000 is from that of 1600. Once the veneer of inhibitions, social and
religious, has been accepted on its own terms, it can be seen
through. What lies beneath it is a tale told not in chapters but sonnet by sonnet, with a discernible beginning, middle, and end; a
narrative that begins innocently enough but soon develops into a
conflict between different kinds of love; a fascinating story familiar to all who have, in Oscar Wilde's phrase, loved "not wisely, but
too well."

CHAPTER 1

Shakespeare in 1609

IN 1609, probably in the summer, the publisher Thomas Thorpe brought out a volume entitled *Shake-speares Sonnets.*[6] (See the facsimile appended to this book.) To anyone who was part of the cultural scene in London the publication of these poems must have been the literary event of the season. In 1609 William Shakespeare, then in his forty-fifth year, was at the peak of his career. He was rich, famous, and at the height of his creative powers. His sizeable income came from his share in a theater company, not from his plays. In 1597 he had purchased a large but rather rundown house in Stratford for £60. The following year he had been in a position to make substantial loans to friends. In 1602 he had acquired 102 acres of land, and three years later he had bought an interest in a lease of tithes that earned him perhaps £60 or £70 annual income.

His playwriting career followed a similar progress. In 1598 his name appeared for the first time on the title page of a play, *Love's Labour's Lost.* Plays of his had been printed before but without any acknowledgement of his authorship. Now his name had drawing power. Already in that same year, he had been placed in the company of the classic authors. The critic and schoolmaster Francis Meres wrote in a literary compendium, "As Plautus and Seneca are accounted the best for Comedy and Tragedy: so Shakespeare among the English is the most excellent in both kinds for the Stage." In a survey of English literature published in 1605, Shakespeare was listed along with Philip Sidney, Edmund Spenser, and Ben Jonson, as one of the "most pregnant wits of these our times, whom succeeding ages may justly admire."[7] He was also well-known as the author of two narrative poems, *Venus and Adonis* and

Lucrece, written in the early 1590s, runaway best sellers, with numerous reprints being called for. Many university students made a pop idol of Shakespeare. "O sweet Mr. Shakespeare! I'le have his picture in my study at the courte," says one of them in *The Return from Parnassus*, a play written by and for students. Outside the nobility and some popular actors there were few people in London in 1609 who would have been better known. In modern terms, he was a celebrity, a fact that the title page of the sonnets acknowledged by blazoning his name at the top in huge letters.

In the year and a half prior to the publication of the sonnets the bookstalls of London were filled with works by Shakespeare, not only re-issued works like *Venus and Adonis*, *Richard II*, and *Henry IV*, but three new plays: *King Lear*, *Troilus and Cressida*, and *Pericles*. Three other plays bearing Shakespeare's name appeared in the years just before the *Sonnets: The London Prodigal* in 1605, *The Puritan* in 1607, and *A Yorkshire Tragedy* in 1608. It is quite improbable that Shakespeare was the sole author of these plays (though he may have had a hand in certain scenes), but attributing the plays to him, as the publishers did, suggests the selling power of his name. By 1609 more editions of Shakespeare's plays had been published than those of any other dramatist.

Five of his poems had appeared in 1599 in a slim volume called *The Passionate Pilgrime*. This meager collection also contained poems by Christopher Marlowe, Sir Walter Raleigh, and Richard Barnfield. Yet although only five of the twenty poems were by Shakespeare, his name appeared alone on the title page. The first three poems were indeed Shakespeare's, and an unwary purchaser might easily assume that he held in his hand a new collection of lyrical poetry by the popular dramatist. Obviously, the piratical publisher was exploiting the name – and the enormous success of *Venus and Adonis*. He appropriated three passages from Shakespeare's *Love's Labour's Lost*, and to eke out the slim pamphlet he included four poems about Venus and Adonis by other authors. The cognoscenti also knew that some of Shakespeare's sonnets had been circulating in manuscript among his friends. A couple of these private poems were included in *The Passionate Pilgrime*, clearly

[15]

without Shakespeare's permission. To those in the know, the volume would be worth purchasing just for these pirated sonnets. Since the issuance of *Lucrece* there had been no authorized publication of any of Shakespeare's more recent non-dramatic poetry, an omission that would have whetted the appetite of the London literati for *Shake-speare's Sonnets*.

Thorpe had never before published anything by Shakespeare. In fact, in the years just prior to 1609, he had issued works by Shakespeare's arch rival, Ben Jonson: *Sejanus* in 1605, *Hymenaei* in 1606, *Volpone* in 1607, and three masques in 1608 and 1609. There may be nothing questionable or suspect about Shakespeare's switching publishers, but in light of the subsequent history of the sonnets, one cannot help but wonder if Thorpe was taking on a book that others had rejected. Moreover, the slim volume, only eighty pages long, was expensive, costing a shilling, when a play in quarto cost half as much. Thorpe must have expected limited sales to a rather small but discerning group of readers, willing to pay more for something special.

It was an unconventional volume, designed to provoke talk, odd in both form and contents. It featured a long strand of over a hundred sonnets devoted to the poet's passion for a very young man, followed by a much smaller string of sonnets largely about fornication with a mature woman. Added to this was a heavy pendant, a poem in an entirely different style about a woman's infatuation with a vain, self-important youth. The homoerotic sonnets were unabashedly frank, much more so than other published poetry of the time, and some of the sonnets to the woman verged on the pornographic. A suitable subtitle for the volume might be "Shakespeare on Love."

Copies of the *Sonnets* were offered for sale by two booksellers; John Wright at Christ Church Gate and William Aspley in St. Paul's Churchyard. Those who first bought copies must have been intrigued and perplexed, as have serious readers ever since, by the preliminary notice immediately following the title page. Instead of the customary flowery and effusive dedication of the work to some prominent nobleman, there was here a rather stark and ambiguous expression of good wishes by the publisher – not the author – to a mysterious Mr. W.H.

TO.THE.ONLIE.BEGETTER.OF
THESE.INSVING.SONNETS
M^r.W.H. ALL.HAPPINESSE
AND.THAT.ETERNITIE.
PROMISED.
BY.
OUR.EVER-LIVING.POET.
WISHETH.
THE.WELL-WISHING.
ADVENTVRER.IN.
SETTING.
FORTH.

T.T. [Thomas Thorpe]

These words conceal as much as they reveal. The use of the word adventurer, which here means someone taking a business risk, suggests that Thorpe did not know how well this volume would sell. But why would a volume of new poems by the celebrated Shakespeare involve much risk-taking?

As strange as the lack of a proper dedication is a peculiar contradiction within the sonnets. Many of the poems are addressed to a young man to whom Shakespeare promises immortality through the power of verse. Yet the young man is never named, never identified. The poet promises immortality, but reneges on his promise.

There is more that is strange. These remarkable sonnets that Shakespeare himself thought would be an enduring monument to his genius did not appear in his collected works, the First Folio published in 1623. Ben Jonson's collected works had appeared in folio in 1616 (the year in which Shakespeare died), and Shakespeare's fellow actors and business partners, John Heminges and Henry Condell, certainly wanted to emulate Jonson in gathering and editing the works of their former colleague. But whereas the Jonson folio contained much of his non-dramatic poetry, the Shakespeare folio contained none of his.

Although any one of these circumstances taken by itself might raise no eyebrows, the combination of them should certainly arouse the curiosity of any conscientious reader of the *Sonnets*. Why this reluctance to endorse or praise or print the sonnets?

There is evidence that the publication of the volume did in fact provoke a minor scandal. Although there is no surviving record or account of what the first readers thought of *Shake-spears Sonnets*, there is evidence that in the estimation of some these sonnets were in bad odor. In 1639, twenty-three years after Shakespeare's death, John Benson published an edition of the sonnets (dated 1640 on the title page), and in his epistle to the reader he noted that these poems had not been as well received as the plays. "They had not the fortune by reason of their Infancie in his [Shakespeare's] death, to have the due accommodation of proportionable glory, with the rest of his everliving Workes." He assured readers that there was nothing but "perfect eloquence" in these poems and that they "appeare of the same purity, the Author himselfe then living avouched." Here Benson doth protest too much. Reading between the lines, we can see that he feels obliged to do what Shakespeare himself must have done: assure readers that there was nothing impure in the sonnets.

Benson took pains to avoid a repetition of such accusations. He did not reprint the work that Shakespeare had presumably defended. What Benson presented to the reading public was not the original 1609 volume but a thoroughly revised version, with the order of the sonnets changed, poems by other authors included, and, most tellingly, with many of the sexual pronouns altered, "she" often replacing "he," and "her," "him." In effect, Benson censored the sonnets in the hope of making them generally acceptable.[8]

By this time Shakespeare was more read than performed. The Second Folio edition of his plays was issued in 1632, but the dramatist James Shirley could lament in 1642 in the prologue to his play *The Sisters*, Shakespeare "has but few friends lately; think o' that; / He'll come no more."

In the decades that followed the sonnets were subjected to much the same treatment — or worse. Instead of being reprinted time and again, as the plays were, the sonnets were virtually suppressed. Except for an edition published by Bernard Lintott in

1710, the sonnets dropped out of sight, not to emerge into print again until 1766 and then in a very limited edition (included in *Twenty of the Plays of Shakespeare*, edited by G. Steevens). It is one of the anomalies of English literature that for more than a century and a half, readers were debarred by censorious critics from some of the most enchanting poetry in the language. Shakespeare knew that he was creating something marvelous and unique and everlasting. In sonnet 55 he asserts, "Not marble, nor the gilded monuments / Of princes shall outlive this powerful rhyme." This proud and daring claim seems rather ironic in light of how narrowly these poems escaped banishment and oblivion.

Ever since the sonnets first appeared in print a cloud of suspicion has hung over them. All their beauty has been obscured not so much by the convoluted thought and the forgotten allusions in many of them as by the source of that beauty. Although there are many mysteries surrounding the *Sonnets* of 1609, the reason for their disappearance from the public view – and for Thorpe's calling himself a risk-taker – is not one of them.

Most of the sonnets, especially those containing the familiar and much-quoted expressions of adulatory love, are addressed to a young man, young enough indeed to be called a boy in two of the sonnets. That England's greatest dramatist might be a homosexual (a word not then used), and possibly a pederast (a word that was used), was enough to cause a veil to be drawn over these remarkably frank and personal poems. In the course of time, as Shakespeare's reputation grew, the man behind the plays turned into a shadowy divinity, an unfathomable creative genius, approachable but ultimately unknowable, an image fashioned by scholars who often functioned like press-agents eager to prevent any hint of scandal from tarnishing the idol. By the end of the eighteenth century Shakespeare had become one of the titans of English literature, publicly and commercially enshrined in 1769 by the actor David Garrick in the Stratford Jubilee, while scholars sought to entomb the master in conscientiously edited sets of his works. Although they felt compelled to include the sonnets for the sake of completeness, they did so very reluctantly. When George Steevens published in 1766 his edition of twenty plays by Shakespeare, he saw fit to include the sonnets. Subsequently, he had a change of heart, and he left them out of his next edition (1793), justifying this act of literary and scholarly vandalism by saying that "the strongest act of Parliament that could be framed" could not force English readers to turn to these poems.

Eventually, however, the Shakespeare idolaters had to contend with the words on the page and find some way of bringing these sonnets within the range of respectability. One approach was to deny that they were in any way a confession. They were to be understood, like the plays and the narrative poems, to be works of the imagination. In his 1821 edition of Shakespeare, James Boswell (the Younger) declared himself satisfied "that these compositions had neither the poet himself nor any actual individual in view, but were merely the effusions of his fancy, written upon various topics for the amusement of a private circle." [9] Almost a century later, A. C. Bradley effectively ridiculed this notion. "No capable poet...," said he, "would dream of inventing a story like that of the sonnets. ... The story is very odd and unattractive. Such capacities as it has are but slightly developed. It is left obscure, and some of the poems are unintelligible to us because they contain allusions of which we can make nothing." All this is "unnatural, well-nigh incredibly unnatural, if, with the most skeptical critics, we regard the sonnets as a free product of mere imagination." [10]

Certainly the sonnets convey a sense of immediacy, of emotions poured forth from the author's pen, not of emotions recollected in tranquility. At the same time, however, there is a purposeful shape to the published volume as a whole. The result is a work that contains a basic contradiction. As a random collection of poems, it is too artfully arranged, while considered as a conscious arrangement, it reads too much like a diary.

If Shakespeare composed the sonnets addressed to the young man according to some pre-conceived plan, if the artist was in charge from beginning to end, developing his story esthetically, he was an incompetent craftsman. However, if he was a human being caught up in emotions that he could scarcely control, if the intensity of his feelings overwhelmed dispassionate commonsense, if he was simply the poet, his eyes in a fine frenzy rolling, there would be an explanation for the artistic flaws in the sonnet sequence, the irregular flow of the narrative, the hurried quality of the verse in many of the sonnets. In many instances the poet is clearly responding impulsively to shifting changes in his relationship with the young man, over whose attitudes he has little control. At one moment the young man is the rose of perfection (sonnet 10), at another he is compared to a flower that has met with some base infection (sonnet 94). Praised in one sonnet (13) as a man of constant heart, he subsequently is accused of inconstancy (92).

It was not until the nineteenth century that the sonnets began to attract serious attention, as readers came to understand that these remarkable poems revealed the essential Shakespeare, the man himself. It was a poet, not a scholar, who was among the first to appreciate this unique quality of the sonnets. In 1827 William Wordsworth declared, "Scorn not the Sonnet; Critic, you have frowned, / Mindless of its just honours; with this key / Shakespeare unlocked his heart." An anonymous writer in 1857 contrasted the intimate sonnets with the public plays. The latter are "but mere windows and loopholes through which we can catch a glimpse of him. Here in these Sonnets we see him face to face." Out of the plays, said another early critic, we can construct any Shakespeare we desire, but in the sonnets "we have a fixed point." [11]

In the *Sonnets* of 1609, Shakespeare came out of the closet. There was the man behind the plays; the poems formed an extraordinary confession. No writer of his time revealed himself more completely; no one explored – and exposed – the psychological depths of an obsessive love as thoroughly as he did and with as few inhibitions. It is tempting to think that Shakespeare, near the end of his career, deliberately ventured into a new terrain, exploring more deeply than anyone before him the conflicting emotions of a man madly in love at one moment and gallingly disappointed in the next. Anticipating Rousseau, he entered on an enterprise that was without precedent, showing his fellows a man as nature made him, that man being himself. And it was not until the age of Romanticism, the age of confession and psychological probing, that these sonnets finally emerged from obscurity.

But what kind of man emerges from the sonnets? What is that fixed point? It turns out that they depict more than a poet infatuated with an attractive youth. The 126 sonnets that concentrate on the young man are followed by a series devoted mainly to the poet's lusty affair with a mature woman. There is nothing feigned or false about them. The passion in them is as real as the passion for the young man, only the passion takes a different direction, aiming at purely physical sex. And in the original 1609 volume this is followed by a longish poem, "A Lover's Complaint," in a style entirely different from that of the sonnets, in which the story of the poet's obsessive love for the young man is retold as the tale of a woman's infatuation with the young man's double. Although many modern editions of the *Sonnets* omit this poem, it was clearly intended to be a meaningful part of the full story. The original readers would have ingested the whole book and seen the "Complaint" as a satiric commentary on what had come before. To them the 1609 Quarto would have offered three stories. The passion of a mature man for a much younger man, the subject of the first 126 sonnets, is followed by the love of a mature man for an earthy woman, and this in turn is followed by a woman's prostrating herself before an uncaring young man. Though the whole work is very roughly hewn, it does have a distinct shape. In a way, the volume seems to consume itself, ending as it began with the young man, but now pictured in an unflattering light. The genuine passion of the first sonnets, containing some of the most beautiful lines, is undercut by the craggy, comparatively unpoetic "Complaint" at the end, providing a sharp and abrasive contrast to what had gone before. The overtly homosexual passion of the long first sequence is blunted by what comes after.

When this volume is read with a scrupulous concern for what is actually said, there does not seem to be any "fixed point" that clearly identifies the poet as transgressing the sexual conventions of his time. Some commentators have argued that the sonnets must have been published against Shakespeare's wishes, since he would hardly have wanted to confess himself a "sodomite" when the laws of the land imposed serious punishment on those who committed homosexual acts. But the opposite position is more tenable: he let his passion for the young man become known because he knew no harm could come to himself. He must have felt fairly secure. Although critics in the past sought to dissociate Shakespeare from "A Lover's Complaint" and to argue that the sonnets were issued against his wishes, the consensus now is that the 1609 volume is entirely his and that he authorized its publication. The most recent editors agree that the arrangement of the poems was Shakespeare's, that the compositors worked from Shakespeare's own copy, and that Shakespeare approved its publication, thereby seconding what common sense has all along decreed.[12]

The sonnets to the young man are almost as much about the poet's creation of immortal verse as they are about the young man's beauty. The one was of course meant to match the other. An impartial reader might sense that the central concern of the sonnets is not love itself but the link between eros and esthetics. The young man takes on the role of the poet's muse; his physical beauty is transmuted into verbal magic. "Shall I compare thee to a summer's day? / Thou art more lovely and more temperate" are the opening words of sonnet 18, which ends with the couplet, " So long as men can breathe or eyes can see, / So long lives this, and this gives life to thee." Early in the sequence the main theme coupling verbal with physical beauty is sounded, and what happens to it subsequently constitutes what might be called the plot line of the sequence as a whole.

There is no sense of religious sin in them, no self-accusation for having loved immorally or impurely, no remorse for the poet's infatuation. Instead the young man turns out to be the one in the wrong. The poet accuses him of not being worthy of the immortality that the poet wishes at first to confer on him. The young man vanishes, leaving generations of scholars and literary detectives puzzling over who he was.

In publishing the sonnets in 1609 Shakespeare must have felt that there was a sizable number of readers who shared or at least appreciated his views on sex and understood the nature of his love for the handsome youth. They would have been part of a sexual culture that not only had its roots in the past but that was also subject to shifts in fashion. There was unquestionably a tectonic shift when the court of King James I replaced that of Queen Elizabeth. In the 1590s, some of Shakespeare's sonnets, the "sugared" ones, as Meres called them, were hand-copied and passed from friend to friend. It is unlikely that the sonnets addressed to the young man could have been published in the 1590s during Elizabeth's reign, and we know they were suppressed after King James died. It was the particular freedom of James's court and the tone he set for it that provided what can be seen in the historical perspective as a window of opportunity for these homoerotic sonnets. As a member of the king's company of actors, Shakespeare would have been fully aware of how James's sexual preferences colored all the conventions about male friendship. Shakespeare's own sexual orientation as revealed in some of his plays and in the hugely popular poem *Venus and Adonis* would have made him feel at home in the court of King James. Given those circumstances, the publication of the *Sonnets* in 1609 might have been less a daring confession than an affirmation of the king's life style.

Fully to understand the sonnets and to sense the undercurrent of thought that flows through them, giving order to what may seem like randomness, one must enter the minds of those first readers. They would have had some familiarity with Shakespeare's works as a whole, would have been aware of the king's predilections, and would have had some knowledge of the historical and cultural background on which the gay men of the time justified their special place in society. Although they had their own vocabulary, writers in Shakespeare's time were far from silent on the subject of gay sex and homosexuality. But like members of any sub-culture, they spoke their own language, and in reading what they have to say lies a dangerous temptation to import the gay attitudes of a modern metropolis in the year 2000 to the London of 1609. We should let Shakespeare's contemporaries speak for themselves.

CHAPTER 2

A Curse on Love

I N the 1590s gay readers must have been getting a tingle of delight from Christopher Marlowe's narrative poem *Hero and Leander*. Left unfinished at his death in 1593, it was circulating in manuscript and finding readers who took a subversive pleasure in those passages in which Marlowe describes how Neptune attempts to seduce Leander. Hero is a priestess of the love goddess Aphrodite; Leander is a young man who must swim across the Hellespont to meet her. But the sea-god Neptune at first mistakes the youngster for Ganymede, cup bearer to Zeus, and tries to seduce him.

> He clapt his plumpe cheekes, with his tresses playd
> And smiling wantonly, his love bewrayd.
> He watcht his armes, and as they opend wide,
> At every stroke, betwixt them would he slide,
> And steale a kisse, and then run out and daunce,
> And as he turnd, cast many a lustfull glaunce, —
> And threw him gawdie toies to please his eie, —
> And dive into the water, and there prie
> Upon his brest, his thighs, and everie lim,
> And up againe, and close beside him swim,
> And talk of love: Leander made replie,
> You are deceav'd, I am no woman I.
> Therat smilde Neptune (second sestiad, lines 181-193).[13]

The love rivalry in this episode is of a special nature. Ordinarily, boy chases girl and has to outrun a male rival. In Marlowe, the young man strives to reach the love goddess but is nearly violated by a male god. Homosexual longings contend with heterosexual passions. Instead of being about love in the usual sense, *Hero and Leander* sets one kind of sexual passion against another.

Shakespeare's early narrative poem *Venus and Adonis* explores the same territory and was addressed to those who were titillated by Marlowe's poem. It was dedicated to Henry Wriothesley, third earl of Southampton, and it is doubtful that the young playwright would have chosen to write on the subject of Venus's seduction of a beautiful boy unless he knew that it would appeal to his patron. And appeal it did. Southampton reputedly bestowed £1000 on Shakespeare for this poem and for its sequel, *Lucrece*.[14] It was an extraordinary sum, quite unbelievable in fact, roughly the amount that Leonardo da Vinci was paid each year while he was engaged in painting *The Last Supper*. Nicholas Rowe, who passed along this information in 1709, found that it was indeed a very great bounty, almost equal to that shown in his time to French dancers and Italian eunuchs. Rowe also mentions that the money might have been a loan. This makes some sense. A loan would have enabled the young actor/ playwright to purchase a share in the Lord Chamberlain's acting company, which he seems to have done at about this time. Southampton would have been only nineteen when *Venus* was printed and not yet the heir to the estate. A little later, however, after the publication of *Lucrece*, Southampton would have been in a position to assist Shakespeare in the theatrical venture.

Shakespeare needed Southampton's patronage. Because of the plague that struck London, he had had to abandon the theatre for a while. By order of the City Council, beginning in August 1592, and continuing throughout 1593, all theatres were closed as the devastation swept through the city. By the year's end, 10,000 Londoners had died,[15] about eight per cent of the city's population. Shakespeare might have made a sensible retreat into the countryside, an appropriate setting for the story of a boy who loved to hunt. The plague continued to rage in the following year, when Shakespeare wrote *Lucrece*. Both poems were bestsellers. *Venus* was reprinted twelve times up to 1636 and was the best known and most widely read narrative poem of the pre-Cromwellian period. Marlowe's poem ran it a very close second, with three separate editions in 1598 and nine more printings from 1600 to 1637. *Lucrece* was another bestseller – eight printings up to 1655. The readers of *Venus and Adonis* adored "honey-tongued" Shakespeare. In a contemporary play, one character asks, "Who loves not Adon's love or Lucrece rape?" and another exclaims, "Let this duncified world esteem of Spencer and Chaucer; I'll worship sweet Mr. Shakespeare, and to honor him will lay his *Venus and Adonis* under my pillow."[16] Yet, in spite of his unique success with these poems, Shakespeare did not on his own publish any other non-dramatic verse until 1609.

What is interesting is that the sonnets published in that year explore the same sexual territory as *Venus and Adonis*. The same outré amatory sensibility suffuses both works. The difference is that the sonnets transpose the Greek myth into real life. The purpose of myth is to teach us more about human existence than daily experience does, just as our dreams may tell us more about ourselves than our waking thoughts. While *Venus* probes the essential nature of his yearnings, the sonnets capture the poet's emotions from day to day,

In this early poem, written when he was twenty-nine, Shakespeare concealed his personal sexual preferences by retelling, in lushly erotic language, the story of Venus's infatuation with young Adonis, a classic tale of heterosexual love known to every educated person. At the same time Shakespeare betrays what his best friends must have known about him by grafting onto the Venus-and-Adonis myth significant elements from another myth, that of the nymph Salmacis and the beautiful boy Hermaphroditus. Both tales are in Ovid's *Metamorphoses*, but there they have nothing to do with each other. In effect, Shakespeare uses the Salmacis story to explain the Venus story. and thereby provides insight into a certain type of sexual sensibility.

The Venus story by itself can be read simply as a seduction gone wrong. The goddess of love pursues a young, beardless boy, who wants nothing to do with her, not even when she offers herself to him.

In what presumably passed as soft-core pornography in the 1590s, Venus murmurs, "Graze on my lips, and if those hills be dry,

/ Stray lower, where the pleasant fountains lie" (lines 233-4).

He remains unmoved.

"Thou art no man," she taunts him, "though of a man's complexion" (214).

Shakespeare's Adonis, however, young as he is, knows that love "is a life in death" (413). Overcome by her unquenched passion for him, Venus faints. The boy seeks to revive her with a kiss. She takes advantage of the moment and presses him to her bosom. Incorrigibly unseducible, Adonis is still not aroused. He leaves her to follow his own passion, hunting, and is killed by a boar.

To explain the unmanly behavior of Adonis, Shakespeare turns to the story of Salmacis and Hermaphroditus. The latter's father was Hermes, the messenger of the Olympian gods, and his mother, Aphrodite, the goddess of love. As Ovid tells the story, the nymph Salmacis espied the fifteen-year-old boy, with white skin and pink cheeks, bathing in the nude. She was enraptured by the sight. Leaping into the water, she sought to gather him into her arms. He resisted, she would not let him go, and their two bodies merged together to become one — that of a hermaphrodite, neither boy nor girl but a union of the two. As he was being transformed, the boy pronounced a curse on the pool of water, condemning all who swim in it to the fate he suffered.

Shakespeare gives the myth a different moral. For him, the teenage androgyne is the ideal of physical beauty. His Adonis is a bisexual creature, one in whom male and female characteristics blend perfectly, the masculine features predominating. In real life this ideal is embodied for him in a beardless lad, aged about fifteen. (In Ovid, Adonis is "between state of man and lad.") His form, boyish but with hints of the man to come, incorporates a passion that is not earthy. He is irresistible to both Shakespeare and Venus because he is the embodiment, the physical encasement, of a spiritual love, the body being the book of the soul. Adonis rejects Venus, as Hermaphroditus spurns Salmacis, because she wishes to possess him physically. He tells her, "Love surfeits not, lust like a glutton dies; / Love is all truth, lust full of forged lies "(803-4).

At the end of the poem, the death of Adonis, which Ovid describes simply as the result of one great thrust by the wounded animal, is transformed by Shakespeare into a grotesque act of love. "Nuzzling in his [Adonis's] flank, the loving swine / Sheath'd unaware the tusk in his soft groin" (1115-6). Venus, like Racine's love goddess, *"tout entière à sa proie attachée,"* confesses that she would have killed Adonis with her kisses if the boar had not killed him with its tusk. Having lost her Adonis, she pronounces a curse on love. From now on it shall be "fickle, false and full of fraud" (1141), "waited on with jealousy" (1137), suspicious and riotous, the "cause of war and dire events"(1159). Henceforth, "they that love best, their loves shall not enjoy" (1164).

As a complement to *Venus and Adonis,* in which there is no sexual intercourse, Shakespeare wrote *Lucrece,* which focuses exclusively on the rape of a pure woman. (It was entered for copyright in the Stationers' Register on May 9, 1594 under the title "the ravyshement of Lucrece.") In the first half of the poem Tarquin cannot subdue or rein in his lust for the virtuous and beautiful Lucrece; in the second half, she reveals to her husband what happened, demands the death of Tarquin, and then kills herself. The two poems are companion pieces, Lucrece picturing the beast in man; Venus, the divine element. In neither one does Shakespeare show us conventional love relationships, as in *As You Like It* or *Romeo and Juliet.* In the narrative poems, written, one may assume, with Southampton's sexual preferences in mind, romantic love of the boy-meets-girl, girl-meets-boy sort does not exist. Instead, love between the sexes turns out to be a one-sided affair, ending in either disappointment or rape.

In the *Ssonnets,* published fifteen years later, Shakespeare's philosophy of love is unchanged.[17] There is the same purity in the sonnets devoted to the Fair Youth, in which there is no sexual consummation; and in the rest of the sonnets there is the same destructive lust of heterosexual intercourse as in *Lucrece.* There may be no rape, but the sex is illicit and is described as hellish. And the woman, the Dark Lady, is almost as aggressive as Venus. She succeeds where the goddess failed, but only because her victim, the poet, is no pubescent boy, only an easily aroused mature man.

In both the narrative poems from the 1590s and the sonnets published in 1609 one finds the same unusual, perhaps abnormal, sexual preferences. The poet finds perfection in a beautiful teen-age
boy, an ideal that consists in physical attraction combined with
spiritual radiance. It is a perfection that is inevitably short-lived.
As soon as the boy becomes a man, as soon as he succumbs to the
female and has intercourse with her, his beauty fades. The irony is
that the love for the boy cannot be consummated. Sexual consummation is the opposite of enduring love. The boy ideal is hermaphroditic, a union of the male and female, a fusion of the two, not a
penetration of the loved one. As soon as there is penetration, the
hermaphroditic being splits apart and the battle of the sexes begins. The Salmacis myth points to the underlying meaning of the
death of Adonis.

In the sonnets no myth is necessary. The gradual transformation of the boy into early manhood and the poet's disenchantment
are recorded almost moment by moment, from the first sonnet, in
which the poet expresses his adulation of "beauty's Rose" and
hopes it might live on in the boy's progeny, to the last of the Fair
Youth sequence, the 126th, in which the poet bids farewell to him
who has now, after about three years' acquaintance, become no-
ticeably the "minion" of time's pleasure.

In the sonnets, woman represents the earthly element; the boy's
beauty, the transcendental spiritual element. To preserve that
beauty, however, the boy must lower himself to mate with woman,
while the woman must seduce the man in order to maintain the
species. Love of the body (Venus) demands consummation, whereas the higher love (Adonis) refuses to be pulled down by base desires. There is no way in which the two can be fully reconciled with
each other. Venus's curse on love is her recognition of the eternal enmity of the sexes. Shakespeare's own answer lay in the androgyne,
the human being who combined both sexes. In real life he found that
figure in the boy of the sonnets, "the master-mistress of my passion," a man in hue, but with a woman's face (sonnet 20).

This concept of the role of the sexes is at least as old as ancient
Greek civilization, probably as old as patriarchal society. But

Shakespeare's variation of it puts an unusual emphasis on the pubescent boy as the perfect image of love before the idealized human being divides itself into male and female. His close identification with the concept, apparent in the narrative poems and in the autobiographical sonnets, suggests that Shakespeare did not find it in his reading of Ovid. His mind was already receptive to the idea. It may have grown out of his personal experiences as a young man. He was only eighteen when he married in haste a woman eight years his senior. Their first child was born only six months after the church wedding. After three years of marriage and the birth of twins, the couple produced no more children. William spent most of his time in London, where, if his sonnets may be accepted as reflecting actual experiences, he took a mistress. At the end of his life, in his will he left his spouse his "second best bed." Although most scholars have insisted that there was nothing unusual in the will and that Anne Hathaway would automatically inherit her fair share of the estate, it is hard to read through the list of bequests without feeling that Shakespeare treated her in a perfunctory and dismissive manner, mentioning her only once and that at the end of the document. "I give unto my wife my second best bed" was inserted after the will had been drafted. At first, he left her nothing. E. K. Chambers speculates that the bed came from Anne Hathaway's "old home at Hewland."[8] Katherine Duncan-Jones adds a touch to her portrait of an "ungentle" Shakespeare by picturing him in his last moments "being nursed in the best, or 'master' bed" . . . "determined that Anne should never occupy it, even after his death." If so, then perhaps one may speculate further that it was the bed in which young Will first learned about sex, a teen-ager seduced by an older, passionate woman, desperate to find a husband before she reached the age of spinsterhood? And did the memory of that sexual encounter, perhaps the young man's first, provide matter for the scenes between the predatory Venus and innocent Adonis, the hunter turned hunted? "Measure my strangeness with my unripe years," says Adonis. "Before I know myself, seek not to know me" (lines 524-5). Actors often relive past experiences to make their scenes on stage more convincingly real. Was Shakespeare the actor relying on emotional memory when he re-enacted the myth, calling to mind himself as a boy who hunted deer and fell into the willing arms of a well-to-do woman? Although the bare facts alone may not justify such speculation, the facts and the tenor of the poems neatly complement each other.

With regard to sexual dispositions, the signal difference between the narrative poems and the sonnets is that in the latter the boy is loved by a man, not by a woman. It was the difference between the socially acceptable and the legally unacceptable. What made the change possible was the tone of court life under a new monarch. It was apparent to everyone that the times were changing. The narrative poems were published in the reign of Queen Elizabeth, when sexual acts between men could be severely punished, according to the law. In 1603, with the accession of James I to the throne, men who liked their own sex began to come out of the closet.

"The legal codes and religious discourses" of Elizabethan England "could not accommodate the vice they abhorred," as John Kerrigan remarks in his edition of the sonnets. "The age was, to that extent, neither sympathetic nor antagonistic towards inversion, but pre- homosexual."[19] To engage in hard-core sexual acts with such men was to degrade oneself physically and socially. The atmosphere in England, especially at court, was more complaisant about homoeroticism and more conducive to public expressions of it than at any other time. The love life of King James provided a climate hospitable to the publication of the sonnets. And it must be kept in mind that as a member of a theatrical company, the King's Men, Shakespeare was under the direct patronage of James and involved in court entertainments when the sonnets were printed in 1609.

The question is, how far did the king and the playwright go in expressing their love? Both men had ample opportunity to meet the sort they desired. In the theater Shakespeare was constantly instructing the boys who played the female roles in his plays, and in the court ambitious young men would vie for the king's attention. However, where there was desire, there were also inhibitions. Between the lover and the young man loomed the specter of sodomy. Homosexuals of a certain type understood sodomy to be sinful, or at least indecent and demeaning, while at the same time insisting that male bonding was preferable to heterosexual love. The union of man and woman was fundamentally a physical one, whereas the love of a man for another man could be construed as fundamentally spiritual – as long as the male partners did not do to each other what men did to woman. Out of this paradox comes the contradictory nature of Shakespeare's philosophy of love, the tension between Venus and Adonis, and the sexual ambiguity of the sonnets, most strikingly expressed in sonnet 20, in which the beloved boy is the poet's "master-mistress." That which makes him a boy is the very thing that makes him as untouchable as Adonis was to Venus.

CHAPTER 3

The Gay Court of King James

A FTER *Lucrece*, fifteen years elapsed before Shakespeare published another volume of poetry, the *Sonnets* of 1609. Shakespeare dedicated both *Lucrece* and *Venus and Apollo* to the earl
of Southampton. *Venus* on the title page bore the inscription: *Vilia
miretur vulgus: mihi flavus Apollo / Pocula Castalia plena ministret aqua.*
Let the common herd be amazed by worthless things; but for me let
golden Apollo provide cups full of the water of the Muses. Or in
Christopher Marlowe's translation: "Let base conceipted witts admire vile things / Fair Phoebus lead me to the Muses springs." From
the juxtaposition, so to speak, of this inscription and the dedication,
a reader might reasonably infer that Southampton was not only
Shakespeare's patron but also his inspiration. It is likely that the
promising dramatist quickly acquired a knowledge of the manners
and customs of the nobility through his friendship with Southampton, and he certainly would have had access to the nobleman's library. And, as we have seen, it may have been through Southampton's bounty that Shakespeare was able to buy himself a share in the
Lord Chamberlain's acting company in 1594 or thereabouts.

Although separated by class differences, the nobleman and the
poet had much in common. The young actor-dramatist on the rise
would hardly have dared to dedicate the rather salacious *Venus and
Adonis* to Southampton if he did not know that he and his patron
shared the same sentiments about sex. They both were strongly
attracted to young men. For both of them, marriage was a necessary inconvenience, not a deeply loving union. In 1594 or 1595,
Southampton refused to marry Elizabeth Vere, the grand-daugh-
ter of Southampton's guardian Lord Burghley, and for his contrari-

ness he had to pay a fine.[20] In 1598 he once again tried to avoid marriage, this time with his mistress Elizabeth Vernon, one of Queen Elizabeth's maids of honor. Southampton was so reluctant to take her as his wife that he went abroad before the date set for the wedding. He soon had to return to England to marry her. He had been trapped by her becoming pregnant before he left for the continent, a situation that Shakespeare would have been familiar with.[21]

No other nubile woman played a part in Southampton's life. By contrast, there is anecdotal evidence of his fondness for young men. In Ireland he was observed embracing his corporal general, hugging him in his arms and playing "wantonly" with him.[22]

The earl of Southampton was also the recipient in 1597 of what a literary historian has called "perhaps the most extended defence of homosexual pleasure in early modern English." This was William Burton's translation of a second-century Greek novel, *The Most Delectable and Pleasaunt History of Clitiphon and Leucippe*. Dedicated to Southampton, the tale includes an extended passage in which the love of boys is declared to be more nearly perfect than the love of women. And for two principal reasons: "their beautie is of more force to delight the senses with pleasure," and homosexual desire is more "vehement" than that of a man for a woman.[23]

In the world of this Greek novel, boys, simply as esthetic objects, are more physically beautiful than women. The great appeal of the young boy lies, however, not just in his attractiveness but in his boyishness. The fact that his beauty will soon vanish causes the pleasure to be mingled with a kind of sorrow.

"For those thinges which sometimes are taken away, are always newe and do daily flourish: and as much as is taken away from them by the shortnesse of time, so much is added to the greatnesse of the desire, and theyre pleasure doth not fade: and whereof is the Rose accounted the fairest of all plants, but because it soonest doth fade away."[24]

This explanation of the allure of boy love could serve as an introduction to Shakespeare's sonnets. Not only is the young man of the sonnets immediately addressed as a rose, but one theme that pervades the sequence as a whole is the impermanence of youthful beauty.

FIGURE 1. Henry Wriothesley, third earl of Southampton. Portrait attributed to John de Critz, the Elder.

When the sonnets became the subject of intensive study in the nineteenth century, it was not long before Southampton was named as the young man who enchanted Shakespeare. The poet of the sonnets is considerably older than the young man, and the two are separated by the class barrier. So it was with Southampton and Shakespeare. Some of the sonnets (those that appeared in *The Passionate Pilgrime*) were definitely written in the 1590s. If, say, the bulk of the sonnets was composed in 1594, the thirty-year-old actor-playwright would have been writing to a nineteen-year-old aristocrat. And Southampton as a youngster would have had the sexually ambiguous features of the "master-mistress" of sonnet 20. A portrait of Southampton (attributed to John de Critz) as an adolescent could easily be taken for the portrait of a woman. And so it was until 2002, when a portrait presumed to be of a certain Lady Norton was identified, though not with absolute certainty, as a portrait of Southampton. (See Figure 1.)

Moreover, the mysterious Mr. W.H., to whom Thorpe dedicated the *Sonnets*, could with a little ingenuity be seen as a discreet reference to Henry Wriothesley, the given name of the earl of Southampton.

If Southampton was in fact the adored youth, that might explain why the publication of the sonnets was delayed for so many years. They revealed too much about the nobleman, and in the mid-1590s, almost everyone among the literati would have known how close Southampton and Shakespeare were to each other.

Venus and Adonis obviously catered to the nobleman's predilections, and the dedication to *Lucrece* is uncommonly effusive: "What I have done is yours, what I have to do is yours, being part in all I have, devoted yours." *Lucrece* was published in 1594, and when a year or so later Shakespeare wrote *A Midsummer Night's Dream*, he may have had in mind the conflict within Southampton between his emotional desires and his social and familial obligations. The play with its highly suggestive sexual imagery centers on two marriages. In the framing story Duke Theseus is about to wed the Queen of the Amazons; in the parallel story, set in fairy land, Oberon and his wife Titania quarrel because she will not surrender to him "a lovely boy."[25] In the last years of the sixteenth century, Southampton was often out of favor with Queen Elizabeth because of his friendship with the rebellious Essex. After the accession of James to the English throne, and with both Essex and Elizabeth gone, Southampton was made welcome at court, and he quickly ingratiated himself with the royal couple. At the Christmas revels of 1604-1605, he arranged a private performance of *Love's Labour's Lost*, for the new Queen, Anne of Denmark, at his house. This highly sophisticated satire may indeed have had its first performance at Southampton's house ten years earlier, as A.L. Rowse has suggested.[26] With its many allusions to contemporary events, to personages, to the latest schools of thought, and its often precious language, it was unfit for the public theater, and for those same reasons very well attuned to aristocratic tastes. By having the play revived soon after James came to the throne, Southampton may have sought to re-establish a bond with the poet that had been broken during the intervening years. If so, that bond must have been sorely tested with the publication of the *Sonnets* a few years later. Before the sonnet sequence comes to an end, the beautiful youth is harshly criticized as vain, aloof, unfaithful, and unkind, and in sonnet 126 the poet bids him a rather bitter adieu. Would Shakespeare have ever used such dismissive tones in addressing his generous patron, the man to whom he owed so much ("What I have done is yours, what I have to do is yours"), the man who certainly gave him a start as a narrative poet and possibly as an investor? It is a question that the supporters of the Southampton theory have never adequately dealt with. It is true that love has its ups and downs, but would Shakespeare, years after the event, wanted to leave this uncharitable impression of his benefactor – and dedicate it to him?

The difference in life among the nobles between the late 1590s and 1609, the date of the publication of the *Sonnets*, is the difference between Queen Elizabeth and King James, the queen who ruled like a man and the king who had too much of a queen in him. She oversaw England at war with the Spaniards; he was proud of himself as a peace negotiator.

His timidity may well have stemmed from his childhood in Scotland. He was the son of the ill-fated Mary Stuart, and for the first ten years of his life he was caught up in the religious and political turmoil of his mother's struggles to claim the throne of England. European intelligence regarded him as a possible successor to Elizabeth. An imaginative novelist could hardly devise a more harrowing and lurid plot than the one the young James lived through or observed at close hand.

In a very real sense his perilous adventures began while he was still in his mother's womb. Queen Mary had married Lord Darnley, her second husband and a Catholic, but she soon tired of him and took David Rizzio, a musician, as her lover. Darnley and his followers murdered Rizzio while Mary looked on, the murderers hoping that they could frighten her into miscarrying the unborn child. James was born a few months later, in June 1566, and not surprisingly proved to be a physically weak child, who suffered all his life from an unsteadiness in the legs. He was cowardly, constantly feared being physically attacked by his enemies, and would turn pale at the sight of a weapon openly displayed. He remarked once that more than most kings he had been subject to "daily tempests of innumerable dangers" ever since his birth, and added, "even as I may justly say, before my birth and while I was in my mother's belly."[27]

When Mary was compelled to abdicate, the young James became a figurehead King of Scots, while others ran the government. The conflict between the Catholics and Protestants made the child the pawn between contending forces, and his education became a matter of political and religious infighting. To counteract the Protestant influence, the Catholic faction in 1579 appointed Esmé Stuart, sixth sieur d'Aubigny, a Scottish nobleman and cousin to the king, as special tutor, in which capacity he became a significant influence on his early life. Esmé was brought from France, where he had been reared and educated. He had been a gentleman of the bedchamber in the flagrantly gay court of Henri III. He became the young king's closest friend, a faithful servant, a reliable advisor, and an understanding confidant. He was the only person James trusted. The young boy would often put his arms around d'Aubigny's neck and kiss him. The earldom of Lennox was conferred on him, and later he was promoted to duke.

Esmé brought with him the charm and culture of the French court, a geniality and grace far different from the gruffness of the Scottish noblemen who had been James's only company. But his virtues were his undoing. His closeness to the king and his Gallic refinement made him disliked and distrusted, and the Scottish Protestants went about removing him from the scene. In spite of his protests, Esmé was suspected of harboring Catholic sympathies and indoctrinating the child-king with them. He was sent back to France, leaving the young James desolate. Those three years under the tutelage of a wise, handsome, well-built older man, who treated him with just the right mixture of deference and authority, were the happiest years of his life. His relationship with Esmé, however brief, exerted a lasting influence. Virtually a motherless child, he had found solace and safety with this older companion, only to have him taken away. Not only had Esmé done something to repair the psychological and physical damage that James suffered at birth and in childhood, but Esmé had also provided physical intimacy and emotional warmth, perhaps going so far as to initiate the boy into the pleasures of male sex. It was a classic instance of pederasty in the Greek sense, a thirty-seven- year old man serving as counselor and sexual partner to a thirteen-year-old lad.

It is impossible to tell whether or not Esmé gave a direction to James's sexual life that it might not have otherwise taken. By all accounts James was innately homosexual. As he grew older, he became more staunchly gay, taking advantage of his position as ostensible ruler of the land to express his true feelings more openly. He made no secret of his sexual inclinations, declaring that he married purely for reasons of state and the need to provide the kingdom with a legitimate heir. Before he sailed to Denmark to meet his queen, he wrote in a letter to the Privy Council that his long delay in getting married "bred in the breasts of many a great jealousy [suspicion] of my inability, as if I were a barren stock. These reasons and innumerable others . . . moved me to hasten the treaty of my marriage; for, as to my own nature, God is my witness I could have abstained longer." [28]

Such frankness shows that James was not a closet homosexual ; he never hid his preference for handsome young men. But as king, he had to try to act like one, and he had to produce an heir to the throne. After the queen's last pregnancy in 1606, James left the marriage bed, and he exercised his royal prerogatives by bringing attractive men into his bedchamber or his hunting lodge. (See Figure 2: King James in 1605.)

FIGURE 2. King James I of England in 1605. Artist unknown.

FIGURE 3. Robert Carr. Artist: Nicholas Hilliard

LIFE IN THE COURT of King James makes for an illuminating chapter in the history of sexual mores. The king's behavior in public shocked and offended many people, but there was never any serious thought of arraigning him on charges of sodomy. Here we have a fine example of what happens when a subculture becomes mainstream. One historian describes the situation:

"The court and the nation were scandalized by the king's unwillingness to keep his physical love of men in the closet. . . . There was something gross about his constant playing with himself and fondling his favorites in public. His large eyes ever rolled 'after any stranger that came into his presence, insomuch, as many for shame have left the roome, as being out of countenance.' Then too, there was always something extravagant, some obsessive psychological need, that gave James's masculine affairs an unhealthy air."[29]

In 1609 his current favorite was Robert Carr, who was the power behind the throne. Carr had been an unnoticed underling in James's court in Scotland until he caught the king's eye when he fell from his horse and broke a leg. The king ordered his own team of doctors to tend to the young man. Concern about the seriousness of Carr's injury quickly turned to infatuation with his person. James solicitously visited Carr daily, and before long he was teaching him Latin. Carr followed James to London in 1603, and by 1607 he had risen to the rank of a gentleman of the bedchamber, which meant that he was always in attendance on the king. He quickly became the sovereign's closest advisor and the most influential figure at court. Carr himself was not homosexual. But he knew that his compact body, comely features, flaxen and tightly frizzled hair, drew the king's eyes and hands, and he made the most of his physical assets, allowing if not encouraging the king to caress him. A contemporary noticed how the king "leaneth on his arm, pinches his cheeks, smoothes his ruffled garment, and, when he looketh at Carr, directeth discourse to divers other."[30] (See Figure 3: Robert Carr.)

There were others like him in the court, the equivalent of modern-day hustlers, whom James would openly fondle, "kissing them," as one observer gasped, "after so lascivious a mode in publick, and upon the theatre, as it were, of the world [that it] prompted many to imagine some things done in the tyring-house [back-stage in a theater] that exceed my expressions no lesse then they do my experience."[31] One courtier who rejected the King's advances, spit "after the King had slabbered his mouth." Visiting the court, the governor of the Isle of Wight exclaimed, "I never yet saw any fond husband make so much or so great dalliance over his beautiful spouse as I have seen King James over his favorites."[32] In the House of Commons he was openly compared to King Edward II (1284-1327), whose devotion to his lover, the Gascon knight Piers Gaveston, helped bring about his ruin. Marlowe dramatized this story of sex and politics in his extraordinary tragedy, *The trouble-some raigne and lamentable death of Edward the second*, printed in 1594.

King James had a more recent counterpart in Henri III of France (1551-1589), who was notorious for his effeminacy and for surrounding himself with his male favorites, his *mignons* — as well as for his timorousness. Thunderstorms terrified him. His enemies denounced him for maintaining a court of sodomites. Not surprisingly, Marlowe found attractive matter in the rise and fall of this king, too, and put him and his minions on stage in *The Massacre at Paris* (ca. 1589-1593).

King James ruled over a land in which, since the time of Henry VIII, sodomy was a felony punishable by hanging. James himself in his writings denounced sodomy and buggery. Yet the sight of men kissing men in a more than friendly fashion, which would have been unthinkable under Elizabeth, became a not uncommon sight. Under James a new order prevailed. Men became more effeminate, paying more attention to their hair and clothes, while the women became more masculine.[33] One observer at court said the king "dwelleth on good looks and handsome accoutrements" and discharged many servants who were "not to his liking in these matters."[34]

An outsider looking in on this court would have found extraordinary contradictions. While the king was unabashedly gay, he viewed sodomy as an abomination. He wanted the young men around him to be dressed with a feminine extravagance, designed to set off their best features, and yet he cautioned his son against such clothing. These contradictions may not have run very deep; the king may have, for the sake of convenience, maintained a double standard about sexual behavior. Yet the more one learns about this unusual monarch, the less likely it appears that he was equivocating or being insincere. It might be more fair to say that he was a man who, because of the conflict between social conventions and his innate sexual orientation, had to wait a long time before he could be at one with himself. By 1609 he had succeeded, but at a great price.

It is ironic that with a homosexual king on the throne, there was a family in residence at the royal court for the first time in many years. But what a family. By 1609 James had become estranged from his wife and alienated from his eldest son. In this splintered family, father, mother, and son each had his or her own support group within court circles. James wanted a peaceful, Protestant England, and male companions; his wife had Catholic sympathies and lived apart from her husband; the son, who had his eye on his father's throne, had to negotiate between his parents.

In 1609, he wrote to his father: "According to your Majesty's commandement I made your excuse unto the Queene for not sending her a token by me, and alledged your Majesty had a quarrel unto her for not Wryting an answere unto your second letter from Roisten when your foote was sore, nor making mention of the receiving of it in her next letter sent some ten days after, whereas in your Majesty's former iorney to Roisten when you tooke first the paine in your foote she sent one of purpose to visite yow. Here answere was that either she had wrettin or dreamed it, and upon that apprehension had told first my lord Hay and next Sir Thomas Somerset that she had wrettin before. I durst not reply that your Majesty was affeared least that she should returne to her old byasse, for feare that such a Word might have sett her in the Way and made me a peace breaker." [35]

By this time Queen Anne had little respect for her husband. She found some redress for his abandonment of her in seeing him ridiculed as an effeminate man. The French ambassador to the English court remarked in 1604 on the plight of a king, "whom the preachers publicly from the pulpit assail, whom the comedians of the metropolis bring upon the stage, whose wife attends these representations in order to enjoy a laugh against her husband." [36]

She must have tolerated or even encouraged the production of John Day's play *The Isle of Dogs*, a clever satire of life in James's court. It was performed in 1606 by her company of boy actors, the Children of the Queen's Revels. In the play the Duke of Arcadia, whose main pastime is hunting, falls in love with a man disguised as a woman. The audience at the private theater would have seen the king behind the duke, and Arcadia as James's feminized court. A woman in the play complains about her husband's indifference to her, attributing it to the new fashion at court.

"Nowe hee will not lie with mee forsooth and why? Tis the Court fashion. He will not love mee, and why? Tis the Court fashion. I must not come neere him at his downe lying, nor his uprising" (Act 4).

Not only was James separated from his wife; he was increasingly alienated from his own first-born son. From early on, Henry and his father had been on very uneasy terms with each other. James entrusted Henry to the guardianship of John Erskine, earl of Mar, to prevent Anne from using the boy against his father, as he himself had been used against his unfortunate mother. Anne had little access to him when he was a child, but that changed when he became a political power in his own right. The abandoned queen opposed her husband on important political matters and wanted to be involved behind the scenes, primarily by influencing Henry. She maintained her own circle at Somerset House in London, which attracted those who felt uncomfortable with the king's gayness and who were opposed to his pacifist political agenda.

Queen Anne was interested in theater and literature to the same extent that James was interested in religion. She sponsored writers like John Donne and Ben Jonson and regularly attended plays. Shakespeare as playwright and actor would have often conversed with her. Her husband cared little for plays and nodded through them, a glass of wine perched perilously on his knee. His intellectual passion was theology and in debates on the subject he was indefatigable, attacking the Vicar of Christ in Rome, both in speeches and in writings. Soon after being proclaimed king of England, he became the driving force behind the new translation of the Bible that would bear his name.

He also possessed a formidable knowledge of demonology, displaying his expertise in a treatise on the subject printed in Scotland in 1596. He took an avid interest in witches; and they in him. On their return from their wedding in Denmark, he and his bride had been stalled for weeks because of storms in the North Sea, conjured up by a coven of witches in Scotland who employed bits of human corpses tied to a cat, a Christened cat, to rouse the elements. James learned about this when he attended the trial of the chief witch, Agnis Tompson, who revealed all – under torture.[37] She confessed that she and two hundred other witches had gone by sea, each in her own sieve, landing near the kirk at Lothian, where they linked hands, danced, and sang to a tune played on a Jew's harp. King James listened with delight to a performance of this witches' reel.[38]

Still more troubling to King James than these witches in Scotland was his relationship with his eldest son, Prince Henry. Trials against witchcraft, in which James actively participated, could keep the demons under control. Politics was another matter. As heir to the throne, the young man quickly became the rallying point for those who opposed the king's international and religious policies. From the moment James made his formal entrance into London as King of England in 1604, the looming rivalry of father and son was apparent. The nine-year-old boy charmed the multitude in the streets, smiling and bowing, while his father sat stiffly by his side and gritted his teeth.[39]

The physical contrast between father and son was startling. The boy was the prince in a fairy tale, while King James was the least kingly person imaginable. His weak legs left him leaning on other's shoulders. His skin was soft and effeminate; his heard was straggly; and his fingers were always fiddling with his codpiece. His doublet was thickly padded and quilted as protection against an assassin's stiletto.

As an intellect and conversationalist, however, James could easily hold his own. He had a generous heart, a kindly disposition, and an honest nature that won him many admirers. But these were virtues that did not particularly appeal to those who wanted an aggressive ruler on the throne. They saw England's future embodied in the young prince.

When James became king of England, his son was already a political icon. To the empire builders James was only an intermediary between Queen Elizabeth and the future King Henry. When Queen Anne and the young prince proceeded from Edinburgh to London to join James, they were entertained in Warwickshire in June 1603 by a wealthy sheep breeder, Robert Spencer, who commissioned an "entertainment" from Ben Jonson for the occasion. In what was intended as a departing speech, Jonson addressed the nine-year-old Henry in words that looked to the future – and overlooked the present.

> O shoot up fast in spirit, as in yeares;
> That when upon her head proud *Europe* weares
> Her stateliest tire, you may appeare thereon
> The richest gem, without a paragon.
> Shine bright and fixed as the Artick starre:
> And when slow Time hath made you fit for warre,
> Looke over the strict Ocean, and thinke where
> You may but lead us forth, that grow up here
> Against a day, when our officious swords
> Shall speake our action better than our words.[40]

His supporters promoted him as a warrior prince, and he was portrayed as such in paintings, the earliest in 1603, when he was only nine.

The prince's cabal was already grooming him for a war on the continent; he was to lead the Protestant forces against the rising tide of Catholicism. To many he was a reincarnation of his namesake Henry V, who had defeated the French forces at Agincourt, and he was even thought to resemble him in looks.[41] The dramatist John Webster said, "Men thought his star / Had markt him for a just and glorious war."[42]

By 1609, when he was fifteen, he had become a formidable political power, reveling in the role he knew he was meant to play in England's history. Naturally, he regarded Robert Carr, only seven years his senior, as a hostile presence, who enjoyed what Henry wanted – the king's close companionship and the king's ear.

James, ever haunted by his childhood experiences, was his son's opposite, a peace-loving monarch, dubbed "the wisest fool in Christendom," who actively participated in negotiations between Spain and the Netherlands in their unending battles with each other. Where Queen Elizabeth had tried to force Spanish troops out of the Netherlands and failed, James eventually succeeded by bringing the warring countries to the conference table and laying the groundwork for the peace treaty signed in 1609, committing the signatories to a ten-year truce, a notable diplomatic achievement for which he wanted to be remembered.

Among the war-mongers was Sir Walter Raleigh, a hold-over from Elizabeth's reign. James knew of Raleigh's close association with the queen and of his desire to prolong the war with Spain. Because of his suspected involvement in conspiracies against the throne, James had him imprisoned in the Tower in 1603. That was a mistake. Raleigh's spirited defense at his show-trial made him a hero to the war faction, and especially to Prince Henry and Queen Anne. The young prince, setting himself up as a warrior in opposition to his conciliatory father, became Raleigh's patron, in touch with him through letters and friends who visited him. Beginning in 1608, Raleigh wrote several treatises presenting "Arguments for War," addressed to the young prince. "None but my father would keep such a bird in a cage," commented Henry.[43]

Thus the two people who should have been closest to the king, his wife and his eldest son, were largely antagonistic to him. In this royal game of sex and politics, King James and his compeer Robert Carr were set against Queen Anne and Prince Henry, with Henry trying his best to moderate the tensions between his parents.

Understandably, James became attached to the young men in his court, men with whom he found himself in rapport, both temperamentally and politically. As far as public relations was concerned, teaming up with young men was a bad move, but one that was probably necessary for James's psychological wellbeing. These men provided the comfort and easy company he could not find in his immediate family, and Carr in particular provided a still, quiet, and reassuring presence.

This was the atmosphere in which Shakespeare's volume of sonnets was published. Its heady male amativeness could hardly have found a more appreciative and indulgent readership than at this time.

As a member of the king's company of players, Shakespeare would have been in a position to observe palace intrigues from the very beginning of James's coming to London. As one of the king's servants, a groom of the Privy Chamber, Shakespeare was allotted four and one-half yards of scarlet red cloth to be used for his livery in the royal procession through London on March 15, 1604.[44] Shakespeare would have been a keen observer of the palace intrigues and sympathetic with the king's difficult position. As a productive playwright and member of the king's company of actors, he would have been a familiar figure in the court, with many more plays being presented at court than during Elizabeth's reign. In the winter season of 1604-1605, seven of his plays were staged in the royal presence, including revivals of *Merry Wives of Windsor*, *Measure for Measure*, *Comedy of Errors*, *Love's Labour's Lost*, *Henry V*, and *Merchant of Venice*. There was also a new play, *Othello*. Already in 1603, the year that James came to the English throne, Shakespeare's company had staged *Hamlet*, perhaps as a welcoming gesture to the queen. And a few years after the Danish play came the Scottish play, *Macbeth*, a tragedy specially aimed to please King James with its witches and hyperborean setting. Moreover, and perhaps more pointedly, *Macbeth* reinforced James's claim to rule by divine right in tracing his ancestry back into distant history.

The Fair Youth sonnets picture an emotional world not too far removed from the king's. Both Shakespeare and his sovereign were about the same age, and both were drawn to members of their own sex. They were also acutely aware of how society in general condemned them. Anonymous tracts charged the king with a "horrid filthinesse within his Bed, his Ganimedes Pallet, or his Closets. . . . But he could not contract it there; He must have the Publique to be witnesse of his lascivious tongue licking of his Favourites lips, and his hands must . . . bee seen in a continual lascivious action." [45]

Shakespeare must have been the subject of similar incriminations, if not from his theatrical cronies, then from hangers-on at court. How else can one explain sonnet 121, in which he seems called upon to defend himself against charges that he is abnormal and sinful? In language that seems strangely modern – the use of "straight" and "bevel" – Shakespeare turns the charges against his accusers, accusing them of hypocrisy and adultery. Note that "wills" would carry the suggestion of sexual desire.

> For why should others' false adulterate eyes
> Give salutation to my sportive blood?
> Or on my frailties why are frailer spies,
> Which in their wills count bad what I think good?
> No, I am that I am, and they that level
> At my abuses, reckon up their own;
> I may be straight, though they themselves be bevel.
> By their rank thoughts my deeds must not be shown.

Recent bibliographical studies concur in pushing the dates of some of the sonnets out of the 1595-1603 period to which they have usually been assigned and forward to the period when King James sat on the throne of England. The tenor of this sonnet, which comes late in the sequence, accords with the moods and attitudes of the controversial court of the king.

Not only did the king and the poet have in common a liking for young men, as well as a defensive attitude about it; they also took pains to set themselves apart from the stereotypical homosexual boy-lover. They made it very clear that they were not sodomites. In sonnet 20 Shakespeare pointedly differentiates himself from the conventional gay man by denying any interest in the young man's genitals. He wins the attention of the young man by first complimenting him on his physical attractiveness and then keeping his confidence by saying in effect, "I'm not a sodomite." The sense of the sonnet is: "You are the epitome of youthful male beauty. But since you are masculine, women will embrace your beauty, while I as a man can only love, that is, admire and adore, you as an icon." Louis Crompton in his history of homosexuality emphasizes the strangeness of the poet's proposition. "The young man should have sexual relations with women but love only him. 'Mine be thy love and thy love's use their treasure.' Love only me, but sleep with women: that is the radical proposal from which modern readers are likely to recoil with confusion."[46]

This confusion may be the main reason why we find it difficult to comprehend the underlying thought in the sonnets. Did the poet's proposal strike the young man as radical and perplexing? Or were the poet and the youth part of a sexual culture quite different from ours? The confident tone of the sonnet gives the impression that the proposal was something the young man would have understood, even half anticipated. Shakespeare's proposal was not idiosyncratic; it was a sexual overture in keeping with the mores and manners of the time.

There is a similar paradox in the case of King James. In his writings he denounced sodomy and buggery, cautioning the teen-age Henry against fancy clothing that might be too flagrantly and sexually suggestive. He specifically had in mind codpieces "bearing the pensel of Priapus," part of a "Paynted preined [adorned] fashion [that would] serve for baytes for filthy Lecherie."[47] It would be easy to reconcile the contradictions in James as a manifestation of public policy in conflict with private practice, except that his homoerotic behavior was very much in the open.[48]

This paradox – a strong impulse toward male sex and simultaneously a reaction against or repulsion from it – lies at the heart of Shakespeare's sonnets. It is impossible to appreciate them properly, to read them in the same spirit as his first readers did, without somehow converting this paradox into a paradigm. For Shakespeare and King James and the many who thought as they did, the kind of sex they imagined and wrote about was the expression of some ideal relationship. Alan Bray sees the paradox as a "hidden road: . . . the unacknowledged connection between the unmentionable vice of Sodom and the friendship that all accounted commendable."[49]

The road is hidden to us because it is overgrown. Time and changing attitudes have done their work. It is still possible, however, to track its course, especially so because of all the roads and paths traveled by homosexuals this was the one most written about in Shakespeare's time.

CHAPTER 4

Ganymede

T HERE must have been many men in the London of Shakespeare's time who sought out sex with boys and young men and whose consciences were not much troubled, even though they knew they were committing an illegal act. Christopher Marlowe and Francis Bacon might be counted among them. But the historical record, sparse as it is, leaves the impression that many educated gay men struggled with the contradictions imposed on them by religion and deep-seated prejudices. King James abhorred sodomy, and he vehemently denounced it. Yet he adored young men and made no secret of it, kissing them in public and sharing his bed with them. Shakespeare adulated the young man of the sonnets, his "master-mistress," but disavowed any desire to embrace him sexually. Behind these paradoxes lies a special kind of love, represented in myth by the love that Zeus bore for Ganymede, the boy who was his cupbearer.

Francis Osborne, who was privy to much of what went on in King James's court, wrote a play, *The true Tragicomedy formerly acted at Court*, in which King James kisses Robert Carr, Earl of Somerset. This work was not intended for the stage; it was a scandal sheet in the form of a play, and the title considers life at James's court as a tragicomedy. The king addresses Carr, "'Tis thou alone, dear Ganymede, shall quench the thirst of my —."[50] Of all the possible kinds of homosexual love, James would tolerate only the love of Ganymede in its purest form.

One of the difficulties in discussing the behavior of gay men in past times is that the language of homosexuality has changed over the years. Even the term homosexuality is of fairly recent coinage.

Before the nineteenth century gay men were called pederasts or pedophiles or sodomites or lovers of Ganymede or Platonists. These terms were generally applied to men who loved boys. Sodomite was the most pejorative and usually implied anal penetration. Ganymede was the most poetic, and though the mythical Ganymede was a young boy, the term was broadened to include the younger partner in a sexual relationship, even if he was in his twenties. According to the historian John Boswell, ancient "Ganymede" and modern "gay" are near synonyms.[51] On the most elevated level was the Socratic lover, who converted physical attraction into a spiritual power.

The cult of Ganymede has a long history in myth and legend, a history that helps to explain both the limits placed on homosexual love in James's court and the baffling tone – baffling to present-day readers – of Shakespeare's sonnets. The beautiful Ganymede was the son of Tros, the founder of the city of Troy. Enchanted by the boy, Zeus gave four horses to Tros in exchange and made Ganymede his cupbearer. As a consequence of this transaction, Troy became the equine capital of the world (its inhabitants known formulaically in the *Iliad* as "horse-taming Trojans"), the link between the horse-rich Asian plains and the centers of commerce dotting the Mediterranean coast. In the sexual sphere, Ganymede replaced the young maiden Hebe as Zeus's cupbearer, a noteworthy change suggesting that pederasty was becoming socially acceptable. In Homer, the gods carry off Ganymede to serve Zeus. In later legend, in a significant addition, Zeus himself in the guise of an eagle captures Ganymede and transports him to the heavens.

Although the symbolism of this points to the social sanctioning of pedophilia, the acceptance placed limits on boy-love. It had to be secondary to the conventional love of man and woman. Ganymede was only a cupbearer, only a pleasant companion to Zeus, without any independent power, a thing of beauty to be enjoyed while it lasted, not a permanent interest. Zeus's appreciation of Ganymede put the stamp of approval on marital relationships in which the man could have both a wife and a boy companion, the wife for procreation, the boy for pleasure. In the *Aeneid*, a boy is one of the causes of the Trojan War. The goddess of marriage, Juno, hates the Trojans not only for harboring Paris and Helen, but also for paying honors to Ganymede. And as we have seen, this is the arrangement Oberon wants in *A Midsummer Night's Dream*, and he and his wife Titania have a falling out when she refuses to yield her attendant, "a little changeling boy," to be his page. Oberon's response provides the mainspring of the action.

Although the Ganymede has only a slight bearing on the story of Aeneas, Christopher Marlowe exploits it to the fullest in his *Tragedy of Dido, Queen of Carthage*. In the opening scene, Jupiter dandles Ganymede on his knee, listens to the boy's complaint that Juno has slapped him, and assuages the boy's hurt pride by offering him the jewels that Juno wore on her wedding day. The gesture affirms the relative positions of wife and boy. Juno remains Jupiter's wife for practical reasons, but the adornments go to the pretty boy. In the usual arrangement, the husband would have a wife and a mistress. In Marlowe's ideal marriage, the husband has a wife to breed his children and a boy to give him pleasure.

In ancient Athens, Socrates and Plato added another dimension to boy love. The youth was no longer thought of as merely an enchanting creature, a source of pleasure. Knowledge was to be instilled in the boy, the boy paying for it with his charming presence. In this exchange quality of mind supplemented physical attractiveness, and pederasty was defined as a teaching relationship. This elevation of the youngster from the beautiful to the intellectual was signified by Zeus's rapture of Ganymede, an assumption from the terrestrial to a higher realm.

This ascension endowed the boy with a double nature, and it was this that gave rise to a problem in ethics and morality which might have been easily resolved if it had not occurred in a highly patriarchal society. The idealization of the young male, not the young female, reflected the prejudices of a society in which woman was seen as inferior to man. She was an earthy vessel necessary for the propagation of man's seed, and for that purpose she had to be penetrated. Subjecting a male to anal penetration was to reduce him to the level of woman, and not for a utilitarian purpose but mainly for selfish indulgence. Having transported Ganymede upwards to make him something more than a toy, boy lovers like Socrates could not debase him by treating him as a female. The sexual bond between two males had to have a spiritual element; otherwise it was barbarian, uncivilized, and too feminine. The problem confronting Greek pederasts was how to satisfy their physical urges without besmirching the ideal. The beautiful and the coprophilic made a disturbing combination.

Fortunately, man's capacity for inventing new social prohibitions and religious taboos has always been matched by his ingenuity in circumventing them. The Greek solution was first of all to insist that the two men should be in the relation of teacher and student to each other, with a considerable difference in their ages. That implied that the foundation of the relationship was primarily educational, not exploitative or physical. The older man would offer gifts, but he would also invite the younger man to symposia, banquets or drinking parties, where he would imbibe wine while taking in the thoughts of clever and influential men. Secondly, the younger partner should be in his teens because males were considered to be most beautiful at that age, their physical charm being a projection or radiation of their soul. At this age they were most androgynous. This meant that the union of the two men was not completely masculine, not male with male. The gently aggressive lover saw himself as communing with the boy's masculine soul while engaging physically with a somewhat effeminate body, thus maintaining a sense of his own masculinity.

Under the conventions of these delicate rituals, the line between acceptable sexual behavior was crossed when the male organ penetrated either the mouth or anus of the sexual partner. The most extreme act allowable was intercrural copulation, the insertion of the penis between the boy's thighs. This was seen as preserving the dignity of both parties by striking a balance between brutish sex and genuine fondness, between man's higher and lower centers. It was a fine compromise, well attested to in ancient literature.[52]

With the spread of Christianity, the tolerant attitude of the pagans gave way to a harsh condemnation of homosexual acts. For the

Greek pederast the problem was how to preserve the ideal from con-
tamination by lust; for Christian boy-lovers the problem was how
to save themselves from eternal damnation. The Greeks could write
about anal penetration and joke about it; for Christians the subject
was too damnable, too awful to be discussed or even described.

ALTHOUGH the inhabitants of Sodom were punished by a wrath-
ful god for their sinful ways, an innocent reader of the Old Testament would find it difficult to specify what they actually did. Lot
surely sinned by offering his two daughters, who "have not known
a man," to the angry men storming his house. But that was not
what aroused God's anger. What sinful act the Sodomites committed was evidently far worse, something that merited the shower of
sulfur and fire that the Lord rained on the city. Exactly what they
did is not mentioned. Those who defined their sin as unnatural sex
had to connect dots that are greatly separated in the Bible. The sin
of "lying with a man as with a woman" is mentioned in Leviticus,
not in the story of Sodom. According to John Boswell, the eminent
authority on Christianity and homosexuality, a purely homosexual interpretation of the Sodom story is relatively recent.[53]

In the universe of human behavior, sodomy is a black hole.
Within it the gravitational pull of social and religious taboos, of ignorance and prejudice, prevent much light from escaping. In the
early days of Christianity it was difficult to find a clear definition
of sodomy. To know what sodomy was was already to know too
much. Anyone who wrote about it had to assert his ignorance of
the subject or find himself highly suspect. Yet the guardians of the
moral order recognized the horrible sin even if it came disguised as
ordinary sex. Giovanni Della Casa (1503-1556), bishop of Beneven-
to, Italy, was the author of some unremarkable books on proper social conduct and of some sonnets distinguished for their melancholy tone, which, as one critic noted, may have been "engendered
by the follies of his youth."[54] Unwanted notoriety came his way
with *Il forno*, ostensibly about sex with a woman, the furnace
(*forno*) being the woman's vagina. But he wasn't explicit; the
vagueness implied sodomy, and the furnace was understood to be

the male anus. Della Casa was denied admittance to the Sacred College because of this.

Hovering over the subject was the fear that writing about it might encourage it. The subject was to be avoided at all costs. The church preferred ignorance to knowledge, following the example of Solon, the lawgiver of ancient Athens, who set down no law against parricide, fearing that it might give unhappy sons some horrible ideas. (Consider Samuel Pepys in seventeenth-century London who upon hearing that buggery was becoming very common among the gallants of the town professed not to know what buggery was. His professed ignorance is belied by his going on to say that he did not know who was the "agent" and who the "patient" in the commission of this sin.[55])

Not until the eleventh century did Christian theologians specify homosexual mating as sodomy. It was then that Peter Damian, a friar in a community of hermits, addressed Pope Leo IX in a booklet in which he described four varieties of what he considered sodomitic acts: masturbation, mutual masturbation, intercrural copulation, and anal penetration. Damian aggressively expanded the definition of sodomy and argued that even masturbation should be sufficient cause for dismissal from the clergy.[56]

Church doctrine and banishment was one thing; the Bible and damnation was another. What Christian homosexuals had to contend with was the real possibility of the eternal fires of damnation. However, the Christians, like the Greeks, soon found that just as there were varieties of sodomy, there were different degrees of punishment. Looking for loopholes in the register of sins, they saw that it might be possible to express their love physically without going to hell. There was, if Dante may be taken as an authority, a sharp distinction to be made between those who would plunge into the abyss and those who would stand on the very edge of it. In his treatment of the sin of sodomy in *The Divine Comedy*, Dante consigned his admired friend and teacher Brunetto Latini to the seventh circle of hell, the place for those who sin against nature (*Inferno*, cantos 15-16). Yet he committed the gay poet Guido Guinicelli to Purgatory, where sins could be purged away. Why the different judgment? It was because Brunetti was a sodomite pure and simple, lusting after boys for sexual release, whereas Guinicelli loved boys solely for their beauty.

In the seventh circle of Purgatory, Dante pictures two groups of gay men. They are moving in opposite directions, blowing kisses, some shouting "Sodom!" in acknowledgment of their errors. One group consists of active homosexuals, the other of passive homosexuals (tops and bottoms in modern gay jargon); hence they move in opposite directions. In the latter group are beautiful teen-agers, hermaphroditic in appearance, and they are likened to the mythical Queen Pasiphae, immortalized as the incarnation of unbridled lust. For her the fabulous artificer Daedalus constructed a wooden cow in which she might conceal herself. "Pasiphae enters the cow that the young bull may hasten to her rut," writes Dante (canto 26). In this passage Julius Caesar is called a queen and equated with Pasiphae, since as a boy he was sodomized by King Nicomedes of Bithnyia.

In the other group, which includes Guinicelli, are the worshippers of beauty. Though the two groups are opposite in one sense, they are united in Purgatory through beauty, either embodying it or idolizing it. Since physical beauty was seen as a reflection of heaven, these two groups are raised above those who like Brunetto Latini are destined for the Inferno.[57]

Guinicelli made his reputation as the poet of a refined love. "Love comes always to the gentle heart" ("*Al cor gentil ripara sempre Amore*"), he wrote in his most famous poem, which inaugurated a new style in Italian poetry. For him and his fellow poets in Bologna, love, in the words of John Addington Symonds in his history of the Italian Renaissance, "became the form of transcendental science; and here the Italian intellect touched, by accident or instinct, the same note that had been struck by Plato in the 'Phaedrus' and 'Symposium.' . . . For them it was natural that . . . love should be confounded with the movement of the soul toward truth; that beauty should be treated as a manifestation of a spiritual good."[58]

Attractive boys like the young Caesar, who was lusted after and seduced, were not damned, only punished. This was also true of the seducers, the aggressors, whose sin was not that they adored youthful male beauty but that they lost control of themselves. They confess that their love went beyond the spiritual. They violated the conventions of Platonic love – "We observed not human law" – and in doing so, they find themselves in Purgatory.

Both the ancient Greek and the medieval Christian gays managed to find a *modus vivendi*. The mental conflict that they had created for themselves by buying into and accepting the moral code and religious prohibitions of their times had to be resolved in one way or another. On the intellectual level there could, theoretically, be a rapprochement between physical sex and "the movement of the soul toward truth," an ascension of sorts to the divine, like Zeus's rapture of Ganymede. It meant settling for something less than anal penetration.

In the Christian era, the church drew a clear distinction between anal penetration and other kinds of male cohabitation and devised punishments commensurate with the sin. What in Dante was the difference between hell and purgatory, and in Peter Damian the difference between ostracism and ordination, became in church law the difference between fifteen years of penance and ninety days.[59] Naturally, the penalties varied from time to time and place to place. One penitential from the Middle Ages assigned seven years' penance for sodomy, four to seven years for fellation.[60] Since it was so difficult to make the punishment fit the crime, the penalties exacted were probably much less severe than the penalties prescribed.[61]

With the rebirth of the classical world, the educated and well-read gay man of Shakespeare's time would have a double view of sexual morality. In the church, he would find homosexuality to be an abomination; at university he would learn that it was a natural phenomenon. What the church condemned in the harshest terms, the classic poets and philosophers tolerated and even encouraged. In Aristotle's *Problems*, pretty much required reading for university students, he would read that anal penetration was a matter of individual preferences and natural constitutions, more specifically, a matter of fluids in the body. When the sexual fluid "finds its way to the fundament only, there is a desire to submit to sexual intercourse; but if it settles both there and in the sexual organs, there is a desire both for performing and submitting to the sexual act, and the desire for one or other is greater as more semen is present in either part. This condition is sometimes the result of habit; for men take a pleasure in whatever they are accustomed to do and emit semen accordingly. They therefore desire to do the acts by which pleasure and the emission of semen are produced, and habit becomes more and more a second nature. For this reason those who have been accustomed to submit to sexual intercourse about the age of puberty and not before, because recollection of the past presents itself to them during the act of copulation and with the recollection the idea of pleasure, desire to take a passive part owing to habit, as though it were natural to them to do so; frequent repetition, however, and habit become a second nature. All this is more likely to occur in the case of one who is both lustful and effeminate."[62]

University men who knew what the Bible said about sodomy would also be aware of what natural science said about it: that there are many men in whom the carnal itch is often anal.

For a gay man in Shakespeare's time, as for Hamlet, the time was out of joint, with pagan tolerance clashing with Christian condemnation. Shakespeare's sonnets cannot be fully understood without a knowledge of the ways men of a certain class in the time of Elizabeth and James thought about sex and of the ways in which belief and practice diverged from each other. The question is, how different was gay life in 1609 from what it is now. The general sexual nature of human beings probably has not changed much in a period of four hundred years, but sexual habits almost certainly have.

In the 1890s, when Oscar Wilde was on trial for homosexual offenses, Mrs. Pat Campbell, the unbigoted English actress, was asked what homosexuals do. She famously replied, "I don't care what they do, as long as they don't do it in the streets and frighten the horses." Her broadmindedness about intimate homosexual activity and her indifference to it were commendable but hardly typical at the time and have never been so. Historians of social culture have always been curious about abnormal and deviant sex, and the guardians of public morals, both in the courts and the churches, have always been greatly concerned. As for the lovers of Ganymede in Shakespeare's time, what they did to each other was of critical importance not only to the officers of the law but to themselves.

What men and boys have in ages past done to one another sexually in the privacy of their homes must remain something of a mystery, since the evidence is usually scanty and always of questionable reliability. Whatever evidence can be gleaned from legal records, personal letters, and journals has been sorted out and evaluated pretty thoroughly during the past half century by historians specializing in sexual culture. Not surprisingly, their findings fall into two schools, the one saying that homoerotic desire and practice have not changed radically since the early Renaissance, any more than the human being as a physical being has, while the opposing school insists that homoerotic practice, if not desire, has been affected by changes in social habits and conventions.[63]

Homosexuals of the past, says B. R. Burg, "engaged in patterns of sexual gratification widely different from those employed by present-day groups." He attributes the differences mainly to habits of personal cleanliness. The availability of more soap and water along with the spread of the practice of circumcision meant that the private parts became less distasteful in every sense. "The distinct preference of Americans for fellatio may be due in part to the universal practice of infant circumcision in the United States," says Burg. The English, in contrast, "prefer genital apposition or very close body contact without penetration as a means to achieve ejaculation. The terms 'ruboff' and 'slicklegging' are usually used to describe their practices."[64] Another investigator says this practice was called the English method because of its "common occurrence among boys in British 'public' schools."[65]

If physical cleanliness and fastidiousness were in fact the primary considerations affecting sexual activity, Burg's theory might afford an insight into the sexual culture of the court of James I. But sexual practices have as often as not been associated with uncleanliness. Yeats expressed poetically in "Crazy Jane Talks with the Bishop" what every human being has noticed at one time or anoth-

er: "Love has pitched his mansion in / The place of excrement."
The house of sex seems to have remained the same over the years,
regardless of changes in the surrounding landscape. In fifteenth-
century Italy, especially in Florence, which was notorious
throughout Europe, sodomy, taken to mean either anal coitus or
fellatio, was not uncommon, with adolescents almost always being
the passive participants. And in sixteenth-century France, in the
court of Henri III, homosexuality in the modern understanding
was pervasive. "Ganymede" was the term for a young man who
took part, actively or passively, in anal intercourse. The king himself had numerous male lovers; marriage among courtiers was frequently a front for homosexual partnerships; and anal penetration
and mutual masturbation were the acts of choice. Apart from a lack
of interest in fellatio, the gay men in the court of Henri III would
be at home in an American metropolis in the year 2000.[66]

London, however, was different. It was neither Florence nor
Paris. There is nothing in the English annals comparable to what
one finds in Italian legal documents or French memoirs. Yet London, like any large city, had an active homosexual subculture, not
only in the court of King James but in the purlieus of the theaters.
There were even male brothels, "malekind Stewes," as Michael
Drayton called them (in "The Moone-Calf"), where boys were
available for sex. Pathic and catamite were terms for the passive
partner, catamite being a corruption of the name Ganymede, just
as the boy for hire was a degraded version of Zeus's cupbearer.[67]

However difficult it may be to determine exactly what was
practiced among the English nobility, it is easy to determine what
was professed. The poets of the time wrote about Socratic love,
and King James in his letters and in his public behavior expressed
the Ganymedean credo: the simultaneous avowal of love of young
men and the disavowal of coition with them. It was sex not only
sanitized but enshrined. The English Ganymede might resemble
the French Ganymede, the *mignon*, in being young and pretty, but
he differed in being impenetrable. He was as much soul as body.
Although he could be adored, embraced, and kissed, copulation
could not go beyond thighs and lips. There was a great gulf fixed

between anal and interfemoral copulation, as great as between Aphrodite Pandemos and Aphrodite Uranus, as between fleshly and spiritual love. (Gay men were called Uranians before they were labeled homosexuals.[68])

Whatever part cleanliness played in formulating this code of homoerotic love, the main influence was the Christian division of body and soul. The ideal was the union of the two, a restoration of the original oneness, and the closest one could come to this on earth was the androgynous teen-ager, innocent in thought, with a face angelic and beardless. To love him without violating him afforded the highest ecstasy.

When Shakespeare published his collected sonnets, he would have known members of the king's circle and been imbued with its homoerotic atmosphere. There is nothing in the sonnets addressed to the Fair Youth that ran counter to the beliefs entertained by the Ganymedeans.

To the gay males of today, those beliefs may seem incredibly puritanical and restrictive. Consequently, when an interpreter of the sonnets reads twentieth-century attitudes and practices into them, the results are far-fetched and inconsistent with what is known about Shakespeare's time. Joseph Pequiney, who assumes that the poet not only desired the Fair Youth physically but also satisfied that desire, finds hidden allusions to carnal copulation where no one has found them before. In the innocent lines, "So am I as the rich whose blessed key / Can bring him to his sweet uplocked treasure" (52), Pequiney sees the "blessed key" as the poet's penis and the "uplocked teasure" as either the boy's posterior or his semen.[69] Cardinal Richelieu boasted, "Give me half a page of any man's writing, and I'll find matter in it to hang him." Two lines suffice for Pequiney to convict Shakespeare of sodomy.

Sonnet 20, the "master-mistress" sonnet, poses a real problem for those who believe that the poet went all the way physically with the young man. "Prick" cannot be decoded, and the poet's denial that it was the object of his passion cannot be glossed over. The historical survey of sexual customs confirms what an unforced reading of the sonnets tell us. What Shakespeare says in this sonnet is entirely in line with what he says throughout the Fair Youth sonnets. The poems mean what they say, and what they say is consistent with the sexual credo and mores of the court of King James.

If masculine embraces could go only as far as interfemoral copulation without overstepping the limits of Socratic love, it would go a long way toward explaining the fine line that Elizabethan and Jacobean society drew between the barely tolerable and the totally unacceptable in homosexual activity. It would help to reconcile King James's condemnation of sodomy with his blatant displays of affection for men.

It might also explain the curious death of Adonis in Shakespeare's poem. *Venus and Adonis* relies for much of its effect on the use of polite and refined language to create highly erotic images. Easily identifiable parts of the goddess's body are likened to hills, fountains, and valley grass (lines 229-238). This kind of sexual symbolism is at work in Adonis's death scene. He dies when the boar he has been hunting nuzzles as with a kiss his tusk into the boy's flank. "The loving swine / Sheath'd unaware the tusk in his soft groin" (lines 1115-6). If orgasm is the little death – Venus says, "With kissing him I should have kill'd him first" (line 1118) – then Adonis "dies" while engaging in intercrural intercourse, in the contemporary English fashion, with the boar's deadly thrust made to seem gently invasive. The gay readers of the poem, having put up with a thousand lines of heterosexual amorousness only by identifying with Venus, were finally rewarded for their patience at the end by a consummation that only they could fully savor. Loving swine! — sheathed unaware!! – his tusk!!! – in his soft groin!!!! As a realistic depiction of a hunter being gored to death by an enraged beast, the words make no sense. Only as an explicit image of gay sex does their meaning leap from the page.

Shakespeare was not the first to see the sexual symbolism in the peculiar death of Adonis. The Greek pastoral poet Theocritus (3rd century B.C.) in one of his idylls pictured the boar as madly in love with the very sight of Adonis. He rushes to kiss his naked thigh, forgetting that his tusk might do irreparable harm. Cursed by Venus for killing Adonis, he tries to explain. "I minded not to kill,

/ But as an image still, / I him beheld for love, / Which made me forward shove / His thigh, that naked was, / Thinking to kisse alas." Translated anonymously in 1588, this idyll, along with five others, probably became familiar fare to the gay set in the 1590s.[70]

WHEN intercrural copulation becomes an accepted practice between an older man and a youth, the center of attraction is displaced from the genitals to the thighs. According to Aeschylus, when Patroclus was slain by Hector in a duel that might have been avoided, the bereaved Achilles upbraided his lover: "You did not care about my reverence for your thighs. How badly you have returned my many kisses!" In a fragment of a lost play by Sophocles, it was especially Ganymede's thighs that aroused Zeus.

In spite of the severe law against sodomy, there were very few convictions or even indictments for the crime during the reigns of Elizabeth and James because the legal definition of sodomy explicitly stipulated penetration. If a man had an orgasm in the company of another man, he might be innocent of any crime against nature. Amplifying the old English prohibition against sodomy and buggery, the lawmakers in the early seventeenth century noted that "emissio seminis maketh it not Buggery, but is evidence in case of Buggery of penetration: and so in Rape the words be also carnaliter cognovit, and therefore there must be penetration: and emissio seminis without penetration maketh no Rape."[71] Unless the lovers were caught *flagrante delicto* or one partner informed against the other, it was difficult to prove that penetration had occurred. The result was that very few men were prosecuted and condemned for sodomitical practices, a fact that makes it impossible for the historian of sexual customs to ascertain how much homosexual activity, and of what sort, actually took place. Oddly enough, the line that an English jurist drew between what was indictable and what was not was very close to the line that the Greek pederast drew between permissible and impermissible sex. Though they differed totally on the moral aspects of sodomy, they were essentially in agreement as regards non-criminal sexual practices.

WHEN James slobbered over his male favorites in full view of people at the court, a true believer in the purity of male love would take the fondling and the kisses as no more than the mundane manifestation of the higher love, in the same way that the selection of the prettiest lads as altar boys is taken as a recognition of spiritual qualities. Others, however, would take it as blatant evidence of a perverse, unnatural affection, a public manifestation of heinous acts performed in private, just as over-elaborate clothing, frizzled hair, excessive jewelry, and languid gestures would point in the same direction.

If the term "gay" is taken to cover the broad spectrum of male love, it is impossible to say how many gay men in Shakespeare's time actually engaged in homosexual acts involving penetration and how many would have been disgusted with such acts. How many gay men of the time were deeply conflicted and self-deluded? Were they in fact using ideal male love as a cloak to conceal their deepest urges? When King James warned his eldest son Henry against "filthy Lecherie" and when he reinforced the laws against sodomy while at the same time installing handsome young fellows as gentlemen of his bedchamber, was he being consciously duplicitous, exploiting his position of power to do what was forbidden to others? Did Shakespeare compose his sonnet 20 in order to fend off any suspicion of sodomitical inclinations? Or were they all being quite sincere?

They probably were. Like many cultured gay men of the time, living during an era and in a society in which Christian values were increasingly being challenged by a resurgence of ancient pagan attitudes, they developed a special complex that allowed them to reconcile the sin of liking their own sex with the Christian preference for the soul over the body. Marlowe, an exception, took male sex unadulterated and uninhibitedly tossed Christianity out the window; avowed that John the Beloved was "bedfellow to Christ" and that "he used him as the sinners of Sodoma."[72] Instead of nuzzling young men as King James did, Marlowe apparently bedded the boys he took home. (His daring frankness in talking in public about his love for adolescent males was more dangerous than what he actually did in bed. The deed could not be proved without an eyewitness, but his public braggadocio was a confession.) More typically, Elizabethan gay men found in Ganymede, the beautiful Trojan boy, an icon that resolved the basic contradictions and embraced both Christian soulfulness and pagan sensuality. To enlightened gay men in Shakespeare's time, Ganymede represented "a wise and understanding Soule, uncontaminated with the vices of the flesh;" hence he was "rapt" into heaven by the Olympian god.[73] Ganymede was transported into the empyrean because of the beauty of his mind, so certain gay men in Shakespeare's time believed. As one of them wrote, "For who that hath read Plato . . . may easily perceive that such love is much to be allowed and liked of, specially so meant as Socrates used it: who saith that indeed he loved Alcibiades extremely, yet not Alcibiades' person but his soul, which is Alicibiades' own self. And so is pederasty much to be preferred before gynerasty, that is the love which enflameth men with lust toward woman kind."

But the writer is very careful to distinguish pederasty from sodomy. "Yet let no man think that herein I stand with Lucian and his devilish disciple [the Italian libertine] Unico Aretino in defense of execrable and horrible sins of forbidden and unlawful fleshliness."[74]

CHAPTER 5

Socratic Love

T HE FULL spectrum of meaning in the sonnets cannot be appreciated unless they are seen through the prism of Socratic love. Shakespeare was so well known to his friends for his sexual inclinations that he is described on his funeral monument as a Socrates in disposition. The teachings of the Greek philosopher underscore the frequently emphasized connection in the sonnets between immortality and beauty, and they also furnish the background to the dramatic conflict that forms the central part of the sequence. Another poet is vying for the attention of the young man, competing with Shakespeare in verse of intimidating power. Did that rival share Shakespeare's view of love? Was he competing for the attentions of the Fair Youth on the same playing field of homoeroticism, or was he countering Shakespeare with a more conventional philosophy of love? Readers of the sonnets in 1609, most of them, surely, would have sensed how Shakespeare was presenting himself as a Socrates to the young man.

From the priestess Diotima, Socrates learned that there are two Aphrodites, two kinds of love, the heavenly and the earthly. The heavenly love has a noble purpose, is not wanton, and does not change with time. The earthly love is the love of the physical body. This is true of both heterosexual and homosexual love. The love of man for woman has as its main purpose the breeding of children, the preservation of the bloodline and the race. In contrast, the love of a man for a man is the attraction of one soul for another, and consequently it partakes of the divine.

Although this vision of perfection is not unlike Dante's Paradise, there is a crucial difference. For Dante, God is Love, the power that moves the stars. For Socrates, love is a daimon, neither mortal nor immortal, but something between the two. Love desires the beautiful, just as it desires happiness. More specifically, it desires the birth of beauty; it seeks to preserve it and make it eternal. Men "are ravished with the desire of the immortal." (Plato, *Symposium* 208.)

In the practical application of this philosophy of love, an older man takes into his care for guidance and tutoring a teen-age youth in whom he senses a noble soul and teaches him a philosophy that unites esthetics and morality. From fair forms to virtuous actions, from virtuous actions to noble thoughts, and from noble thoughts to absolute beauty – these are the steps to the paradise envisioned by Socrates. This is the educational process that affords a closer, more spiritual friendship and attachment than that which begets mortal children.

The higher love envisioned by Socrates, the mingling of male beauty and divine wisdom, runs through Western culture from its ancient sources up to the present era, with its currents usually purling through subterranean caverns hidden from the view of most citizens. It is always present but comes into view when artists extol its virtues. This was the case in Shakespeare's time, with other poets beside Shakespeare expressing the Socratic ideal. It was again very much a part of cultured life in the Romantic era.

Richard Wagner, aspiring to bring modern culture to the level attained by the ancient Greeks, praised "the love of man to man," averring that it "proclaims itself as the noblest and least selfish utterance of man's sense of beauty, for it teaches man to sink and merge his entire self in the object of his affection. . . . The higher element of that love of man to man consisted even in this: that it excluded the motive of egoistic physicalism. Nevertheless it not only included a purely spiritual bond of friendship, but this spiritual friendship was the blossom and crown of the physical friendship. The latter sprang directly from delight in the beauty, aye, in the material, bodily beauty of the beloved comrade; yet this delight was no egoistic yearning, but a thorough stepping out of self into unreserved sympathy with the comrade's joy in himself, involuntarily betrayed by his life-glad, beauty-prompted bearing. This love, which had its basis in the noblest pleasures of both eye and soul . . . was the Spartan's only tutoress of youth, the never aging instructress alike of boy and man, the ordainer of the common feasts and valiant enterprises; nay, the inspiring helpmeet on the battlefield."[75]

To make the process effective required a mature man full of noble thoughts and a young man in the formative stage of his life, susceptible to the older man's teachings, while the older man must be susceptible to the charms of the youth. Just as the sexual activity itself had to balance the carnal against the spiritual, resulting in sex without penetration, so the ages of the two men had to demonstrate the tutelary aspect of the relationship. The older man had to be fully mature in mind and body, the younger should ideally be on the verge of manhood. Pre-pubescent boys were strictly off-limits. An incipient beard, nothing more than light down on the cheek, provided the outward sign of inner readiness, an indication that the youth has attained the age of reason. After the beard sprouted, physical intercourse was deemed improper and unseemly. The relative ages of the two was so vital to the relationship that Plato had to revise and correct Aeschylus who described Patroclus as the beloved of Achilles. This could not be the case, said Plato, because Achilles was the younger of the two, and hence he must be the beloved (*Symposium* 179). From his older companion, Achilles learned true virtue, and on that account he was bound to avenge the slaying of Patroclus, and for that deed the gods awarded him a place in the Isles of the Blessed. (Homer offers no clear evidence as to which is the older.)[76] In Homer, the charm of youth is fairest when the first down appears upon the lips (*Iliad* 24: 347-8).

The "rose" of the *Sonnets* is just such a young man when he first appears, "the world's fresh ornament / And only herald to the gaudy spring" (1), while the adoring poet portrays himself as in his forties (2). The sense of age difference runs through all the sonnets written to the Fair Youth. The poet is the older man, offering the gift of immortality through his verse in exchange for a vision of the divine. There could be no talk of patronage; the relationship could not be tainted with material interests. "Mutual render, only me for thee," says the poet (125).

The best concise description of the emotions felt by Shakespeare in his sonnets to the Fair Youth is to be found in Socrates' explanation, given to Phaedrus, his fair youth, of the origin of love. He speaks of the love of masculine beauty as if it were the only love, a power stronger than devotion to family, desire for children, respect for social proprieties, or the companionship of friends. Its power comes from its being a recollection of the origin of the human soul in heaven.[77]

If the poet's soul is relatively uncorrupted by its descent to earth, if its memory of "the many glories in the other world" is still fresh and pure, the poet will be "amazed when he sees anyone having a godlike face or form, which is the expression or imitation of divine beauty; and at first a shudder runs through him, and some 'misgiving' of a former world steals over him; then looking upon the face of his beloved as of a god he reverences him, and if he were not afraid of being thought a downright madman, he would sacrifice to his beloved as to the image of a god." The shudder of delight causes wings to grow, and that is why Eros is depicted with wings, wings that are meant to carry him upward to the divine, the source of all beauty. (Plato, *Phaedrus*, 251, Jowett translation.)

To some these views were enlightened and admirable; to others they were unnatural and detestable. This difference in moral outlook has always affected the way in which the sonnets have been read. Sex obsessed roués who regularly committed adultery and ravaged women might be immoral, but men who loved men with a divine love passed beyond immorality into incomprehensibility. The special nature of this love and the claim that it was superior to other kinds set its believers apart from the rest of society. It also imparted to Shakespeare's sonnets that strange aura in which it is difficult to tell whether an excessive adulation encroaches on the forbidden or the divine.

The niceties of homosexual congress were part of an intellectual and social construct that was meant to deal with certain natural but relatively uncommon urges by making them appear to be lofty and ethical. The Ganymede worshipper knew he was different from others. He had to accommodate his transgressive desires to society's standards of proper behavior. The result of this strata-gem was that he created a challenging situation for himself by in-sisting that he was first of all a teacher or substitute father, not a predator. Like Socrates, he replaced the civic and religious inhibi-tions against sodomy with a philosophical prohibition, placing himself on a higher moral plane than the ordinary man, all the while prudently allowing himself some room for error, for some in-advertent lapse when the horses of desire slipped their reins. If the older male succumbed momentarily to his baser impulses, he still might find a place in heaven, but man and boy could then never be as dear to each other as purely philosophical lovers. If in some care-less hour, caught off their guard, they behave like wanton animals and "accomplish that desire of their hearts which to the many is bliss," they are no longer philosophically minded and can never soar to heaven. Only the desire for the divine gives one the neces-sary wings, the wings of Ganymede.

If the lovers "leave philosophy," says Socrates, " and lead the lower life of ambition, then, probably in the dark or in some other careless hour, the two wanton animals take the two souls when off their guard, and bring them together, and they accomplish that desire of their hearts which to the many is bliss; and this having once enjoyed they continue to enjoy, yet rarely because they have not the approval of the whole soul. They too are dear, but not so dear to one another as the others, either at the time of their love or afterwards. They consider that they have given and taken from each the most sacred pledges, and they may not break them and fall into enmity."(*Phaedrus*, 256.)

This combination of philosophy and sex made for a subtle dis-tinction between sodomy and other amatory activities, drawing a line that could not be crossed without shattering the philosophical ideal. Between the desire and the fulfillment loomed the specter of sodomy. Both the refined gay man of Shakespeare's time and the Greek pederast of a Socratic persuasion often settled for intercrur-al copulation in which the physical act reflected the balance between contemplation of the divine and copulation with it. Cicero, remarking on the tolerance of pederasty in some parts of Greece, described precisely what was tolerated. "How free and easy are their contacts and love relations! To say nothing of the Eleans and Thebans, among whom lust is actually given free rein in the relations of free men, the Spartans themselves, who give every freedom to love relations with young men except that of actual defilement, protect only by a very thin wall this one exception; for, providing only that cloaks be interposed, they allow embraces and the sharing of the bed."[78] That thin wall made all the difference; safe sex required its protection.

In the Christian era when sodomy was totally proscribed and its practitioners condemned by Dante to the seventh circle of hell, would-be sodomites knew that their inclinations brought them close to perdition. Yet many of them could not resist their passions. Men like Christopher Marlowe were the exceptions, at least among the educated classes. The others, those with a strong sense of sin, indulged in sex practices or sexual imaginings that lacked fulfillment, perplexed and troubled either by their longings or by their consciences. From their writings it is hard to tell whether they were having sex without enjoying it or enjoying sex without having it.

It is easy to read the sonnet cycle as the confession of a homosexual man with a passion for pubescent boys and a concern for his public reputation, that is, as the insincere confession of a Ganymede worshipper. The often fulsome language of the poems, the servility of the poet toward the boy, and the concomitant lowering of the woman to the status of a convenient sexual receptacle, all support this interpretation.

However, with the Socratic doctrine in mind, another reading is possible. The sublime lyricism along with the occasional severe criticism of the Fair Youth, putting the poet in the position of tutor or counselor (as in sonnets 69 and 94) or a father figure (as in sonnet 37), and the association of physical sex with the plain woman and not with the boy, suggest that the poet worships physical beauty only as a manifestation of the divine, as the incarnation of ultimate truth. This interpretation is consistent with the cycle as a whole. Its framework is philosophical, and the narrative it contains describes a frantic longing for truth and beauty – and its futility. Looking into the boy's eyes, the poet believes for the moment that "truth and beauty shall together thrive" (14). He places his faith in his imagination, and, as in Keats, "what the imagination seizes as beauty must be truth – whether it existed before or not."

This fantasy, embraced as if it were religious dogma, calls to mind Thomas Mann's poet, Aschenbach, in *Death in Venice*, and, by way of contrast, Marcel Proust's Baron de Charlus. Aschenbach and Charlus occupy opposite points in the gamut of homosexual experience. Proust's decadent aristocrat secretly pursued pugilists and bus conductors. Their sweaty odor and their proletarian coarseness made them particularly alluring to the effete baron, whose sexual excitement came from lowering himself to their social and hygienic level. Shakespeare was the opposite. He abased himself with women, finding in some of them what the baron found in certain men. With men, Shakespeare looked upwards. His Fair Youth was of the nobility, spiritually and socially.

Reading the sonnets as arranged in the 1609 Quarto, one cannot help but feel that Shakespeare intended, either early or late in the project, to run the whole gamut of sexual passions. Read cursorily, they can seem repetitious and monotonous; read carefully, they reveal an inexorable movement from the brightest aspects of sexual attraction to the darkest.

Charlus was one of those whose love "springs not from an ideal of beauty which they have chosen but from an incurable disease."[79] Nothing could be further from Shakespeare's estheticism. But Mann's hero lives in the same ethereally erotic atmosphere as the poet of the sonnets, pursuing the same dream, entranced by the same kind of youngster, transported by the same Socratic sentiments. Aschenbach finds in the fourteen-year-old Tadzio the "expression of pure and godlike serenity. Yet with all this chaste perfection of form it was of such unique personal charm that the observer thought he had never seen, either in nature or art, anything so utterly happy and consummate." What Shakespeare saw in the

[73]

Fair Youth, Mann saw in Tadzio: "beauty's very essence; form as divine thought, the single and pure perfection which resides in the mind, of which an image and likeness, rare and holy, was here raised up for adoration."

For Mann, living in an age when the heavens had been nearly emptied of the divine element, this love of beauty is a form of death in life. On this point Mann departs from the ancient Greeks, and from Shakespeare. The apartness of Aschenbach, his solitariness, and his inability to seize beauty bring him each day in cholera-ridden Venice closer to an acceptance of death. The worship of beauty does not lead to a higher sphere, only to nothingness. He would "snatch up this beauty into the realms of the mind, as once the eagle bore the Trojan shepherd aloft."[80] But in fact he never takes any action; he never approaches the teen-age boy; never writes a poem to him. Shakespeare, on the other hand, did what Zeus did; he swept his Ganymede up to the heavens on his wings. At least, he tried to.

Plato's *Symposium* became known in England principally through the lengthy commentary on it, published in the fifteenth century, by the Italian philosopher, teacher, astrologer, and Grecophile Marsilio Ficino. During the reign of James I, the theologian Thomas Jackson made this commentary the subject of his lectures at Oxford. Ficino, who took holy orders, neatly blended together Christian and Socratic concepts of the higher love and established a connection between sensual delight in beauty and access to God. In Ficino's interpretation of Neoplatonism, the ray of beauty emanates from God, passes through the soul as if it were glass, and floods into the body prepared to receive it. From the body of the younger male, it shines out, especially through the eyes, which are the windows of the soul, and thence penetrates the eyes of the older man, pierces his soul, and kindles his appetites. The wounded soul then seeks to heal itself by reaching back to the place from which it descended and in which it had its origin, God Himself. The soul and the body are joined together by means of the spirit — a very thin and clear vapor produced by the heat of the heart from the thinnest part of the blood.

Those who seek the heavenly love, quite distinct from carnal love, prefer men to women, and adolescents to pre-teenage children. Actual copulation would of course destroy the whole fragile scheme. Love is understood to be the desire for beauty; but the desire for gross sexual congress is the opposite of love. Although the attraction felt by the older man for the younger occurs through the five senses, the attraction must be fundamentally an intellectual one. The appeal to the mind comes through the eyes and the ears, whereas the senses of taste, touch, and smell, being entirely physical, can only appeal to lust.[81]

Such beliefs constituted the faith of many of the devotees of Ganymede. They were a varied lot, ranging in their actual behavior from the meritorious to the flagitious. What defined them as a group was their conviction that divine beauty was incarnated in the androgyne – not a pure androgyne, however, but one in whom male attributes were dominant. Altogether representative of this Ganymedean ideal was the incomparable youth of the sonnets, a mingling of Adonis and Helen (sonnet 53). What made this teenager representative of the ideal was that he was more Adonis than Helen. It was his boyishness, his masculinity, that presented a dilemma for the Ganymedeans. For them, the idol had to be essentially male because females lacked soul (although, paradoxically, the soul was often thought of as feminine). Taking as their gospel the teachings of Plato and Socrates, they separated heavenly love from the terrestrial, the noble from the vulgar. In the former, two souls embraced each other; in the earthly love one body physically invaded the other. What created a problem was that the Ganymedeans connected beauty of soul with beauty of form. When the souls embraced, the senses could not be dismissed. They had to be accepted and transcended, treated as a means to an end.

From Plato they derived the concept, typical in Renaissance writings, that the beauty of a young man is more likely to excite "the amorous desire of the intellect" than the physical attractions of a young woman.[82] This philosophical view of male attractiveness clashed with what society considered normal and acceptable. To those who did not share the esthetic view of the Platonists, all talk about male souls embracing each other seemed like a nefarious, underhanded scheme that sought to give legitimacy to a depraved kind of fleshly love. The ordinary man, eager to raise a family and not strongly drawn to beautiful things, would regard the infatuation with boys as at best an anomaly and at worst a terrible sin, condemned by both Christian teachings and English law. It was difficult for him to believe that the act of love as he understood and practiced it would not be pretty much the same with the Ganymedeans, copulative and orgasmic. A love that began with sensual excitement but that deliberately avoided the satisfaction of sensual fulfillment, a love that was all longing and always incomplete, seemed either perverse or incomprehensible or both. To bring it within the understanding of the ordinary man, it had to involve sexual release, and that made it corrupt and degenerate. For him, Platonic love was Ganymedean palaver, a cloak for sodomy, pure and simple.

Even the ancients, tolerant as they were of homosexuals, saw what lay behind the replacement in Greek mythology of the young maiden Hebe by the young boy Ganymede as cupbearer to Zeus. They shared Cicero's skepticism. "Why is it no one is in love with either an ugly youngster or a beautiful old man? For my part I think this practice had its origin in the Greek gymnasia where that kind of love-making was free and permitted. Well then did Ennius say, 'Shame's beginning is the stripping of men's bodies openly.' . . .Who has . . . any doubt of the meaning of the poet in the tale of the rape of Ganymede. . . . What disclosures . . . do men of the highest culture and poets of supreme merit make about their own life in their poems and songs."[83]

Undoubtedly, there were always Ganymedeans who were active pederasts and who concealed their activities under the transparent cloak of Platonic ideas. In the court of James I they might feel fairly comfortable, more inclined to "come out" than at any previous time in English history, with the king himself caressing handsome young men for all to see. In effect, the court of King James was a revival of the Greek symposium. However, that royal sanction did not deter some observers from issuing warnings against this depravity. In a volume of moralizations, *Minerva Britanna*, dedicated to Henry, the king's eldest son, Henry Peacham, whose profession was tutoring young men for university, specifically cautioned the teen-ager against these Ganymedeans, who were all around him.

Upon a Cock, heere *Ganimede* doth sit,
Who erst rode mounted on JOVES Eagles back,
One hand holdes *Circes* wand, and joined with it,
A cup top-fil'd with poison, deadly black:
   The other Meddals, of base mettals wrought,
   With sundry moneyes, counterfeit and nought.

These be those crimes, abhorr'd of God and man,
Which Justice should correct, with lawes severe,
In *Ganimed*, the foule Sodomitan:
Within the Cock, vile incest doth appeare:
   Witchcraft, and murder, by that cup and wand,
   And by the rest, false coine you understand.[84]

FIGURE 4. Ganymede upon a Cock. From Henry Peacham, *Minerva Britanna*, 1612.

For skeptics like Peacham, not inclined to be beguiled by Platonic cant, the bird carrying Ganymede aloft was not Zeus's eagle but a cock! (See Figure 4.)

A learned man, Peacham probably knew his Greek; etymologically, Ganymede could mean "rejoicing in his genitals."

For the true Ganymedean, however, Jove's eagle was just an elevating spirit, and it transported him to heaven. The mind of the philosopher-lover acquired wings when it contemplated earthly beauty, and it took flight when it recollected heavenly beauty.

Still, the intimate relation of a mature man and a young boy was always socially questionable and morally problematic. Richard Barnfield in a poem, "The Complaint of Daphnis for the Love of Ganimede," written at about the same time as Shakespeare's *Venus and Adonis*, declares his love for a "sweet-faced boy", whose "ivory-white and alabaster skin / Is stained throughout with rare vermilion red," and offers him gifts of all sorts to woo him away from a woman. He knows that his love is unorthodox and socially unacceptable. "If it be sin to love a lovely lad; / Oh then sin I, for whom my soul is sad." Nevertheless, he justifies his love because the boy's beauty is a distillation of the boy's soul. "I love thee for thy gifts, she for her pleasure; / I for thy virtue, she for beauty's treasure," lines faintly echoed in Shakespeare's sonnet 20. ("But since she pricked thee out for women's pleasure, / Mine be thy love, and thy love's use their treasure.") Physical contact between the poet and the boy only goes so far, even in his imaginings, only to the point of making "my bosom thy bed."[85]

CHAPTER 6

Body and Soul

THE heterosexual male and the Ganymedean gay man had one important thing in common: they shared the same religious values and beliefs. They both had to contend with the Christian dichotomy of body and soul, hell and heaven, damnation and salvation. They both believed that in the act of love, body and soul should be made one. And they both believed that men possessed more soul than women did. However, the simple union of body and soul was complicated by another factor: the belief that men were more like angels than women were. "Just such disparity," said Donne, "As is 'twixt air and angels' purity, / 'Twixt women's love and men's will ever be."

The situation of the homosexual was more awkward than that of the straight man. For him the problem of body and soul was complicated by the fact that both church and state condemned his liking for handsome young men as ungodly and unnatural. In tracing the progress of the human soul, John Donne went out of his way to denounce men who were captivated by beautiful boys. Their fondness for the features of teen-age lads could only lead to sodomy. "Sins against kind," he wrote, "they easily do, that can let feed their minds / With outward beauty; beauty they in boys and beasts do find."

The Ganymedean tried to accommodate himself to society by insisting that his kind of love was as pure as the normal man's devotion to the Madonna. In both cases, the human being was attempting to raise himself above his animal nature. In the sex act, however, the soul had to lower itself. "So must pure lovers' souls descend / To affections and to faculties," said Donne. For just that reason, the Ganymedeans considered themselves superior to the average male. They didn't descend into the flesh quite so far.

STILL, for homosexual men there was always the difficulty of keeping their sexual drives within the proper channels. When did two men embracing each other become too much like sex with a woman? What the Bible forbade was a man lying with a man as with a woman. For men like King James there was no sin in lying with a man as long as there was no penetration. This meant that there could be an intimate form of physical contact leading to orgasm without a terrible sin being committed. It all depended on how narrowly one defined sodomy. When James explicitly warned his eldest son Henry against sodomites and when he defined sodomy as a crime that a king was "bounde in Conscience never to forgive,"[86] he must have seen a crucial difference between the biblical sin of sodomy and his own behavior with young men; for him sodomy must have meant anal penetration. This seems to be the most reasonable way of accounting for his expressed abhorrence of sodomy and his public display of homoerotic love.

There was a fine line drawn between what his conscience could tolerate and what it abhorred, between what his moral guide shied away from and what his temperament or physical constitution longed for. The intimate terms that King James used in his private correspondence shows how fine that line was. He ended a letter to his dear friend George Villiers, Duke of Buckingham, with "And so bless you, my sweet child and wife, and grant that ye may ever be a comfort to your dear dad and husband." The historian David Bergeron sees these family terms as raising "marriage to some higher power, earthly yet spiritual: a same sex marriage that James sees as wholly desirable." As to what lies behind these words, there is, as Bergeron notes, "a vexing problem of interpretation," of "trying to determine when metaphor ceases to be metaphor."[87]

These terms, wife and husband, dad and child, which in a homoerotic context must seem strange to a modern reader, formed part of the vocabulary of men whose friendships bordered on the forbidden. These metaphors revealed the ambiguity of their position on the sexual spectrum. There was both male bonding and sexual desire. The combination created an electric charge: the devotion of husband and wife, and of father and child, was intermingled with a physical desire for the masculine body. What generated the electricity was the underlying sexual desire that had to be simultaneously expressed and denied.

In the play *The Two Noble Kinsmen* (acted in 1613), co-authored by John Fletcher and Shakespeare, Arcite tells his close companion Palamon, "We are an endless mine to one another; / We are one another's wife, ever begetting / New births of love; we are father, friends, acquaintance, / We are, in one another, families"(2.2. 79-82). This passage suggests that when James calls Buckingham his wife, he was not being idiosyncratic; nor was he writing in a secret code. He was speaking a language that would have been understood by the broad theater-going public.

What sexual practices Arcite and Palamon indulged in when locked together in the same prison cell is clearly hinted at early in the play. There the friends of Greek mythology Theseus and Pirithous are described as ideal lovers, mature and rational in judgment, and "Their needs / The one of th'other may be said to water / Their entangled roots of love" (1.3.57-59). The image suggests genitals rubbing together, "slicklegging," as Burg calls it.

King James probably kept his Christian conscience clear while consorting with his favorites by indulging in intercrural sex and mutual masturbation, creating an atmosphere of permissible and regally sanctioned male love. In the hotbed of King James's court, gay men were more free to let their true feelings blossom and grow than they had ever been before in England. But these gay men were hardly all alike in their preferences.

There was, to take the most prominent examples, a difference between Shakespeare and King James as regards the objects of their affections. James's male companions were always mature men, whereas Shakespeare was drawn both to men his own age and to teenagers. Robert Carr was in his early twenties when James fell in love with him. He found in Robert Carr a near perfect friend and a willing sexual partner. But Carr was bisexual, at least in practice, if not by nature. While serving as the king's closest advisor, he became involved in a disastrous love affair with Frances Howard, the wife of the son of Elizabeth's former favorite, the earl of Essex. According to Francis Osborne, that invaluable purveyor of court gossip, Carr exhausted himself attending to the needs of both Frances Howard and the king. Osborne has Carr complaining, "I am so stifled with the unnatural heats of the old king – that I would exchange it for the fires on this side Hell."[88] Carr fit a type that obviously appealed to James. The king seems to have preferred men who were not exclusively gay, possibly because the man who, by most accounts, introduced the young James to male sex, Esmé Stuart, had been a thirty-seven-year-old married man with four children. A palpable masculinity evidently made these men more attractive to James; not for him the passive catamite, who participated in the horrible sin of sodomy. His male companions were not adolescents, not pubescent boys, but grown men who would become husbands and fathers. In his mind this legitimized the relationship by keeping it free of the taint of pederasty and its association with sodomy.

All the contradictions apparent in the sex life of the worshippers of Ganymede – the passion for young boys but without any tactile description of their bodies, King James's condemnation of sodomy while keeping male lovers, Shakespeare's adoration of the Fair Youth while disavowing any phallic interest in him, his disgust with the woman who aroused him sexually while he was the one who was unable to control his lust for her, copulating with the woman while hating her, loving the boy while avoiding sex with him – all these paradoxes were resolved by dividing the male being into two, making it a composite body and soul, while the woman was in essence only body. The masculine soul wanted to ascend, while the male body threatened to drag it down to the earthly level of the woman. That which made the man a man, the penis, was that which made him terrestrial. That paradox could not be resolved, but it was kept out of mind as much as possible. However, when the boy grew a beard, it could not be kept out of sight. The body exerted its dominance over the soul.

The ideal youth in ancient Athens had a small penis, while

satyrs and comic figures had large organs, which signified a lack of control and a submission to bestial, irrational drives.[89] The men in King James's court who loved adolescents as Socrates did probably entertained the same association of ideas. The exaltation of the soul was accompanied by a compensatory diminution of the penis. Shakespeare in sonnet 20 disclaimed any interest in the phallus of the Fair Youth, yet he would not have found him equally attractive as a prepubescent boy. The mindset of the worshippers of Ganymede was peculiarly ambiguous about the phallus. Typical of this ambiguity was James's behavior. He cautioned his son against eye-catching codpieces while constantly fingering his own.

The ideal erotic state found the lover suspended between admiration for the beauty of the adolescent boy and the embrace of it, between the desire and the deed. It was foreplay of the imagination. It was sex in the head, with women being degraded and treated as sex objects and teen-age boys glorified as angels. To keep their divine status, they had to be perceived as celestial non-sexual beings, who could only be described in rather abstract terms. Goethe's Mephistopheles, ready to claim Faust's soul, is deprived of his reward by being distracted at the moment of his triumph by the buttocks of angelic boys. Nothing like that is allowed to manifest itself with the Socratic worshippers of Ganymede.

THE POET of the sonnets was infatuated with a young man who, by all signs, was in his teens. Shakespeare chides him "for having traffic with thyself alone" (4), that is, masturbating, and thus "spend[ing] / Upon thyself thy beauty's legacy." . . . "[Thou] feed'st thy light's flame with self-substantial fuel" (1). (Notice that no stigma is attached to this teen-age habit.) And, as we have seen, he has an adolescent's build, as slender as a girl's, and with a "woman's face" (20). This sonnet was meant to please the young man, and what follows in the sequence suggests that he was in fact delighted. Now a thirteen or fourteen-year old boy in the year 2000 would probably be somewhat hurt or disappointed by such a description of himself. In 1600, however, standards of ideal male attractiveness were different, at least for most gay men.

Wherein lay the appeal? Not in the hermaphrodite in the modern sense, that is, someone possessing both male and female organs. This young man was not physically abnormal; he was the perfection of male adolescence. His attraction lay in his promise of spiritual uplift. There could be no true beauty without a sense of the divine. A muscular physique brought maleness down to earth. So did a beard. The teen-ager, however, was a combination, a fusion, of the earthly and the heavenly. Desire had to be kept relatively free of lust. It was a floating eroticism suspending the lover somewhere between heaven and earth, a balancing act between what was subconsciously desired and what was socially and culturally permitted. Physical beauty drew the lover, but it also elevated him. His attraction for the physical was sublimated, a transformation depicted by Michelangelo in his drawing of Zeus's rapture of Ganymede. (See Figure 5.)

The ideal of beauty was masculine, not a nubile girl, nor a boyish figure equipped with a clitoris. It had to be a girlish figure equipped with a penis. In his *Tragedy of Dido* (printed in 1594), Christopher Marlowe described Ganymede as a "wanton female boy," not as a wanton boyish female. The androgyne represented this transformation, just as in alchemy the sublimation of matter was analogous to a fusion of the male and female. To a modern Jungian psychoanalyst this union of the sexes is "an ideal of desexualized self-containment, a fantasy capable of offering relief from the incessant impulses of carnal desire by transforming them into a wealth of spiritual wholeness. . . . For alchemists and Neoplatonists, Ganymede stood for the same ideal: the questing spirit seized and taken away by the promise of knowing God."[90]

Much of the charm of the adolescent lay in his ephemerality. His divine beauty would shortly and inevitably turn terrestrial as his arms and legs thickened, and a beard sprouted on his chin. The perfect symbol of the transience of beauty was the rose, and in the very first of the sonnets the Fair Youth is evoked as "beauties *Rose*" (the word is italicized), and one of the principal themes of the sequence is the fugitiveness of his beauty and the need to preserve it as far as possible. The first thought is for the young man to marry

FIGURE 5. Michelangelo. Rape of
Ganymede. Pencil drawing.

FIGURE 6. *David*. Artist:
Donatello. Bronze Statue, 1430-1432?

and pass his handsomeness on to a son, a thought quickly succeeded by the poet's promise to accomplish the equivalent through imperishable verse. Even if the youth will not overcome time by fa-
thering a son, the poet will immortalize his short-lived beauty in
verse. The principal themes of the Fair Youth sequence are sounded here in the first sonnet. As Helen Vendler says, "[This] sonnet
can be seen . . . as an index to the rest of the sonnets, or as a diapa-
son of the notes of the sequence."[91]

The male teen-ager was the perfect combination of the physical
and the spiritual. Beauty of face and form betokened beauty of
soul. As Spenser said, "For of the soule the bodie forme doth take;
/ For soule is forme, and doth the bodie make." ("An Hymne in
Honour of Beautie.") In this ideal union, the immaterial soul
would outweigh the body, for the spirit was seen as the ultimate
source of strength.

The artworks of the Renaissance render the words of the poets
in physical form. Donatello's bronze statue of the boy David,
which dates to about 1430-1432, shows a very slim, undeveloped
body. (See Figure 6.)

Symonds described this nude (the first nude David) as "the boy-hero of a marvelous romance," in which the body "is but the shrine of an indwelling soul, the instrument and agent of a faith-directed will."[92] God is on David's side; it is not physical strength that triumphs but an inward-dwelling spirit. A generation later, however, about 1466, Verocchio sculpted David as "a lad of some seventeen years" with "the heavy-veined arms of a stone-hewer or gold-beater"[93] This was a sign of changing times, with pagan values asserting themselves more and more. As Christian doctrine began to lose its hold on the minds of Europeans, the physical element made itself increasingly prominent. Finally in 1504, Michelangelo created his huge muscular David. Unlike the previous Davids, this one carried a potent sexual charge. With its oversized hands and head, it captures an eruption of matter from a spiritual center. The young man of sonnet 20 is definitely not Michelangelo's assertively masculine figure: it is Donatello's *David* that portrays the adolescent Shakespeare describes.

Although the sensual pleasure taken in the sight of the boy was the source of attraction, the physical details that made up his allure had to be played down to prevent the link between body and soul from snapping, letting the body plunge to the beastly level. This concern accounts for a peculiarity of the sonnets written to the Fair Youth: they are strikingly free of tactile impressions. His hair is the color of marjoram (99), but apart from that, none of his physical characteristics are ever specifically mentioned. The poet admires his build, the "composed wonder of your frame" (59), but leaves it at that. Was he tall and slender? Were his movements those of an athlete or a dancer? As J. B. Leishman remarked, Shakespeare never attempts "anything like a series of evocations of his friend's youness : does not say 'I shall never forget the moment when I first saw you', . . . or 'the way you suddenly looked up', or 'the way you tossed your head.' . . . In fact, we know nothing at all about his friend's 'ways'."[94] The boy never takes on the qualities of a uniquely identifiable individual. There is here no portrait of the young man as Adonis. The poet admits that he lacks the tongue to praise the boy (106) and that he is incapable of describ-

ing his fair face; instead he urges him to look in the mirror (103).
Yet he is haunted by the boy and shapes everything he sees into an
image of him (113). The poet intends his verses to build a monument to the boy, yet the monument is strangely featureless. He exists like the Christian god in some paintings – a shaft of light and
nothing more. Perhaps this was part of a conscious artistic strate-
gy. To single out particular features of the boy's beauty might
make him less ideal, since beauty is in the eyes of the beholder, and
ideals of male beauty change with time. If the boy was to represent
the finest and highest aspects of the human being – in action like
an angel, in apprehension like a god, the beauty of the world, the
paragon of animals —it would be best to leave the details to the
reader's imagination.

To see how strangely abstract the Fair Youth is in Shakespeare's description, how lacking in the tactile sense, one need only compare him with the seductive young man in Marlowe's *Hero
and Leander*, written at about the same time as Shakespeare's *Venus*,
both poets, like Chapman, too, being caught up in the Ovidian
temper of the times. Marlowe dwells on the physical aspects of Leander's attractiveness and does not shy from making him as entic-
ing to men as to women.

> His bodie was as straight as *Circes* wand,
> *Jove* might have sipt out *Nectar* from his hand.
> Even as delicious meat is to the tast,
> So was his necke in touching, and surpast
> The whtie of *Pelops* shoulder. I could tell ye,
> How smooth his brest was, & how white his bellie,
> And whose immortall fingars did imprint
> That heavenly path, with many a curious dint,
> That runs along his backe, but my rude pen
> Can hardly blazon foorth the loves of men,
> Much lesse of powerfull gods: let it suffise,
> That my slacke muse sings of *Leanders* eies,
> Those orient cheeks and lippes, exceeding his
> That leapt into the water for a kis
> Of his owne shadow, and despising many,

Died ere he could enjoy the love of any.
Had wilde *Hippolitus Leander* seene,
Enamoured of his beautie had he beene,
His presence made the rudest paisant melt,
That in the vast uplandish countrie dwelt,
The barbarous *Thratian* soldier moou'd with nought,
Was moou'd with him, and for his favour sought.
Some swore he was a maid in man's attire,
For in his lookes were all that men desire (lines 61-84).

It must be kept in mind that Shakespeare was writing directly to the Fair Youth, not about him, and that he wanted him to be kept at some distance, seen but not touched. Nevertheless, it is decidedly odd that Shakespeare does not portray the handsome blond in some physical detail when the Ganymede ideal was so often represented in paintings, usually as a pubescent boy, gracefully posed, with an angelic face, slim arms, and light musculature.

The one physical aspect of the Fair Youth that Shakespeare does dwell on is the beauty of his eyes, as in sonnets 17, 49, 78, 83. For lovers of Ganymede, the eyes were entries to the soul, and to sing of their radiance was to raise the loved one above the terrestrial element. Michelangelo, who saw with his hands as much as with his eyes, and who was probably even more susceptible to physical perfection that Shakespeare, prudently tells his beloved young man, "My eyes did not see any mortal object, when I found complete peace in your beautiful eyes."[95]

CHAPTER 7

Descent into the Inferno

T O ANYONE looking for perfection of form, the 1609 Quarto is very disappointing. First come 154 sonnets that seem to meander without any clear sense of direction, and then comes a longish poem, "A Lover's Complaint," entirely different in tone and technique. Compared with other sonnet sequences, Shakespeare's is, at first glance, esthetically unsatisfying. Ever since they were first re-issued in 1640, editors, scholars, and printers have tried to improve on the original by re-arranging the poems and by leaving out the "Complaint."

Many commentators blamed profit-seeking publishers and unscrupulous pirates for the patchwork quarto – the sonnets stolen from Shakespeare's friends and thrown together haphazardly, the "Complaint" acquired from another author and tacked on to fill out the slim volume. It took a good many years before editors began to accept the 1609 Quarto as authentically Shakespeare throughout. One of the first was George Wyndham who in 1898 wrote that the "quarto was not carelessly issued," nor was it "a pirated edition published without Shakespeare's knowledge or against his wishes." There is throughout the "presumption of design."[96] Since then there has been has been some slow progress, glacially slow, in scholarly appreciation of the Quarto's design and purpose. Almost all the editions of the sonnets before the 1980s ignored the "Complaint" and had little to say about the arrangement of the sonnets. The editions prepared by John Kerrigan (1986) and Katherine Duncan-Jones (1997) signaled a major shift in the critical acceptance of the integrity of the 1609 Quarto. Kerrigan sensibly observed that although " modern critics may be baffled by the heterogeneity of the volume, Shakespeare's audience had a framework for reading it. . . . They would have read the volume as a volume, and their sense of the parts would have been modified by the whole."[97] Finally, a careful scholar like MacDonald P. Jackson, after many years of studying the sonnets, could write, "Once we focus on aesthetic reasons for the numbering of the sonnets in the 1609 Quarto, we see, not accident and disarray, but more and more signs of authorial purpose, pattern, and control."[98]

A number of sonnet cycles had been published before Shakespeare's. They were epidemic in the mid-1590s: Philip Sidney's *Astrophil and Stella* (1591), Samuel Daniel's *Delia* (1592), Barnabe Barnes' *Parthenophil and Parthenophe* (1593), Thomas Lodge's *Phyllis* (1593), Michael Drayton's *Idea's Mirror* (1594), William Percy's *Coelia* (1594), and Edmund Spenser's *Amoretti* (1595).[99] Sidney may have started the vogue; he certainly set the standard by which the other sequences were measured. They all had a philosophical framework, usually Platonic, and they could rightly be called sequences because there was a narrative thread leading from sonnet to sonnet.

Sidney's *Astrophil* tells the story in 108 sonnets of a brash and brilliant courtier (Sidney himself) who missed his chance for happiness when he fell in love with a married woman. In poems addressed to her (but probably never sent), his passion for her is pitted against what society and reason demands.

Shakespeare's Fair Youth sequence tells a somewhat similar story, with the poet sending sonnets (certainly delivered) to the loved one who is beyond his reach. But there are crucial differences. Sidney tells his story looking backwards; Shakespeare writes his impassioned sonnets while his ardor is most intense. Both describe how passion infected their lives. Sidney says early in *Astrophil*, "I a lesson new have speld, / I now have learn'd Love right, and learn'd even so, / As who by being poisond doth poison know" (no. 16). He writes as one who has lived through the experience, recollecting it in a mood of resignation. Shakespeare writes as one who has just ingested the poison and is in agony. ". . . [T]hence I learn, and find the lesson true, / Drugs poison him that so fell sick of you. . . . What potions have I drunk of siren tears / Distilled from limbecks foul as hell within, / Applying fears to hopes and hopes to fears, / Still losing when I saw myself to win!" (118, 119).

Nothing suggests that Shakespeare set out to compose a cycle of sonnets. What happened was beyond his control. His affair with the Fair Youth began with a few sonnets urging the young man to get married. This was not a conventional theme for sonneteers. Moreover, he encourages the young man to marry in order to perpetuate his good looks, not his family line. This, too, is odd. The poet is unconcerned about the family name, the family fortune, or any such mundane, practical matters. His thoughts soar upwards, lifted by a transcendent spirituality that he finds in the young man. Soon he is pulled into an orbit circling around him, unable to escape the attraction of the "sweet boy" (108), an attraction that held many others besides Shakespeare in its spell. "What is your substance, whereof are you made, / That millions of strange shadows on you tend?" (53). He is unable to sleep at night. "[T]hus by day my limbs, by night my mind, / For thee, and for myself, no quiet find" (27). He is fully aware that his love cannot be consummated. "Let me confess that we two must be twain, / Although our undivided loves are one" (36). He is racked with jealousy when he finds another poet is praising the young man. "O how I faint when I of you do write, / Knowing a better spirit doth use your name" (80). Finally and inevitably, the enchantment comes to an end. He bids farewell to the boy by returning to the theme of the first sonnets: beauty and the corrosive effects of time. Nature blessed him, but what nature gave, nature will take away. "[F]ear her, O thou minion of her pleasure: / She may detain, but still not keep, her treasure" (126).

All this made for a good story in and of itself, a story with a beginning, a middle, and an end. Shakespeare could offer his readers a unique chronicle of a mad infatuation, a story of enchantment and disillusion, unlike other sonnet sequences in its immediacy, intensity, and frankness. However, it lacked one thing that most of the Elizabethan cycles provided: a philosophical or religious framework. He quickly made up for this by incorporating the Fair

Youth sequence in a larger scheme, one that continued the love story and brought it to a surprising conclusion (though perhaps not so surprising to the first readers).

One striking feature of the sonnet sequence is the sharp contrast between the first 126 sonnets devoted to the Fair Youth and the last twenty-eight sonnets centering on the poet's mistress, the Dark Lady. Immediately after the poet has dismissed the "lovely Boy" with the ominous warning that nature will not preserve his blond beauty, he begins the next sonnet by praising the lady's dark complexion. "[N]ow is black beauty's successive heir" (127). The contrast could hardly be made more effective. Turning from the Fair Youth to the Dark Lady, one sees a diptych of opposites – the youth's fair locks set against the "black wires [that] grow on her head" (130), his handsomeness against her plainness, his angelic remoteness against her easy accessibility, his androgyny against her total womanliness, his heavenliness against her earthiness. Underlying it all is a series of deeper oppositions, of man and woman, of unrequited love for the youth and his quickly satisfied lust for the woman, of Aphrodite Uranus and Aphrodite Pandemos. This blatant contrast of black and white serves as a background for the story line in which the initial radiance of the youth is gradually darkened and finally extinguished.

The first readers would have brought to the Quarto the beliefs and prejudices of Elizabethan and Jacobean culture and would have apprehended the design of the full work. They would have seen that the sequence expressed a familiar philosophy of love based on the pagan and Christian ideas of body and soul, angels and demons, male superiority and female inferiority.

As we have seen, the dominant note in that philosophy is struck in the first few sonnets. The poet encourages the boy to produce offspring in order to preserve the boy's beauty, "now the worlds fresh ornament" (sonnet 1). Beauty is the first theme, with the second following immediately. He must "breed another thee" before "winters wragged hand" mars the beautiful face of youth in its summer (6). Beauty must be made to live forever, although time will not have it so. Time becomes the demon that haunts the first part of the sonnet sequence, an inescapable force that makes itself felt not only in the form and features of the Fair Youth but also in the relationship of the youth to the poet.

At first Shakespeare can claim his attention by promising him immortality, with lasting fame etched in the poet's lines. That hope is shaken by another poet who appeals to the boy for patronage, offering him the same kind of literary immortality. Shakespeare is genuinely troubled although he knows he is by far the better poet. He is disingenuous when he writes, "O how I faint when I of you do write, / Knowing a better spirit doth use your name" (80). He is being careful not to belittle the talents of a poet whom the young man admires.

A woman, a shadowy figure, appears briefly behind the scene and attempts to seduce the boy. Because of the woman and the rival poet, the poet's admiration of the young paragon becomes tainted with envy and disgust. "Thou dost common grow" (69) is his scathing comment.

This is hardly the way a poet writes to his patron. The tone is that of a hurt lover, in this case that of a lover who has expected too much of his ideal. The Rival Poet may have been looking for monetary support from the Fair Youth but the tone of this sonnet makes it plain that Shakespeare wasn't.

This raises a question about the sonnets that critics, Auden being an exception, have ignored. The sonnets give an ultimately unflattering picture of the boy, and it is difficult to imagine Shakespeare sending sonnets 69 and 94 ("Lillies that fester smell far worse than weeds") to a nobleman like the earl of Southampton or the earl of Pembroke while expecting to stay in his favor. Taken in the context of the poems that praise the young man, the harsh criticism of these sonnets seems like the heartfelt utterance of someone who cares deeply and feels confident that the hard words will be taken as an expression of love, like that of a stern father admonishing a wayward son. Auden did not believe that these sonnets would actually be sent. But it is obvious from the sequence as a whole that they were passed on to the young man. What is astonishing is not that they were sent but that they were eventually published. Certainly those in the inner circle of court and theatrical gossip would know who the boy was.

In the last sonnet addressed to the Fair Youth, the "withering" poet warns the still "lovely boy" (126) that even though he is the "minion" of adoring nature, time will render an accounting. The exalted young man of the first sonnets has fallen from grace, and the poet has fallen with him, becoming envious of a rival, emotionally torn between adoration of the boy and disappointment in his behavior, knowing that "beauty's veil doth cover every blot" (95). In the floral language of the sonnets, the perfect "rose" of the first sonnet has turned into a lily that festers.

This, however, is not the end of the poet's descent. Taking leave of the boy (in the scheme of the sonnets, not in real time), the poet becomes involved with a woman, the Dark Lady. In the last twenty-eight sonnets the poet describes another kind of infatuation. The love for the boy was transcendent; the love for the Dark Lady is completely physical, earthy, sensual, and common. Shakespeare is driven by sexual lust, by what he calls his "will," punning on his name and the Elizabethan word for carnal appetites (135). He cannot free himself from the bondage of the flesh. His love "is as a fever" and the "physician" reason has abandoned him. He curses the woman "who art as black as hell, as dark as night" for her hold over him (147). Having sex with her, injecting his semen in her vagina, is "th'expense of spirit in a waste of shame" (129). A bit of his soul is lost in his ejaculation.

Yet in the very next sonnet, deliberately placed there for the sake of the sharp contrast, the faults of the woman, her bad breath, her darkish skin, her wiry hair, become her attractive features, drawing him down to her level, just as the perfections of the boy drew him upwards. The boy's beauty mirrors the ideal world of the spirit; the Dark Lady's plainness and sexual receptiveness match the poet's craving for basely sensual pleasures.

The poet's disillusionment in the Fair Youth, with idolatry turning into disaffection and infatuation into clear-sightedness, begins a descent into the flesh. In sonnet 20, the master-mistress sonnet, the male organ exerts no power over the devoted poet. But in sonnet 151 the penis proves to be ungovernable and will have its way. His reason, his mind, his higher self protests and should prevent this from happening. But the flesh suborns the warden of his soul, and conscience, which in the Neoplatonic view is "born of love," becomes the occasion for a pun on "con" (French for cunt), converting God-given conscience into knowledge (science) of the vagina.[100] In her sharp and striking analysis of the very sounds of the sonnet, Helen Vendler finds that "the unstoppability of orgasm is certainly imitated here, with 'ejaculation' occurring in the redundancy of proud of this pride."[101] Ingeniously, in the wonderland of sex, the poet has made conscience the spur to lust and copulation.

> . . . I do betray
> My nobler part to my gross body's treason:
> My soul doth tell my body that he may
> Triumph in love; flesh stays no further reason,
> But rising at thy name doth point out thee
> As his triumphant prize; proud of this pride [erection],
> He is contented thy poor drudge to be,
> To stand in thy affairs, fall by thy side.
>   No want of conscience hold it that I call
>   Her love for whose dear love I rise and fall.

As much as any one sonnet can, this sonnet with its extraordinary cynicism captures the drift of the entire sequence.

Taken as a whole, the 1609 arrangement of the sonnets reveals a comprehensive design, which takes the reader from heaven to hell, reversing Dante's progress in *The Divine Comedy*. The Italian went from the inferno of sin through purgatory to end in paradise, gazing at the Holy Virgin while in the presence of the love that moves the sun and the other stars. The rose is the emblem of paradise in Dante. Shakespeare begins with the rose, significantly italicized in the very first sonnet and intended as the emblem of the boy's beauty. From this vision of paradise, the poet plunges into the purgatory of disenchantment to end in the pit of the inferno, the woman's vagina. Dante had a teen-age Beatrice as inspiration for his upward journey of the soul, and Shakespeare had a teenage boy as companion on a descent into the flesh.

A contributor to *Blackwood's Magazine* in 1884 was the first to see Dante's influence in the overall arrangement of the sonnets. "To Dante, the symbol of this wisdom [eternal love]," said this anonymous critic, "was the poetical or figured form called 'Beatrice;' to Shakespeare it was the anonymous form of manly and youthful beauty, figured in the introductory series of the sonnets – a figure for which he was indebted to Dante. For although Dante used the figure of Beatrice as an expression of heavenly wisdom, beauty, and virtue, he represented the heavenly love itself under the form of a young man of matchless beauty and grace, who appeared to him, and, taking possession of his heart, so disposed of it as to place the happiness of Dante where it was, independent of accident, policy, time, force, or change. . . . . Shakespeare selected this figure and made it the 'master' of his 'passion,' the 'lord of his love,' in the first and main series of his Sonnets."[102]

It is wrong to say, as Auden does, that the sonnets "contain no theory of love."[103] In fact they comprise a poetic disquisition on love in the Western world, drawing on both pagan and Christian teachings, more specifically, on Plato and Dante. They are Christian in their belief in man's soul and its descent from heaven, pagan in their adoration of physical beauty, and Christian as well as pagan in their degradation of women.

Fundamentally, however, the tone throughout is more pagan than Christian. There is, as Bradley said, "an almost entire absence of definitely religious thought or feeling."[104] Although the sense of an ideal world is often present, the sonnets picture a world without an omniscient, judgmental god, a universe in which the only afterlife is that eternity promised in the preliminary note and in which the supreme deity is beauty. George Santayana's view that "with the doubtful exception" of sonnet 146, "they are not Christian" seems entirely valid.[105] Nor is there any reason to make an exception of that one sonnet. It begins, "Poor soul, the center of my sinful earth," and consists of a debate between body and soul. It has a Christian aura, but that aura is dispelled by the way in which the debate is resolved. Soul says the body should not be fed richly and adorned ornately. Depriving the body of what it wants will feed the soul: "Within be fed, without be rich no more." Body and soul are seen as engaged in a transaction, an exchange of commodities. "Buy terms divine in selling hours of dross." The purpose of privation is not to win a place in heaven but to make it easier to accept death. If one's life is a sensual riot, if one's sole aim is pleasure and indulgence, then the prospect of death is frightening. But if one cuts back on pleasures or does without them, one has less to lose in death. One slips into death incrementally, denying oneself one earthly pleasure after another.

In the convoluted thought of the sonnet, living is paradoxically seen as the process of dying, each day bringing one closer to inevitable death – giving "birth astride of a grave" in Samuel Beckett's terse formulation. One nourishes the soul, the higher, intellectual element in the human being, by doing less living, by depriving the senses and the passions of what nourishes them. In that way, the soul prospers at the body's expense .

The last couplet of the sonnet reads like a reproof to John Donne. "One short sleep past, we wake eternally," avowed the medieval-minded poet, "And death shall be no more; death, thou shalt die." For Donne, who kept a coffin in his bedroom, death gives way to the eternal life in heaven. His sonnet ends: "So shalt thou [the soul] feed on death, that feeds on men, / And Death once dead, there's no more dying then." The emphasis on dying is significant. For Shakespeare, living is dying, and death ends the process, *tout court*. Nothing more can be said.

Shakespeare's sonnet is humanist in spirit and, in respect to the eternal life, not Christian at all. As J. M. Robertson noted, the sonnet is Shakespeare's response and assent to the stoicism expressed in Montaigne's essay "That to Philosophie, Is to Learne How to Die," which must have been in front of Shakespeare as he wrote the sonnet.[106] The influence of Montaigne on *Hamlet* and *The Tempest* is well attested, and John Florio, Montaigne's English translator, was Southampton's secretary and someone Shakespeare would have known. There are a number of verbal links between the poem and the essay that cannot be attributed to chance, and central to both is the transactional concept of life and death, of body and soul. What the poet set to verbal music is the following passage from Montaigne:

> "All the time you live, you steale it from death: it is at her charge. The continuall worke of your life, is to contrive death; you are in death, during the time you continue in life: for, you are after death, when you are no longer living. Or if you had rather have it so, you are dead after life: but during life, you are still dying."[107]

Some Christian eschatology clings to Montaigne: he would believe that death is the beginning of another life. Nothing like that is hinted at in Shakespeare. The idea that there is a place for souls in some heaven is absent in the sonnets. In them the only heaven is the beauty of the Fair Youth, a recollection perhaps of an ideal Platonic world, and hell is the sexuality of the woman. There is no otherworldly life that can be separated from terrestrial attractions. Shakespeare's angels and evil spirits are human beings, the Fair Youth and the Dark Lady, not winged cherubs or horned fiends. Sonnet 146 is a cautionary sonnet placed among those that treat of sexual love as a fever. It is the poet's admonition to himself not to yield to his lust, albeit a rather ineffective one. Nothing avails against Cupid, the impish love god.

The sonnets are singularly lacking throughout in any reference to the special tenets and doctrines of Christianity.[108] They picture a world without an omniscient, judgmental god, a universe in which the only afterlife is that eternity promised in the dedication and achieved by the poet's immortal words. Some interpreters read sonnet 105 as the poet's dismissal of the Holy Trinity and its replacement by the Platonic Triad of the beautiful, the good, and the true.[109]

> "Fair, kind, and true" is all my argument,
> "Fair, kind, and true" varying to other words,
> And in this change is my invention spent,
> Three themes in one, which wondrous scope affords.

In expressing his love of the youth, Shakespeare makes beauty the supreme deity. The paradisal rose of perfection is not Dante's starlit heaven but the physical radiance of a lovely boy seen on the cusp between puberty and manhood. It is a vision completely in harmony with the Socratic view of male love as expressed in Plato's *Symposium*, once the bible of educated homosexuals, or at least their vade mecum. The *Sonnets* comprises a poetic disquisition on love in the Western world, drawing on both the ancient Greeks and the medieval Christians for its frame of reference, and especially on the teachings of Socrates.

The classically trained scholars of the nineteenth century had a better understanding of the philosophy inherent in the sonnets than more recent interpreters. Reading the sonnets as the direct expression of Platonic love has fallen out of favor with critics in recent years, though there are exceptions like J.B. Leishman. On the other hand, Georg Brandes in his exhaustive, two-volume biography of Shakespeare, published in 1895 and 1896, read the sonnets as the poet's intimate confession and saw them as expressions of the pagan ideal.[110] Earlier in the Victorian age, when Platonic love was taken more seriously as an ideal than it is now, the connection between Socrates and Shakespeare was marked and emphasized, and the sonnet sequence was read as the expression of an otherworldly love that only men, "sensitive" men, could appreciate and respond to. Writing in 1868, Richard Simpson, the most articulate of these philosophically inclined critics, said, "Socrates was supposed to be the first founder of this school of thought [Platonic love], and Shakespeare's adherence to it was so notorious that he was called in his epitaph 'Socrates ingenio,' a Socrates in his turn of mind."[111] A few years later William Minto took the phrase as an undisguised reference to Shakespeare's physical attraction to beautiful young men. "It is difficult to see what can have been meant by the expression 'Socratem ingenio – a Socrates in disposition – in Shakespeare's epitaph, if it does not point to his sentiment for beautiful young men."[112] Both Minto and Simpson misquote the phrase, which actually reads, "*Genio Socratem.*" Many biographers try to remove the taint of gayness from the epitaph by translating the phrase as "a Socrates for his genius," meaning for his intellect. In the Renaissance, however, genius usually meant temperament or true nature. The epitaph reads: "*Judicio Pylum, Genio Socratem, Arte Maronem, /*

Terra tegit, populus mæret, Olympus habet." (The earth covers, the people mourn, and Olympus holds the man who was a Nestor for his judgment, a Socrates by nature, and a Vergil in his art.)

For Simpson the sonnets depicted a step by step ascension of the ladder of love. Physical beauty was the incitement to a contemplation of beauty of the soul, and the aspiration to immortality is the root of the love that moves all things. But to make this Dantesque interpretation consistent with what is actually said in the sonnets, he had to re-arrange their order. Shakespeare's own arrangement begins where Simpson would have it end.

CHAPTER 8

How to Have Sex with an Angel

NOWHERE in these sonnets does one get the impression that the poet ever embraced the Fair Youth. He does not even imagine holding the boy in his arms, unlike Richard Barnfield who did dream of making his bosom a bed for his beloved adolescent. Age and class separate the actor, "chopped with tanned antiquity," from the noble young man. Yet the poet feels close enough to censure the youth's behavior in strong language. And there is one point in the sonnet sequence where he approaches a kind of intimacy. This occurs when he and the youth share the same mistress. Instead of being upset by this situation, he is filled with joy at the thought that he and the youth are as one (42). What lies in the depths of this odd romance comes to light towards the end of the whole sequence, when the so-called Dark Lady replaces the Fair Youth as the object of the poet's interest.

While we get to know rather little about the actual physical aspects of the young man, we get to know a lot about this woman: how she looks and how she acts and what she does and how she smells. Her eyes and hair are black; she plays an instrument, the virginals; her complexion is bad ("colour'd il" [144]); and her breath is foul. In contrast to the boy, she is the sum of all imperfections. She exists entirely on the earthly level and can be held in the poet's arms, while the boy is ethereal, celestial, angelic, seemingly beyond his reach. Sex and adoration exist on separate planes.

The Fair Youth cannot be touched sexually, while the Dark Lady satisfies the poet's lust. The poet's sin as he himself sees it lies not in loving the boy but in copulating with the woman. His eyes feast on the boy, not on the woman. He adores the boy, but seems never to have even touched him. He debases the woman, yet his "foolish heart" cannot resist her. In sonnet 151, the ode to the erect penis and the pliable conscience, this foolish heart is filled with contrary desires, conscience demanding one thing, carnal lust another. With its pun on conscience and its depiction of orgasm, this sonnet is about as pornographic as early modern literature ever gets. But the salaciousness of the poet's couplings with the Dark Lady goes beyond what this sonnet suggests. The poet is irresistibly drawn to having sex with a certain married woman who is simultaneously having an affair with another man. The triangular nature of the relationship is part of its perverse appeal to the poet. By committing himself to it, he confirms his belief that sexual lust is beastly, that it has nothing of the divine about it, that it has its roots in betrayal, exactly as ordained by the disappointed goddess of love at the end of *Venus and Adonis*. The poet acts out his own cynical view of sex, never more bitterly and more paradoxically formulated than in sonnet 129, in which the emission of semen ("spirit") into the vagina ("hell") is man's most degrading and yet most compelling act. "Th'expense of spirit in a waste of shame / Is lust in action. . . . All this the world well knows, yet none knows well / To shun the heaven that leads men to this hell."

Post coitum animae omne triste: after intercourse one feels sad, or more precisely "dispirited," depleted of spirit. Shakespeare found the act revolting; as did Sir Thomas Browne in his *Religio Medici* (1642), who saw it as "the foolishest act a wise man commits in all his life; nor is there any thing that will more deject his cool'd imagination, when he shall consider what an odd and unworthy piece of folly he hath committed." Shakespeare's attitude was certainly not exceptional among educated men of his time.

The nastiness of sex is one reason, the main one, why he betrays his "noble part to [his] gross body's treason" (151). There may, however, be a second reason, stranger than the first, but in conformity with his homoeroticism. The poet is sexually attracted to both the Dark Lady and the man who is physically intimate with her. There is nothing particularly queer about that, though such relationships may not be usual in the life of most men. What is remarkable is that the man is called an angel while the woman is described as the "worser spirit." He suspects that the woman has corrupted his "saint to be a devil, / Wooing his purity with her foul pride" (144).

Now an ordinary man would presumably be jealous, gnawed like Iago by thoughts that a lecherous man "hath leap'd into my seat" (*Othello* 2.1.291). But the poet entertains no thoughts of revenge and expresses no enmity towards the other man. Quite the opposite. He loves the male friend, calls him his angel, his saint, all the while he lusts after the woman, the devil in this sexual triad. When he is away from them, he imagines "one angel in another's hell" – the man occupying the woman's vagina. The guilty party is the woman, the temptress, who corrupts the purity of the friend with "her foul pride," meaning her voracious sexual appetite. In the complicated dialectics of the sonnet, the poet is caught between the soul of the man and the body of the woman, between "comfort and despair." He would be comforted to know that the friend has not succumbed to the temptations of the woman; he would despair if the admired friend has debased himself and sunk to his level. Disappointment, not jealousy, determines the mood of the sonnet.

The poet is lured into an emotional and psychological inferno when the woman seduces the friend; and friend becomes a "fiend," not because the poet hates him but because he knows that the friend has entered the woman's hell. In composing the sonnet the poet agonizes over his double view of the friend and what this tells him about himself. When he makes love to the Dark Lady, her body carries with it in his mind the body of the other man. His soul longs for the man; his body has to be satisfied by the woman. Her demonized organ gives physical access to the male angel. In sharing the foul, dark woman with the "man right fair," the poet is acting out a dangerously tempting fantasy. In penetrating the diabolic woman, he comes as close as is permissible to doing what is impossible: actually copulating with a male angel.

Given the customs of the time and the way in which his psyche was organized, it was impossible for him to have sex directly with the beloved man; he had to invade him through the vehicle of the woman. In modern terms, the poet displayed signs of that aberration known to psychologists as troilism, the desire to possess the female partner of the man for whom he has homosexual yearnings. Helen Vendler, one of the few commentators (the only?) to understand what lies behind this threesome, says, "A psychoanalytical argument can be made that in having intercourse with a woman who has betrayed him with the young man, the speaker is in effect having vicariously that homosexual intercourse which he desires."[113]

This "design for living," given literary currency and notoriety in the twentieth century by Noel Coward, is also evident in the sonnets to the Fair Youth and explains the poet's inconsistent reactions to the boy's sexual escapades. In sonnets 69 and 70 the poet condemns the boy for shaming "the beauty of [his] mind" by having sex with some woman. (The circumstances behind these two sonnets will be considered later.) The condemnation is remarkably harsh, the poet accusing the noble youth of becoming vulgar and "common."

This was not the first time that the poet had heard of the boy's sexual affairs. In sonnets 40, 41, and 42, written when he was away from him, traveling with his fellow actors, he learned that the boy had been wooed and sexually seduced. But here the language is in a different key from that of sonnet 69. He is complaisant and indulgent; he understands why such an attractive lad would be ambushed by some experienced woman, and he obligingly excuses him. Why so severe in the one case and so forgiving in the other? The difference is that the woman in sonnet 69 was no friend of the poet's; the woman in the second was his mistress. Sharing a woman with the Fair Youth was a kind of "flattery."

> Take all my loves, my love, yea, take them all.
> . . .
> I do forgive thy robbery, gentle thief,
> Although thou steal thee all my property (40).

In sonnet 42 the poet tries to sort out the thoughts that both trouble and arouse him. He considers two ways of looking at the boy's involvement with his, the poet's, mistress. It may be nothing more than an expression of teen-age concupiscence, under-standable but regrettable. The other and far worse possibility is that the woman has won the boy's love, has touched his soul. In the first case the male element is dominant; in the second the fe-male. The first lines set forth the alternatives (emphasis added):

That thou hast <u>her</u> it is not all my grief,
And yet it may be said that I loved her dearly;
That she hath <u>thee</u> is of my wailing chief,
A loss in love that touches me more nearly.

The poet tries to make the best of the situation by a strange ra-tionalization, a product of wishful thinking and sleepless nights (sonnets 27 and 28), that makes both possibilities work to his benefit. In the first instance, he imagines that the boy willfully takes the woman because she belongs to the poet, projecting onto the boy what are actually his own troilistic motives. "Loving of-fenders, thus will I excuse yee: / Thou dost love her because thou knowst I love her" (42). The second possibility is even more ingeni-ously handled. On the surface, the woman seems to "abuse" the poet by being unfaithful to him. However, because of the hidden motives at work, she is in fact having sex with the boy for the po-et's sake. Poet and boy are united in her body; she brings them to-gether in a physical sense.

The poet forgives both the boy and the woman because the three of them form a *ménage à trois*, an erotic trinity on a mystical level. Although the poet chides the Fair Youth – "thou mightst my seat forbear" (41) – he ends by accepting the situation with joy because "my friend and I are one. / Sweet flattery; then she loves but me alone" (42). Quite daringly, the poet is implying – and hoping – that the boy's sexual orientation or aberration is the same as his. In the master-mistress sonnet Shakespeare made a partial declaration of his feelings. Now, twenty sonnets later and absent from the boy, he takes a further step toward a complete and mutual understanding.

Shakespeare's fascination with this kind of love triangle was ap-parent early in his career. He presented a variation of it in *The Two Gentlemen of Verona*, written about 1594. Proteus and Valentine are

close friends, both in love with Silvia. After numerous plot complications, Proteus attempts to rape Silvia. Valentine comes to her
defense – and having saved her, forgives Proteus! Clemency and
forbearance can hardly do more. But friendship of the Shakespearean kind can. Valentine not only pardons Proteus, he offers Silvia to
him! "And that my love may appear plain and free, / All that was
mine in Silvia I give thee" (5.4.82-3). As A.C. Bradley says of this
resolution, "We can hardly suppose that it was so absurd to him as
it to us."[114] True. For Shakespeare, the bond between the male
friends was manifestly stronger than any heterosexual attraction,
and stronger even than any sense of justice. If love between men is
earth's highest felicity, the surrender of a woman to the beloved is
not much of a sacrifice; it is only a token of one's love.

IN *The Merchant of Venice*, probably written a few years later, Antonio, sick with love for his friend Bassanio at the opening of the
play, will literally give him his heart, whereas Bassanio's intended
bride can only offer a few ducats to save his life. In the trial scene,
when Antonio is in despair, he attributes his plight to his being an
unhealthy, abnormal kind of man. "I am a tainted wether [a cas-
trated ram] of the flock / Meetest for death" (4.1.114-5). As a perceptive reader of the play has remarked, the ending of the comedy,
"with the consummation of the Bassanio / Portia relationship
hanging unresolved – wreathes the whole triangular relationship
in further enigma. What, the innocent audience might think, is
Antonio doing at Belmont anyway – what kind of man would take
his best friend on his honeymoon?"[115] Perhaps the kind of man who
feels as Oscar Wilde's Algernon does: "In married life three is company and two is none."

The Two Noble Kinsmen, written at the end of Shakespeare's career, offers another variation of the theme. As noted above (in
chapter 6) Arcite and Palamon are sworn blood brothers and
lovers, lovers who stop short of sodomy. Says Arcite, "We are an
endless mine to one another./ We are one another's wife, ever
begetting / New births of love" (2.2.79-81). That all changes when
they become rivals for Emilia. Attracted to both of them, she finds

that the two kinsmen differ from each other in nearly every respect
– in looks, in temperament, in desires. She compares Arcite with
Ganymede: "Just such another wanton Ganymede / Set Jove afire
with, and enforced the god / Snatch up the goodly boy and set by
him, / A shining constellation" (4.2,15-18). The shorter of the two,
Arcite is a muscular athlete ("you run the best and wrestle, / That
these times can allow" [2.5. 3-4]). He is boyish, full of mirth, with
sparkling eyes. As with the young man of sonnet 20, "Nature herself would run mad for this man" (4.2.12). Palamon is Arcite's foil,
"a dull shadow" compared to Arcite, darker in hue, tall and rather
thin, with a manly, unsmiling face, and a melancholy disposition
(4.2.26). If Arcite is another Ganymede, Palamon is another Narcis-
sus, self-absorbed, introspective, and sad (4.2.32).

Once they fall in love with Emilia, they suddenly find themselves quarreling bitterly as to who shall have her, and their differences extend to what having her means to them. Arcite wants to
have sex with her, while Palamon wants to worship her. Arcite
does not mind sharing her, and he upbraids Palamon for behaving
"so unlike a kinsman, / To love alone" (2.2.233-34). "I will not do
as you do, to worship her / As she is heavenly and a blessed goddess. / I love her as a woman, to enjoy her: / So both may love"
(2.2.163-6). However, he insists upon taking her first, asserting his
position as the dominant male.

The Two Noble Kinsmen presents the options available to gay men
who, for whatever reason, shunned sodomy. Before Emilia enters
the story, they are "one another's wife," indulging in interfemoral
sex or mutual masturbation. After Emilia enchants them, Arcite
wants a troilistic relationship. In the sonnets, both in the Fair
Youth sequence and in the Dark Lady sequence, troilism is the only option.

CHAPTER 9

The Rival Poet

IN one substantial group of sonnets, 76 to 93, Shakespeare fears
that the Fair Youth has deserted him and fallen under the spell
of another poet. The rivalry is literary, not sexual. The other poet – and there is only one other (83) – has a powerful style, invents
strange compound words (76), is more erudite than Shakespeare
(78), and writes "above a mortal pitch" (86). Shakespeare knows he
is engaged in a lethal battle with this magnificent wielder of words,
a poetomachia that he compares to a sea battle, in which his own
"saucy bark" takes on the rival's ship "of tall building and of goodly pride" (80). "The proud full sail of his great verse" is "bound for
the prize of all-too-precious you" (86). What is at stake is the power to influence the Fair Youth, to serve as a mentor to him, and in
that capacity to create a poetic monument to him.

We know who won on the literary front, but while the war was
going on, Shakespeare had genuine doubts about the outcome. Indeed he may have felt that he lost out to his formidable rival. It may
have been a factor contributing to Shakespeare's disillusionment in
the adored boy. At one moment he feels faint, realizing that he may
be "cast away" (80); at the next, he asserts that through his verse
the boy's "name from hence immortal life shall have" (81). At first,
his muse is sick at the thought that another poet has taken his place
in the eyes of the Fair Youth (79). Later he admits that he has no
right to think his muse was married to the boy (82); others should
have a chance to capture the boy's grace in a work of art. Again, continuing the marriage metaphor, he feels like a deceived husband,
who cannot believe that the sweet face of the loved one hides a false
heart. Subsequently, he chastises the boy for succumbing to flat-

tery and for being too fond of praise (84), a remarkable statement
from the poet whose own idolatry seems to know no limits and a
sure sign of Shakespeare's passionate involvement. Finally, in two
of his harshest sonnets, 94 and 95, harsh and caustic in their indictment of the boy's emotional coolness and hauteur, the poet adds ar-
rogance to his failings and finds his beauty infected. There is a
"canker in the fragrant rose," an image that perfectly conveys the
poet's disillusionment, his discovery of the boy's false heart and
adeptness at using his charm to get his own way. "O, what a mansion have those vices got / Which for their habitation chose out
thee, / Where beauty's veil doth cover every blot, / And all things
turns to fair that eyes can see" (95). Between the writing of sonnets
96 and 97 the poet leaves home and, being away, is able in his imagination to restore some parts of the fading ideal.

In the underlying drama of the sonnets, a climax of sorts is reached
when Shakespeare is torn between confidence in his own poetic powers and doubts about them. "O, how I faint when I of you do write,
/ Knowing a better spirit doth use your name, / And in the praise
thereof spends all his might / To make me tongue-tied speaking of
your fame" (80). Yet in the next sonnet, Shakespeare asserts, "Your name from hence immortal life shall have. . . . Your monument shall be my gentle verse."

Who was this po-
et who could bring Shakespeare, even if only with false mod-
esty, to think of himself as "a saucy bark" compared to the proud tall ship of his rival? In 1874,

FIGURE 7. George Chapman (c.1559-1634).
Portrait from the 1614 edition of the *Iliads*.

William Minto first proposed that the poet and dramatist George Chapman, born a few years before Shakespeare, was this genius.[116] (See Figure 7: George Chapman.)

In our time Chapman is a nearly forgotten figure whose plays are seldom performed and whose poems, such as *The School of Night*, are unread. In Shakespeare's time, however, he had a formidable reputation as both poet and dramatist. Francis Meres in his 1598 assessment of English writers, *Palladis Tamia*, considered Chapman a better maker of plots than Shakespeare. His highly elevated, artificial, and hieratic language, which is now an impediment to an appreciation of his poetry, made him stand out among his rivals. John Webster (in his dedication to *The White Devil*) praised him for his "full and heightened style." In 1600 eighty excerpts from his poems appeared in the anthology *England's Parnassus*. Two hundred years later he found admirers among the Romantic critics. Samuel Taylor Coleridge thought Chapman excelled Ben Jonson, possessing "more dignity, more lustre, and equal strength."[117] Writing in the early years of the twentieth century, Algernon Swinburne (in the eleventh edition of the *Encyclopædia Britannica*) singled out the qualities that made him a real threat to Shakespeare: "a singular force and solidity of thought, an admirable ardour of ambitious devotion to the service of poetry, a deep and burning sense at once of the duty implied and of the dignity inherent in his office; a vigour, opulence, and loftiness of phrase, remarkable even in that age of spiritual strength, wealth and exaltation of thought and style."

Above all, it was Chapman's translation of Homer that impressed not only his contemporaries but also later generations of readers. Ben Jonson knew parts of it by heart. It earned Chapman the patronage of the earl of Essex, and in 1604 on the basis of it he was appointed to the position of sewer in ordinary (a lowly position) to the ten-year-old son of King James.[118] Later generations remained no less impressed with Chapman's highly individual renderings, with Homer's lines transformed into fourteen-syllable verses. Swinburne declared that "no praise can be too warm or high for the power, the freshness, the indefatigable strength and inextinguishable fire which animates this exalted work and secures for all time that shall take cognizance of English poetry an honoured place in the highest annals for the memory of Chapman."

There can be few poets in any language who have received such praise for their work as translators. Whatever might be said about Chapman's poems and plays, his Homer conjures up a world, strange and real, that Homer himself might have felt at home in. Although few modern readers may have read Chapman's *Iliads*, almost every literate person recalls the impression it made on Keats. When he first "heard Chapman speak out loud and bold, / Then felt [he] like some watcher of the skies / When a new planet swims into his ken." More recently, Gary Wills found wonder and enchantment in this tale of the Trojan war when he got "the knack of reading Chapman's challenging lines. The stretch and leap of the fourteener lifts the poem onto the superhuman level of Homer's warriors. The poet's moralizing disappears into wonder at the blaze of human energy and beauty."[119]

In spite of himself, Shakespeare may have felt like Keats when he first read the opening lines of Chapman's *Iliads*, in fourteeners, which Shakespeare seldom attempted (*Love's Labour's Lost*, 4.2.56-62, and *Cymbeline* 5.4. 30-90 being exceptions), and was caught in the ebb and flow of their majestic rhythms. It was lines like these that befitted Shakespeare's involuntary and reluctant praise, "the proud full sail of his great verse" (86):

> Achilles' baneful wrath resound, O Goddesse that imposd
> Infinite sorrowes on the Greekes, and many brave soules losd
> From breasts Heroique— sent them farre, to that invisible cave
>   That no light comforts; and their lims to dogs and vultures gave.
> To all which Jove's will gave effect; and from whom first strife begunne
> Betwixt Atrides, king of men, and Thetis' godlike Sonne.[120]

Facing Shakespeare were waves upon waves of heptameters of equally commanding force.

The evidence educed by Minto makes for a very strong case for Chapman as the Rival Poet. Most editors of the sonnets have, however, displayed a surprising reluctance to be convinced. Their skepticism is based not on contrary facts but on their sense of things: the supposition that Shakespeare could not possibly have taken Chapman seriously as a rival and the certain knowledge that Chapman, the stern, high-minded moralist, could write lyrics as ardent and luxurious as Shakespeare's. This is a very short-sighted view of the situation that existed in the early 1600s. Chapman did have a formidable reputation as a poet, and his heavy-handed sermonizing could very well have offered the Fair Youth exactly what the sonnets lacked.

Swinburne said that Minto's conjecture was "fortified by such apt collocation and confrontation of passages that we may now reasonably accept it as an ascertained and memorable fact." Shakespeare tells us that the Rival Poet was more learned and that he had a "well-refined" style (85). Shakespeare knew Latin,[121] but he had no command of Greek, as Chapman did. Further, "the proud full sail of his great verse" (86) seems a likely reference to the mighty lines, the fourteeners, of Chapman's Homer.

Yet Minto used only part of the evidence that points to Chapman as the rival. There is another item that eliminates any other poet as the rival and pretty much cinches the case for Chapman. In sonnet 86, Shakespeare asks, "Was it his spirit, by spirits taught to write / Above a mortal pitch, that struck me dead?" The classical scholar J. A. K. Thomson noticed that here was a specific reference to Chapman and to Chapman's translation of Homer.[122] In a long poem *The Tears of Peace*, Chapman relates how the ghost of Homer arose from the past to inspire him. This happened in Hitchins, where Chapman was born.

> I am (sayd hee) that spirit *Elysian*,
> That (in thy native ayre; and on the hill
> Next *Hitchins* left hand) did thy bosome fill,
> With such a flood of soule; that thou wert faine
> (With acclamations of her Rapture then)
> To vent it, to the Echoes of the vale;
> When (meditating of me) a sweet gale
> Brought me upon thee; and thou didst inherit
> My true sense (for the time then) in my spirit;
> And I, invisiblie, went prompting thee
> To those fayre Greenes, where thou didst english me (lines 75-85).[123]

However daunting it must have been to contend with a poet who was in direct communication with Homer's spirit, and thus able to turn Homer's Greek into magnificent English verse, Shakespeare scoffed at the man and his apparition, "[t]hat affable familiar ghost / Which nightly gulls him [Chapman] with intelligence" (86). The tone is slightly but unmistakably disdainful. Ghosts are devilish, this one is friendly with Chapman, and it deludes the poet with information as likely to be false as true. Further than that Shakespeare hesitates to go, well aware that the Fair Youth admires Chapman. Nor is it Chapman's rapport with Homer that dismays him. What does make him weak and fearful is the knowledge that Chapman has written verses praising and honoring the young man.

Knowing that Chapman is the Rival Poet is like being introduced into the circle of informed readers of 1609. It puts us in possession of a great deal of information that is only alluded to in the sonnets. The involvement of Shakespeare with Chapman provides a fascinating back-story to the sonnet sequence that those first readers would have been familiar with. And the Shakespeare-Chapman connection also cannot help but prompt the tantalizing thought that the Fair Youth may not be so elusive after all. How many handsome young men would be receiving adulatory verses from both Chapman and Shakespeare?

By the time the 1609 Quarto appeared, the rivalry between Chapman and Shakespeare, both as playwrights and as poets, was of long standing, dating back to the mid-1590s. It may have begun when Chapman tried to capitalize on the enormous success of Shakespeare's *Venus and Adonis*. As a rebuttal to the eroticism of Shakespeare's poem, which derived from Ovid, Chapman composed *The Shadow of Night* (printed in 1594) and *Ovid's Banquet of Sense* (printed in 1595), both philosophical works in which the senses that inflamed Venus are considered instead as pathways to virtue and philosophical wisdom. In Shakespeare the passions aroused by beauty as perceived by the senses are ends in themselves. Not so in Chapman. He disapproves of "Muses that sing loves sensuall Emperie." In *Lucrece*, the companion piece to *Venus*, the rape takes place at night, when "the flesh being proud [erect], desire doth fight with grace" (line 712). Not so in Chapman. His night is not made for sensual lovers but for philosophers, not for fornication but for lucubration. His motto, inscribed in his portrait, was *conscium evasi diem* (I will escape conscious day).

Supernatural inspiration came to him from night's darkness: "Rich-tapird [tapered] sanctuarie of the blest, / Pallace of Ruth, made all of teares, and rest, / To thy blacke shades and desolation, / I consecrate my life" (*Shadow of Night*, 268-271). He urged those of his readers who sought inspiration to join him.

> All you possest with indepressed spirits,
> Indu'd with nimble, and aspiring wits,
> Come consecrate with me, to sacred Night
> Your whole endevours, and detest the light.
> Sweete Peaces richest crowne is made of stares,
> Most certaine guides of honord Marinars,
> No pen can any thing eternall wright,
> That is not steept in humor of the Night (370-377).

For the philosophic man, love flows not from the liver, the seat of the passions, but from the soul. This emphasis on man's soul brought him close in spirit to those who worshipped the enraptured Ganymede. "The prophane multitude I hate, & onelie consecrate my strange Poems to these serching spirits, whom learning hath made noble."[124]

There is a creditable and beguiling story, first told by Arthur Acheson, that the animosity between Shakespeare and Chapman sprang up when Chapman in 1594 submitted *The Shadow of Night* to the earl of Southampton, hoping for the nobleman's patronage. According to Acheson, Southampton asked his poet-friend Shakespeare for an opinion. Everything in the poem was anathema to Shakespeare, and when Chapman received no help from the nobleman, he knew who had ruined his chances. Embittered by the rejection, Chapman struck back by questioning the nature of Southampton's relationship with Shakespeare. When *The Shadow of Night* was published in 1594, Chapman in his dedication referred to "passion-driven men" who act as it they were "judgment's butchers, or as if the life of truth lay tottering in their verdicts." The dedication was addressed to Chapman's colleague Matthew Roydon, who in that same year published *Willobie his Avisa*, a narrative poem thought by many to contain allusions to Southampton and Shakespeare as both being involved with the same woman (a troilistic relationship fore-shadowing the one in the sonnets). Although there is nothing scat-ological or scurrilous in the poem, it encountered objections from censors when it was reissued, and the 1599 edition was burned.[125] The implication is that Southampton, affronted by what the book implied, used his influence to proscribe it.

What Acheson fails to explain is why Chapman would ever think of appealing to Southampton for patronage. After *Venus and Adonis*, Chapman must have known that he would have to look elsewhere to find a patron with a stern, anti-passionate moral code similar to his own. He quickly took a stand against Shakespeare. As we may recall, on the title page of the quarto is the motto, tak-en from Ovid: "*Vilia miretur vulgus; mihi flavus Apollo / Pocula Castalia plena ministret aqua.*" Let the common herd be amazed by worthless things; but for me let golden Apollo provide cups full of the water of the Muses. Some months later Chapman replied in *The Shadow of Night*:

> Presume not then, ye flesh confounded soules,
> That cannot beare the full Castalian bowles,
> Which sever mounting spirits from the sences,
> To look in this deepe fount for *thy* pretenses (emphasis added).
>
> (*Hymnus in Cynthiam*, lines 162-165.)[126]

An alert reader in 1595 would see that Chapman was deliberate-ly challenging Shakespeare, setting his moralistic verse against the sensuous and voluptuous *Venus and Adonis*.

Chapman having had his say about "serching spirits, whom learning hath made noble," Shakespeare had his. There is a theory, also first advanced by Arthur Acheson (in 1903), that in *Love's Labour's Lost* he ridiculed Chapman's nocturnal school of philoso-phy and that in the character of the pedant Holofernes he caricatured Chapman himself, whose learning and erudition were ostentatiously displayed in the etymological notes he appended to *The Shadow of Night*. Chapman often uses a word in its root sense, rather than with its colloquial meaning. When Holofernes says, "Let me supervise the canzonet" (*Love's Labour's Lost* 4.2.119), using "supervise" to mean "look over," he sounds like Chapman. The failed attempt by the four gentlemen in the play to devote themselves to scholarly pursuits for three years and to shun women during that time does seem an obvious jibe at Chapman's anti-erotic exaltation of the mind and the soul. Moreover, the whole plot of the play is in opposition to Chapman. The protagonist Berowne learns that life in the ivory tower of study and learning, removed from women, inhibits true knowledge. "Without the beauty of a woman's face," the mind withers, says Berowne. "From women's eyes this doctrine I divine: / They are the ground, the books, the academes / From whence doth spring the true Promethean fire" (4.3. 298-301). The last phrase with the emphasis on "true" seems to be a reproof to Chapman, who attributed the advance of mankind out of its savage state to "Promethean Poets with the coles / Of their most geniale, more-than-humane soules" (*School of Night*, 131-132). Chapman would "frame mans figure by his mind," his intelligence enlarged and deepened through learning. Shakespeare has Berowne reply, " Why, universal plodding poisons up / The nimble spirits in the arteries. . . . Learning is but an adjunct to ourself, / And where we are our learning likewise is: / Then when ourselves we see in ladies' eyes, / Do we not likewise see our learning there?" (4.3.301-314). In place of Chapman's intellect and knowledge, Shakespeare-Berowne puts intuition and feeling.

Finally, Shakespeare's phrase "school of night" does not make much sense unless it is taken as a direct reference to Chapman's poem and his philosophy.[127] "Black is the badge of hell," says Berowne, "The hue of dungeons and the school of night; / And beauty's crest becomes the heavens well" (4.3. 251-3). The condemnation exceeds what the plot requires, but it matches the tone of Chapman. For him, the beauty that attracted Shakespeare was not heavenly, and he called upon his readers to "serve the night, / To whom pale day (with whoredom soked quite) / Is but a drudge, selling her beauties use / To rapes, adultries, and to all abuse."[128]

In the 1590s, both Shakespeare in his *Venus* and Chapman in his *Shadow of Night* took the Ganymede type, the adolescent boy verging on maturity, as representing the abstract concept of beauty. The difference between them – a crucial difference that allowed for no compromise, no healing of their strained relationship— was that Chapman insisted that Ganymede signified wisdom, the "beauty of the mind."

> He is Ganemede, the birde of Iove,
> Rapt to his soveraignes bosome for his love,
> His bewtie was it, not the bodies pride [that is, not the genitals]
> That made him great Aquarius [the cup-bearer] stellified:
> And that minde most is bewtifull and hye,
> And nearest comes to a Divinitie,
> That furthest is from spot of earths delight,
> Pleasures that lose their substance with their sight,
> Such one, Saturnius ravisheth to love,
> And fills the cup of all content to Jove.
> If wisdome be the mindes true bewtie then,
> And that such bewtie shines in vertuous men,
> If those sweet Ganemedes shall onely find —.
> (The next line is missing in the original) [129] (462-474).

For Chapman, ugly youths and soulful old men could be lovers because minds and intellects were all that mattered. But in the 1590s Shakespeare saw Ganymede as non-intellectual, as sensually seductive, without any higher qualities apart from a vague soulfulness. Physical beauty was a type of perfection just as beauty of language was. His Adonis, "no man, though of a man's complexion" (line 215), does not arouse Venus because of his fine mind or his wit. It is "the maiden burning of his cheeks" (line 50) that inflames the heart of the lovesick goddess. In Chapman, the eyes of the lover feasting on beauty will stir the mind. In Shakespeare, the ardent embrace of the boy, "more lovely than a man, / More white and red than doves or roses are" (lines 9-10), is all that Venus wants. Beauty is an end in itself. In the sonnets, the poet succumbs to the blandishments of the youngster's form and features, to his being what he is rather than to what he may do. In fact, the deeds would lead to disenchantment.

Some of the sonnets may have been written as a cynical rebuke to Chapman's high-mindedness. Chapman, following Ficino and the Platonists, believed that the five senses when reined in by philosophy would energize the spirit and the soul. For Shakespeare, the five senses become chains that enslave the lover. Speaking of his dark mistress, he said, "But my five wits nor my five senses can / Dissuade one foolish heart from serving thee" (141).

A stern moralist like Chapman could not feel comfortable for long in Ovid's fanciful, imaginative, and sensual world, not even when he tried to make a place for himself in it by combining Ovid with Plato. About 1596 his thoughts took a new turn when he abandoned Ovid and embarked on his translation of Homer. Moving from the sybaritic to the heroic, he found his true self. Two years later he was able to publish *Seven Books of the Iliads*, containing his versions of Books 1, 2, 7, 8, 9, 10, and 11; and in the same year he produced a translation of book 18, "Achilles' Shield," both publications dedicated to the earl of Essex. (Chapman called his version of the epic the *Iliads* in the plural because he believed that the books had existed in several discrete sections before being collected.)

Chapman and Shakespeare had been heading in different directions ever since *Venus and Adonis*, and the philosophical rift between them that had opened up in the mid-1590s grew ever wider. Shakespeare saw man as driven by irrepressible passions, some of which, such as the longing for beauty, were to be admired and cultivated. Taking the opposite path, Chapman grew ever more convinced that valiancy and stoicism were the supreme manly virtues, and that any excess that they might lead to would be held in check by gentleness and temperance, virtues associated with women. The ideal man would combine both these masculine and feminine qualities; hence his interest in the androgynous Ganymede as a symbol.

By the time the first parts of Chapman's Homer appeared in print, Shakespeare was ready to challenge the cult of heroes. Portents of his skepticism are apparent in *Henry V*. The vivid recounting of the savage slaughter of ten thousand French soldiers at the battle of Agincourt and the cut-throat policies of King Henry in his treatment of prisoners of war undercut the heroism and patriotism on display in the drama as a whole, and they have been used by some high-minded but undedicated directors to turn the script into anti-war propaganda. There are numerous parallels between *Henry* V and Chapman's *Iliads*, so many that Gary Taylor in his edition of the play can assert that the "cumulative evidence that Shakespeare read Chapman's *Seven Books* before or while composing *Henry V* seems to me indisputable."[130] The ordinary playgoer would not have noticed these parallels; Chapman, however, would certainly see that Shakespeare was sparring with him.

Henry V was first staged in 1598 or early 1599,[131] and Shakespeare's real onslaught on Chapman's supermen came a year or two later. It was first pointed out by a young Irishman, destined to become the self-appointed heir to Shakespeare's crown as England's greatest dramatist, that *Troilus and Cressida* was aimed specifically at Chapman. In a paper read at a meeting of the *New Shakespere* [sic] *Society* in London in 1884, a young George Bernard Shaw said that Shakespeare "had long suspected Chapman and the ancient poets, and on reading Chapman's 'Iliad' saw that he was right; and hence *Troilus and Cressida*. It was Shakespeare's protest against Homer's attempt to impose upon the world and against Chapman as upholding him. . . . Chapman's 'Homer' appeared, and he saw that it was only his *Henry V*; and it was to expose and avenge his mistake and failure in writing *Henry V* that he wrote *Troilus and Cressida*."[132] (Shaw himself did not read his paper. It was read by a Miss Latham. On February 24, 1884, Shaw was probably lecturing on the socialist circuit.)

That Shakespeare was more interested in attacking Chapman's admiration of Greek warriors than in recounting an episode in the Trojan War accounts for the anomalous nature of the play. It smacks more of satire than history. Shakespeare made his jibes at Chapman doubly trenchant by lifting much of his material from Chapman's translation of the *Iliad* and turning it against him.[133] His mordant and cynical depiction of the ancient

Greeks and Trojans was a counterblast to Chapman's glorification of them in his version of Homer. Where Chapman made Achilles an enraged superhero, Shakespeare depicted him as brutal, treacherous, and ignoble.

THE ALTERCATION between Shakespeare and Chapman was a public affair, and it probably added ammunition to the so-called War of the Theatres, a quarrel among the leading playwrights in London that broke out in 1599. Nobody now knows what the central issue was, or even if there was one. Whatever the original cause, personal animus and injured egos kept the war going. John Marston in his satiric play *Histriomastix* (The Player Whipped) inserted a skit about Troilus and Cressida, staged as a play-within-a-play, in which the knowledgeable audience in 1599 would have caught a hint that Shakespeare had neatly dispatched Chapman. Troilus calls, "Come Cressida . . . behold, behold, thy garter blue / Thy knight his valiant elbow wears, / That when he *shakes* his furious *spear*, / The foe in shivering fearful sort / May lay him down in death to snort" (emphasis added).[34]

That was not the end of the matter, far from it. Although *Troilus and Cressida* was registered for publication in February 1603 and may possibly have appeared in print then, it was certainly published in 1609, the very year in which the sonnets came out. This was not a coincidence. By 1609 Shakespeare and Chapman had become bitter enemies, and their antithetical views of the Trojan War and its heroes must have been a factor in determining who found favor with the Fair Youth.

CHAPTER 10

The Difference a Date Makes

WITH Chapman identified as the Rival Poet, the search for the Fair Youth takes on a different aspect. Shakespeare did not name him, but that is no reason to believe that Chapman was equally reticent or mysterious. Improbable as it may seem, the scholar-detectives have never followed up this promising lead. Instead they have sought for him through the words prefacing the 1609 Quarto and in hints within the sonnets, making their task hopelessly difficult.

Given Chapman's literary reputation, the works that he wrote and dedicated to the Fair Youth must have circulated among the cognoscenti and in all likelihood got into print. Shakespeare certainly read them, since he commented on them in his epistolary sonnets to the Fair Youth. He admitted he was stunned by their poetic power; and then counteracted his praise by noting that his rival catered too much to the youth's love of praise.

> Who is it that says most? Which can say more,
> Than this rich praise: that you alone are you?
> . . .
> But he that writes of you, if he can tell
> That you are you, so dignifies his story.
> Let him but copy what in you is writ,
> Not making worse what nature made so clear,
> And such a counterpart shall fame his wit,
> Making his style admired everywhere.
>> You to your beauteous blessings add a curse,
>> Being fond on praise, which makes your praises worse (84).

The first step in searching for Chapman's potent lines is to establish a time frame for the sonnets. What he wrote should find an echo in Shakespeare, and vice versa. He lauded the young man in lines that struck Shakespeare as "gross painting" (82), fulsome flattery. Such lines, the "dedicated words which writers use / Of their fair subject" (82), should exist in Chapman's writings. Those lines, filled with the boy's "countenance" (86), were probably published. If Shakespeare wanted his verses, which at first circulated only among a select few, to appear in print, why would not Chapman, an eminent and highly respected poet, not want the same? Those lines would have been set down at approximately the time Shakespeare wrote the group of sonnets centering on the "alien pen" (78), the poet of "new-found methods" and "compounds strange" (76). If these sonnets could be dated rather precisely, the search for Chapman's words of praise would be considerably narrowed. And then if some verses by Chapman "dedicated" to a young man turned up, they would go a long way toward identifying the Fair Youth.

MOST of the early attempts at dating assumed that the sonnets were written before 1603. In spite of the poet's portraying himself as getting on in years, many scholars insisted that the sonnets were the work of a man not much older than the Fair Youth. If there was a big age difference, the erotic nature of the sonnets would raise the specter of a pederastic Shakespeare. That had to be avoided, no matter what the sonnets themselves said. Shakespeare and the youth had to be friends, devoted friends, not far apart in age, and the hyperbolic language of the sonnets had to be deemed characteristic of the times. No matter that other examples of such slavish devotion and worship of one friend for another could not be cited; no matter that Shakespeare nowhere asks for the youth's patronage; no matter that he often harshly criticizes the young man; no matter that the poet describes himself as old – the Shakespeare of the sonnets had to be fairly young and indebted to his friend.

This subjective and prejudiced approach to the dating of the sonnets could not stand up to common sense and simple logic. It did not accord with what was explicitly said in the sonnets. It also failed to explain why Shakespeare waited until 1609 to publish them. That they were pirated and published against his wishes was one explanation. But that idea lost any support it might have had when scholars applied new techniques to a study of the 1609 Quarto, techniques that make use of statistics concerning rhymes and the occurrence of rare words. The tendency of these objective studies is to assign the Dark Lady sonnets to the 1590s and the Fair Youth sonnets to a later period, with the possibility that some of the sonnets were put in their final form after 1603, that is, after James became king of England. Katherine Duncan-Jones in her 1997 edition of the sonnets emphasizes that the poems fit in with the world of James I's court and finds "good reason to believe that the whole sequence as published in 1609 was put into its final shape after 1603, and possibly quite close to its printing."[135] A summary of recent findings by other scholars concludes that "there can be no immediate objection to the proposition that Shakespeare was still writing or revising the sonnets up until their publication in 1609."[136]

Both the style and the matter of the Dark Lady sonnets date them to the mid-1590s. The dark-haired, dark-eyed woman who arouses the poet bears a close resemblance to Rosaline, the heroine of *Love's Labour's Lost*, written some time before 1598. Her blackness is harped upon in lines (4.3.245-262) that could easily be substituted for those in sonnet 127, the first of the Dark Lady sonnets.

> In the old age black was not counted fair,
> Or, if it were, it bore not beauty's name;
> But now is black beauty's successive heir.

Some of the sonnets forming part of the dialogue in the play would not seem out of place in the 1609 volume, and some of the sonnets from that volume could form part of the play. *Love's Labour's Lost* and the Dark Lady sonnets are cut from the same cloth.

Francis Meres in his *Palladis Tamia*, which was printed in 1598, refers to Shakespeare's "sugared sonnets" circulating in manuscript "among his private friends." At least two of these for-eyes-only sonnets got into print, the ones numbered 138 and 144 in the 1609 edition. These were published in modified versions in 1599 (perhaps in 1598, since the 1599 issue is a second printing) in a volume of miscellaneous poems by various authors entitled *The Passionate Pilgrim*. These two sonnets circulated widely and were put into print against Shakespeare's wishes.[137] Ten years later he changed his mind. He wanted them published, although in a different context, and he may have revised them for inclusion in the 1609 *Sonnets*.

That leaves the Fair Youth sonnets. They cover a relatively brief period of time, and they are held together by a narrative that begins with the poet's urging the young man to marry and ends with an ominous warning that the boy, like the poet himself, is subject to an audit, a settling of accounts, by time and the force of nature. On the basis of internal evidence these first 126 sonnets are in a proper sequence, more or less, and were written over a period of less than three years. In sonnet 104 the poet repeatedly mentions that he has known the boy for three Aprils, three Junes, three summers, three winters, and three autumns, and it is likely that the poet was acquainted with the boy for some time before he began sending sonnets to him. This means that if any one these 126 sonnets can be accurately dated, most of them could be assigned to a specific three-year period.

Although efforts have been made to bring the Fair Youth sonnets within the time frame of the Dark Lady sonnets, the tone and mood of the first group, 1 to 126, suggests that it was composed at a much later date. The poet's allusions to his age confirm this. In the Dark Lady sonnets, the poet is a highly sexed man, hardly able to control his desires. In the other sonnets, in sharp contrast, the poet describes himself as "beated and chopped with tanned antiquity" (62), "with time's injurious hand crushed and o'erworn," his brow filled "with lines and wrinkles" (63), and in the "twilight" of his life (73). It goes against reason to suggest, as most commentators have until recently, that these sonnets were written in the period 1595 to 1603 when Shakespeare was comparatively young. They were obviously written by a man in middle age, as the poet himself hints when he tells the young man to consider what will become of his adolescent beauty "when forty winters shall besiege

[his] brow" (2). Shakespeare turned forty in 1604, and he was forty-five when the sonnets were published.

Now there is one sonnet in particular, number 107, "Not mine own fears nor the prophetic soul," that has always been considered a touchstone for dating the sonnets. It clearly alludes to a certain contemporary event, manifestly one of some historical importance. If that event can be singled out, this particular sonnet would establish a time line for dating the Fair Youth sequence as a whole. The sonnet contains a number of allusions. The question is, what one event do they all refer to?

> Not mine own fears nor the prophetic soul
> Of the wide world dreaming on things to come
> Can yet the lease of my true love control,
> Suppose as forfeit to a confined doom.
> The mortal moon hath her eclipse endured,
> And the sad augurs mock their own presage;
> Uncertainties now crown themselves assured,
> And peace proclaims olives of endless age.
> Now with the drops of this most balmy time,
> My love looks fresh, and death to me subscribes.
> . . .
> And thou in this shalt find thy monument,
> When tyrants' crests and tombs of brass are spent.

There are a number of reference points here, all of which must point to a specific occurrence or phenomenon that would have been familiar to readers in 1609. To determine what it was a modern literary detective may find the essential clue where least expected. That is what happened when scholars tried to find out when Sidney wrote his *Astrophil and Stella*. It appeared in print in 1591 but had circulated privately for some years before that. To determine the date of composition Sidney experts turned to one of the sonnets in the sequence, number 30, which clearly contained allusions to international politics – seven of them, in fact. One of them referred to a Dutch diet, which did not make much sense until a scholar saw that here Dutch meant German and that the diet was the Diet of the Holy Roman Empire, held at Augsburg in the summer of 1582. All the other six allusions were consistent with this date.[138]

Shakespeare's sonnet 107 with its six allusions to some contemporaneous political event offers a similar invitation to archival research. In 1859 an anonymous commentator ventured the suggestion that the mortal moon was a reference to the virgin Queen Elizabeth, the moon being a conventional symbol of maidenhood.[139] Since then most editors of the text have built their interpretation of the sonnet on this slender implication. The "eclipse" is taken to refer to the end of her reign, the "sad augurs" to the predictions that England would be torn by civil war after the death of Elizabeth, and "the peace of endless age" to the calm that prevailed upon the succession of James to the throne of England. This would set the date of the sonnet at 1603.

This widely accepted interpretation of the evidence can be made to work only by distorting the meanings of some words, ignoring others altogether, and leaving the reader bewildered as to the purport of the sonnet as a whole. With regard to the last, the poet equates a certain political event with his own inner feelings. In the larger arena of world affairs, a terrible disaster of some sort seemed likely. In his own private sphere, the poet feared he was losing the boy's devotion, and that loss would be a kind of death. When he comes to write the sonnet, the disaster has been averted, and he dares to hope that through his verse his warm relationship with the youth will be revived. "Tyrants' crests" in the last line refers back to the mortal moon. Death, war, and tyrants have been defeated. In the personal sphere, love has not lost; in the political, peace has been achieved. Hence neither the poet's fears nor the state of the world is "forfeit to a confined doom."

The topical allusions must support this general sense of the sonnet. The natural, unforced meaning is that the mortal moon has survived a setback of some sort. The basic sense of the word endure is to persist, to suffer through in spite of adversity. Even when endure is used in association with death, as in *King Lear* ("Men must endure their going hence, even as their coming hither" [5.2.9]), the emphasis is not on death but on persistence, on continuance.[140] Furthermore, an eclipse is a temporary phenomenon, not one possessing the finality of death. The moon disappears for a few moments and then re-appears. Taking this into account, some critics have surmised that the sonnet refers to an illness that struck Queen Elizabeth, an illness from which she recovered, and have consequently dated the sonnet to 1599, when there were rumors that she might be near death's door.[141] But talk about her illness does not do much to explain the hosanna to peace and balmy times in the sonnet.

Nor does it agree with the general drift of the sonnet. The eclipse of the mortal moon is connected with the defeat of tyrants. Elizabeth may have been a strong ruler, but it is unlikely that the poet would make her emblematic of tyranny. Nor was she defeated. Nor, for that matter, was she ill in 1599.

For Shakespeare's readers in 1609, however, there was a moon that had recently been eclipsed. Living in a time when England's great war had been fought at sea, they would have known that a moon in the context of battles referred to a massed formation of warships, an armada. Leslie Hotson provided ample evidence showing that fleets in battle array took the shape of a lunar crescent. He cited numerous examples: "The Spanish fleete . . . went into . . . a proportion of a half moone;" "The Spaniards . . . remained gathered on a cluster compass wise like the Moone;" "a fleet of fire . . . through the enemies moone," "a horned Moone of huge and mighty shippes," and so on.[142] He might have added another example: Ben Jonson in 1611 in his masque *Prince Henries Barriers* called the Spanish Armada "the enemies moone, / that wan'd before it grew."

In Shakespeare's time, the mortal moon of sonnet 107 plainly meant an armada of ships in fighting formation. Hotson assumed that Shakespeare was referring to the Spanish Armada of 1588, even though that can hardly have been said to have endured an eclipse. It was roundly defeated. And specialists on prognostications have been quick to point out that in 1588 there were no "sad augurs mock[ing] their own presage."[143]

To determine the historical occasion that inspired 107, it is necessary to take into account all of the allusions in the sonnet, not just those that might support an early date. The mortal moon, the eclipse, the sad augurs, the olives of endless age, the "drops of this most balmy time," and the "tyrants" of the last line must all be associated with one noteworthy occurrence. The defeat of the Spanish Armada in 1588 has effectively been ruled out. So has the death of Queen Elizabeth

Now there is one such event that satisfies all the conditions, an event that occurred not long before the publication of the sonnets. It involved a temporary setback for the Spanish fleet ("the mortal moon hath her eclipse endured") and had repercussions in England. This was the sea battle at Gibraltar between the Spanish and the Dutch in April 1607, in which the Dutch fleet under Admiral Heemskerk destroyed a number of Spanish ships. As a result of that battle, the two sides were persuaded after years of warfare to agree to a truce. The Dutch had exhausted their funds, and the Spanish had suffered the loss of a considerable part of their fleet.

Overlooked by the exegetes, even by Leslie Hotson, is a passage in *Antony and Cleopatra* that echoes the words of the sonnet, "the mortal moon hath her eclipse endured." In act 3, Antony says, "[O]ur terrene moon / Is now eclips'd, and it portends alone / The fall of Antony" (3.13.152). The "terrene moon" is not Cleopatra (hardly a virgin maid), as some editors say, but her fleet of ships, which fled the scene. This defeat heralds the fall of Antony. A bit later, however, Antony says, "Our force by land / Hath nobly held, our sever'd navy too / Have knit again" (3.13.169). The fleet survived, "endured," exactly as did the Spanish fleet in 1607.

Still, it took two years before the peace treaty was actually endorsed. Envoys from England and France pressured Spain (the tyrants) and the United Provinces to come to terms. Finally, the treaty was signed on 29 March 1609; the news reached London on April 3.[144] The treaty stipulated a twelve-year truce, and Shakespeare's "olives of endless age" is doubly apt, considering that the country of olives was a signatory.

This event on the continental side of the Channel had a special significance in England because the peace treaty was brokered by

King James. It was a personal triumph for him, affirming England's position as a leading power among European nations. As a man of peace, he was proud of his accomplishments as a negotiator and wanted to be remembered for them. In 1624, long after the signing of the treaty, it was said of him that he "enters not with an Olive Branch in his hand, but with a whole Forrest of Olives round about him; for he brought not Peace to this Kingdome alone, but almost to all the Christian Kingdomes of Europe."[145]

It was only to be expected that poets in 1609 would praise James's diplomatic feat. The most ambitious and most noteworthy was a poem in 1232 lines entitled *The Tears of Peace*, extolling James as "the great King of Peace," who hath "outlabored Hercules; / And, past his Pillars [Gibraltar]," stretched the victories of peace.[146] It was a virtuoso performance, a learned work longer than Shakespeare's *Venus and Adonis* and composed in just a few weeks' time. This is the poem referred to in sonnet 107 in the phrase "drops of this most balmy time." Shakespeare frequently used "drops" to mean "tear drops."[147]

The poet who accomplished this exceptional feat of versification, which was obviously dashed off to impress his patron, was none other than the Rival Poet, George Chapman. In *Tears of Peace*, Chapman takes on the role of the scholarly philosopher discoursing on the causes of war and of social unrest in general. His credentials as expounder on these matters were impressive. After all, the spirit of Homer had visited him, spoken to him, and given him its blessings for translating the *Iliad* into English. In the poem, the spirit of Homer leads Chapman to the Goddess of Peace, who tells him that the pursuit of wealth and pleasure, and the interest taken in fads and fashions, prevent the attainment of any lasting peace. Man's sensual parts, his appetites, are the cause of a war within the soul, which "earth-bruised and lam'd, . . . with sick feathers . . . and broken pinions" flutters in vain towards heaven and cannot ascend to "the high-heaven-reaching Scale of man's true Peace." As long as man prefers to govern others and not himself, there will be wars. Man can control his passions only through study, for learning is the "soul's actual frame."

This punditic poem (its full title is *Euthymiæ Raptus, or The Tears of Peace*), divided in scholarly fashion into an *Inductio*, an *Invocatio*, a *Conclusio*, and a *Corollarium ad principem*, is dedicated to a young man, who may at any time be called upon to act in affairs of state. Chapman takes upon himself the role of instructor to this young man, who is also his patron. In the final section, the corallarium, Chapman makes a pathetic plea to this "Great Prince of men" for the continued support that would allow him to complete his translation of Homer.[148]

This young man must be the young man of the sonnets, a mysterious figure perhaps to anyone who was not familiar with the times and not part of the literary scene in Jacobean London. But this "prince" was certainly well known to those readers who snapped up copies of *Shake-speares Sonnets* in the spring of 1609. This was the Fair Youth who stood between the two rival poets, one asking for his patronage, the other for his love; one offering philosophy and statesman-like advice, the other verse of beauty great enough to match the boy's handsomeness; one an austere tutor to the boy, the other a devoted slave (57 and 58). The contention between them was not just a matter of pretty words, a piddling poetic contest; it was a deeply felt dispute between two schools of thought, two kinds of living. In sonnet 20 Shakespeare set his "passion" against Chapman's sobriety and self-command; in sonnet 107 his monument in enduring verse against Chapman's political credo.

A mere glance at the dedication to *The Tears of Peace* or to the "epistle dedicatory" prefacing the 1609 edition of Chapman's Homer (which Shakespeare was adverting to in sonnet 82: "the dedicated words which writers use / Of their fair subject, blessing every book") should reveal the identity of this "Great Prince." There are enough clues scattered about in the sonnets themselves, apart from the references to the Rival Poet, to make identification doubly certain.

CHAPTER 11

In Search of the Fair Youth

T HERE ARE those – W. H. Auden is among them – who believe that attempts to identify the protagonists in the drama of the sonnets is an example of "plain vulgar idle curiosity at work." In the efforts to determine who the Fair Youth was,
says Auden, "More nonsense has been talked and written, more intellectual and emotional energy expended in vain, on the sonnets
of Shakespeare than on any literary work in the world." He denies
that identifying the Fair Youth and the Rival Poet "would in any
way illuminate our understanding of the sonnets themselves."¹⁴⁹
By preserving the anonymity of the chief persons in the drama,
Shakespeare would seem to agree. However, he published his sonnets knowing that within his knot – a coterie, in the language of
the time – the persons would be recognized. By publishing to the
world at large what seem like very private and personal documents, he was making a statement that was important to him.
And, as is evident from their imperfections, many of the sonnets
were written under the great pressure of time in order to make his
point and to settle accounts with those who disagreed with him or
who slighted him. Everyone who studies the sonnets carefully
knows that Shakespeare bared his soul in them, and what he revealed cannot be fully known unless we are put in the position of
the readers Shakespeare had in mind. And everyone knows that
that is why so much energy is expended on solving the great mystery of the sonnets: who was the young man? Identifying him is not
merely a matter of scholarly curiosity or of a compulsion to explore
the territory surrounding the sonnets; it might help to explain
why Shakespeare was so entranced by him.

Auden asks, regarding sonnet 57 —"Being your slave, what should I do but tend / Upon the hours and times of your desire?" — whether anyone could imagine actually showing it to the person addressed.[150] But if some biographical fact made it possible to imagine the poet calling himself a servant and the boy his sovereign, would not even Auden be grateful for this bit of enlightenment?

Since those amateur detectives who went in search of the Fair Youth disregarded the identity of the Rival Poet as the essential clue, they created a mystery for themselves that was impossible to solve. After they had spent sixty years without getting anywhere, Oscar Wilde felt he could rightly call it "the greatest mystery of modern literature."

WHAT MAKES the anonymity particularly fascinating is that Shakespeare promised the young man everlasting fame, yet what he left us is something like the tomb of the Unknown Soldier. Everyone knows the monument, but who knows who is buried in it? The situation was different in 1609, when every reader would have known who the young man was and wondered at Shakespeare's temerity.

In sonnet 55 the poet boasts, "Not marble, nor the gilded monuments / Of princes, shall outlive this powerful rhyme." In sonnet 81 Shakespeare writes, "Your name from hence immortal life shall have, / Though I, once gone, to all the world must die: / The earth can yield me but a common grave, / When you entombed in men's eyes shall lie. / Your monument shall be my gentle verse." "Your *name*" shall become immortal through these poems; yet that name has vanished.

At this point, two thirds of the way through the Fair Youth sequence, Shakespeare clearly thought that his sonnets would be the verbal equivalent of a gilded monument, like Michelangelo's tomb of Lorenzo di' Medici, in which the artistic genius of the sculptor outshines the political achievements of the subject. Shakespeare knew that in magnifying the glory of this young man he was creating poetry of a power and complexity unsurpassed in English literature.

Indeed he was right. The poems did become part of our living heritage, with lines such as "When to the sessions of sweet silent thought / I summon up remembrance of things past," familiar to every literate person. But he did not make the Fair Youth part of that heritage. He could have put the youth's name somewhere in the sonnets or on the title page. And if he became disappointed in the youth, as he must have done, and regretted the praise he had lavished on him, he could have done, as Beethoven did when Napoleon's vainglorious excesses dismayed him. He crossed off the emperor's name from the score of the Eroica Symphony, an act that made his feelings clear. But in the *Sonnets* of 1609 there is no scratched out name, and the promised eternal fame turned into oblivion. As Napoleon said, "Glory is fleeting but obscurity is forever." By publishing the sonnets in 1609 without any clear dedication and with no names mentioned, Shakespeare, slipping off into retirement, seemed to be saying, "My name will live on, but yours won't." He refused to pen any obsequious and flattering dedication to match the accolades of the sonnets themselves, as was customary. But he proudly put his own name on the title page, conferring immortality on himself while denying it to the idol of the sonnets. The human and very personal drama of the sonnets lies in that change of heart.

The odd thing is that no one seems to have taken much interest in the identity of the Fair Youth until almost two centuries after the sonnets were published. Perhaps it is not so odd, since the sonnets were not much read and not easily accessible until after 1800. By that time the trail had grown cold, and when the literary bloodhounds tried to pick up the scent, they went off in the wrong direction, several wrong directions, in fact. The result was a mystery filled like all good mysteries with a number of red herrings. Also, as in a cleverly plotted mystery, the essential clue, the one that breaks the case, was in evidence from the beginning, in plain sight, like the purloined letter; in this case, Chapman's poem.

There are two reasons why the sonneteer languished in obscurity while the dramatist prospered. George Steevens, who edited the complete works of Shakespeare, only reluctantly included the sonnets, explaining that they were marred by far-fetched and strained poetic conceits. This was true. The sonnets are often difficult to understand, and commentators have worked hard to coax a consistent meaning out of some of them. They are more convoluted in thought than the sonnets of other poets, and the best of them combine polyphonic music and multi-layered meanings in a way unmatched by other poets of the time. To appreciate the density of meaning in them, one need only turn to Helen Vendler's 500-page magisterial critique, in which, two hundred years after Steevens's complaint, we are afforded new insights into Shakespeare's poetic art.

The other reason is that in one respect the sonnets were not obscure enough. It was apparent to even the most casual reader that these sonnets, however arcane and equivocal the language, were the uninhibited expressions of the love of one man for another. When the poet wrote, "Shall I compare thee to a summer's day? / Thou art more lovely and more temperate," he did not have a young maid in mind. This is what shocked and disconcerted Steevens, who, having once published the sonnets, realized his moral error and declared he would not offer them again to the broad public even if compelled to do so by Parliament. One thing stood out very clearly. Shakespeare, the poet who had explored the heights and depths of the human soul and who was now established as an English institution, was a sexual deviant.

With the coming of the nineteenth century and the advent of Romanticism, attitudes began to change. Obscurity was welcomed, and confession was good. Keats (1817) found that great poets had a "negative capability," which made them "capable of being in uncertainties, mysteries, doubts, without any irritable reaching after facts and reason." If the sonnets had no apparent line of thought, if Shakespeare's habit of playing on the multiple meanings of words, left the reader somewhat adrift in a sea of possibilities, that only made them a more accurate reflection of life and human nature itself with all their contradictions and ambiguities.

Another Romantic poet, William Wordsworth, did much more than Keats to promote interest in the sonnets. Walking along the shore of Rydal Lake, he improvised (so he said) a sonnet in praise of the sonnet form, which had fallen out of fashion. "With this key Shakespeare unlocked his heart," he declared. From that moment the terra incognita of the sonnets began to be explored by everyone who took an interest in Shakespeare the dramatist. Who would not want to know what Shakespeare the man was really like? It was the strong sense of life lived that attracted Wordsworth to the sonnets. He ignored the harsh moral judgment of Steevens, and he made the personality of the poet the center of interest. For Wordsworth, these sonnets were more than literature; they were a revelation. By issuing them near the end of his career, Shakespeare, the elusive genius who had conjured up the great gallery of dramatic characters, stepped forward and unmasked himself. He stood revealed as a man as fascinating and as passionate as any of the heroes he had created.

It was a giant step forward in the history of Shakespeare criticism. The 1609 Quarto was now something more than a collection of love poems. It contained the fragments of an autobiography. In place of the mythical Shakespeare, a shadowy figure fashioned out of a few unreliable anecdotes, there was now a human being, passionate and vulnerable, ecstatic and despairing, the authentic Shakespeare speaking in his own voice, and really in love.

There was bound to be a mixed response. While some critics voiced their acceptance and understanding of Shakespeare's confession, others registered their disappointment. Some went into denial. John Boswell, the Younger, as we have seen, declared they were not personal revelations at all. They were part of a fiction, "the effusions of his [Shakespeare's] fancy, written . . . for the amusement of a private circle." Yet Boswell, contradicting himself, assumed the Fair Youth was a real person, not a fictional character, and he went looking for him.

Most bizarre was the response of Samuel Taylor Coleridge, who opined that "the sonnets could only have come from a man deeply in love, and in love with a woman; and there is one sonnet [the notorious sonnet 20] which, from its incongruity, I take to be a purposed blind."[151] Why a man deeply in love with a woman should address her as a boy is not explained. And why the poet should use this sonnet as a blind, as a subterfuge to mislead the reader about the recipient's sex, is a question that Coleridge does not address. If the poems are written to a woman, why is any "blind" necessary? Looking into the decidedly queer universe of Coleridge's mind, one commentator has tried to follow the convolutions of his thought: Shakespeare "disguises himself as a pederast as a ruse to avoid detection as a man 'deeply in love' with a woman."[152] As a plot for a comedy, Plautus or Wycherley might make something of this imbroglio, but it makes nonsense of the sonnets.

PROBABLY the most representative response was that of the historian Henry Hallam, writing in 1837. He bravely accepted the "genuineness " of the sonnets and tried to be broadminded and understanding. Using the guarded language of his time, he noted that the sonnets were now being warmly appreciated by a certain group of readers. Remarking on the change in taste since Steevens banished the sonnets, Hallam said that "there is now a tendency, especially among young men of poetical tempers, to exaggerate the beauties of these remarkable productions." But inextricably mixed in with these beauties, he went on to say, was an "excessive and misplaced affection," an emotion that tainted the judgment of these young men of poetical tempers. Hallam finally let social morality outweigh esthetics and took Steevens's position, declaring that "it is impossible not to wish that Shakespeare had never written them."[153]

Apart from those like him who wanted the sonnets to disappear, readers were divided into two camps: the gay and the straight. Both wanted to claim Shakespeare as one of their own kind. For the latter group the sonnets addressed to the young man were an expression of an ideal friendship, unusual, but not perverse, in its intensity. The other group saw the relationship as going beyond friendship into amorous passion. In the nineteenth century there was no socially proper term for them. In eighteenth-century London they were sometimes called "monsters" or "finger-twirlers." In the nineteenth century, at least in literary circles, as in Hallam's, they were more kindly, less derisively, referred to as men of a poetical temper. They found in the sonnets what Ralph Waldo Emerson described as a "singular friendship amounting to a passion."[154] Before words like homosexual and gay entered the language, this singular friendship was in Lord Douglas's famous phrase "the love that dare not speak its name." Whatever slang terms were used by ordinary people, esthete was the delicate code word used by the educated and literary set. But other terms, like Socratic love, would convey homosexual interest.

What thoughts they harbored seldom found public expression. There could be no open debate about the subject as long as homosexuals were treated as social outcasts and always in danger of being imprisoned – or worse. In 1811 in London a number of men were pilloried in the Haymarket merely for frequenting a notorious tavern in Vere Street. Louis Crompton in his history of homosexuality reports that English popular feelings against sodomites "attained a kind of hysteria during the regency (1810-1820), when brutal pilloryings in the heart of London drew enormous crowds seething with hostility and all but shut down city business. Between 1806 and 1835 over sixty men were hanged in England and another twenty in the navy, a much greater number than in any earlier century."[155] In America, the young Walt Whitman was tarred and feathered by a mob of churchgoers when he was accused from the pulpit of being a sodomite, which goes a long way towards accounting for his gingerly treatment of male sex in his poems.

Inevitably in the course of the nineteenth century there developed a subterranean quarrel, a shadowy battle, between the esthetes and the hearty types over the true nature of Shakespeare's devotion to the Fair Youth. The battle could not be fought in the open because the esthetes feared for their reputation – and perhaps for their security and safety. Besides, who would publish an outspoken exposé of England's revered dramatist as a man strongly attracted to young men? Consequently, what the advocates of a "normal" Shakespeare had to say appears in the written record, in the chronicles of the time, while what the closeted young men of poetic temperament really thought has to be inferred. There was no public debate and no scholarly exchange of ideas. If there had been, the men of poetic temperament would have had the last word.

When the philistines insisted that the ardent language of the Fair Youth sonnets was characteristic of the language of patronage in 1609, they revealed their ignorance. "Being your slave" (57), "being your vassal" (58), "O, how I faint when I of you do write" (80), "the master-mistress of my passion" (20) – no one has ever found anywhere in Elizabethan or Jacobean examples of patronage anything comparable. Neither recipients of patronage nor close friends went to such extremes of abasement. C.S. Lewis said, "I have found no real parallel to such language between friends in sixteenth-century literature."[156]

Neither the esthete nor the philistine was able to put his prejudices aside and look at Shakespeare's sexuality clinically. Each conjured up an image of the Fair Youth that he could set next to his image of Shakespeare. Those who preferred their Shakespeare straight drew on the Dark Mistress sonnets, and turning from them, imagined that Shakespeare's friendship with the young man was of the ideal kind, extolled by Spenser in Book IV of *The Faerie Queene*. There in the Temple of Venus, but far removed from ordinary lovers, one finds Hercules and Hylas, Jonathan and David, Pylades and Orestes, Damon and Pythias, Theseus and Pirouthus. These were legendary figures, true, but modern times offered the very real examples of Montaigne and Estienne de la Boëtie, Milton and Diodati, Arthur Hallam and Tennyson, Henry Cardinal Newman and Ambrose St. John. These were soulful friendships, and to them should be added that of Shakespeare and the Fair Youth.

However, those young men of a poetic temper, especially those who had delved deeply into the matter, found historical and contemporary examples of male partnering more to their liking. They thought of Achilles and Patroclus, Socrates and Alcibiades, Alexander and Hephaestion, the boy Caesar and Nicodemus of Bithnyia, Michelangelo and Tommaso de' Cavaliere (twenty-three years old when they first met), Lord Byron and the choirboy John Edleston, Walt Whitman and his "Dear Boy" Doyle.

The conventionally minded early set about finding who the Fair Youth was, convinced that identifying him would settle the matter in their favor. But in looking for him, they brought their prejudices into play. They went in search of a man roughly of Shakespeare's age who might have been his patron, totally disregarding the information contained in the sonnets themselves. Their wishes and the plain facts were in direct conflict.

The first attempts to identify the young man date from 1780 when Edmund Malone in the third edition of the works of Shakespeare incorporated the sonnets. In his commentary on them he considered two possibilities: Thomas Tyrwhitt's suggestion that the Mr. W.H. mentioned as the "begetter" of the sonnets was William Hughes, a name conjured up from the wordplay on "hues" in sonnet 20; and Richard Farmer's that Mr. W.H. was William Harte, Shakespeare's nephew. Neither suggestion had much to recommend it, and nobody seemed to care.

The search for the elusive youth did not become serious until the nineteenth century, after Wordsworth's sonnet. In 1817 Nathan Drake (in his *Shakspeare* [sic] *and His Times*) put forward the earl of Southampton. Two years later B.H. Bright proposed and in 1832 James Boaden seconded the earl of Pembroke. Why these two names? W.H. were the initials of William Herbert , earl of Pembroke, and, reversed, they were the initials of Henry Wriothesley, earl of Southampton. Beginning in the early 1590s Wriothesley had been a prominent figure in Shakespeare's career. Herbert was a patron of the arts, a devotee of the theatre, and in 1623, long after the publication of the *Sonnets*, aided the publication of the First Folio of Shakespeare's plays. These two theories picked up momentum in the course of the nineteenth century, as the commentators who concerned themselves with the identity problem adopted either Southampton or Pembroke as their man. Both theories originated in the desire of orthodox Bardolaters to keep the Fair Youth and the poet fairly close together in age. There could be no hint of pedophilia. There was also the equally strong need to see the relationship of the two as that of patron and poet.

This error was absolutely fundamental. It lay in assuming that the publisher's dedication to the *Sonnets* referred to the object of the poet's devotion. "Begetter" was taken to mean the person who inspired the sonnets. But to beget meant either to procreate or to gather; it did not mean to inspire. Even if it was argued that the meaning of the word was stretched to include the sense of "to give birth to," there remained the insurmountable fact that a nobleman could not possibly be addressed as Mr. (as in Mr W.H.), that is, mister or master. That would have been a star-chamber offense, audacious beyond belief, according to scholars.[157] Conceivably, Shakespeare, who eventually fell out of love with the youth, might have been daring enough to call him mister, but certainly the publisher who wrote the dedication would not have put his business and his reputation at considerable risk.

Most of the discussion throughout the nineteenth and twentieth centuries had the Pembrokists and the Southamptonites at each other's throats. They effectively destroyed each other – just how effectively can be seen in the neat table of arguments pro and con drawn up by Raymond Macdonald Alden in his 1916 edition of the sonnets, where the inadequacies of both schools are best displayed. His summary: "The whole body of evidence is seen to be circumstantial and inferential." Moreover, both candidates lacked the crucial distinguishing traits of the young man described in the sonnets. Surely, the fact that neither Pembroke nor Southampton was fair-haired and the fact that neither would have been addressed as a boy would have been enough to put to rest both theories. William Herbert had dark hair and beard, and Henry Wriothesley had red hair; both were of the nobility, not Misters; both were mature men.[158]

Yet each side insisted that its candidate was indeed the youth. The lack of a signal and conspicuous characteristic, such as blond hair, posed no problem for them.

(One other point, seldom mentioned, that tells against Pembroke is that the Shakespeare First Folio, which was dedicated to him, does not contain the sonnets!)

While the defenders of Shakespeare's reputation were busy chasing their own tails, the men of poetic temperament were slowly gathering courage, getting their views into print, and making incursions into conformist territory. Richard Simpson in 1868 (earlier in *The Chronicle*) published *An Introduction to the Philosophy of Shakespeare's Sonnets*. As we have seen, this was a significant contribution to Shakespeare studies, significant in that it raised the very real possibility that the sonnets constituted something more than a day-by-day chronicle, that they added up to a philosophy of love. To Shakespeare the sublime lyricist Simpson added Shakespeare the thinker. He brought out the connection between the sonnets, Dante's *Divine Comedy*, and Platonic love.

"All the great sonnet writers affected one particular philosophy," said Simpson, "which was derived originally from the Banquet of Plato. Socrates was supposed to be the first founder of this school of thought, and Shakespeare's adherence to it was so notorious that he was called in his epitaph 'Socrates ingenio' [sic], a Socrates in his turn of mind. . . . From the Platonic schools and books this science passed to Dante and Petrarch, and became a distinguishing characteristic of the Italian revival of the sixteenth century. From Italy it radiated through Europe, and was taken up by Surrey and Spenser. But it was treated by none with such depth and variety as by Shakespeare."[159]

Simpson defended the particular kind of love that animates the sonnets and touched on the delicate subject of the poet's adoration of male beauty.

"Beauty is the only metaphysical quality which can become an object of the physical sense. Thus it is both physical and metaphysical; and love, the passion which it excites, appertains to both spheres – that of matter and that of spirit. It is this community of love which enables it to assume the character of universality."[160]

By viewing the sonnets as deriving from Plato, Simpson was able to see how the Dark Lady sonnets with their implicit misogyny, had a place in Shakespeare's philosophy. There are three exemplars of love, he said: of woman to man (Alcestis and Admetus), of man to woman (Orpheus and Eurydice), and of man to man (Achilles and Patroclus).

"In the general Greek notion, the last was the highest love; it was not feminine but masculine beauty that fired the imagination with the glowing sentiment and idealizing passion which was the stimulus of philosophy, and which raised a man above the vulgar and selfish pursuits of live, and even above the fear of death."

Simpson circumspectly dissociated this ideal friendship from "Greek corruption," proffering Montaigne's affection for Estienne de la Boëthie as the "perfect community of soul and will, passing the love of women."[161] Simpson was part of that shadowy Victorian gay subculture inhabited by classicists like Walter Pater and A.E. Housman, a closeted society in which Greek philosophy was admired and Greek practice teasingly hinted at. It was a society very much in tune with Shakespeare's sonnets.

Simpson's essay was a landmark in that it opened up a channel for public discussion of Shakespeare's eroticism. In 1873 in an essay in *Academy*, John Addington Symonds, who was to become a leading spokesman for the esthetes, endorsed Simpson's Platonic interpretation of the sonnets. A few years later, in his hugely influential multi-volume study of the Italian Renaissance, he discussed and translated some of the sonnets of Michelangelo, sonnets that invoke the beauty of a young man.

"That to beauty in all its human forms [Michelangelo] was throughout his life a slave," wrote Symonds, "we have his own sonnets to prove."[162] Symonds obligingly translated and appended a few of them. Esthetes reading these passages could not help but see the parallel between the Italian artist writing poems to his adored Tommaso and the English poet composing sonnets to the Fair Youth, with the similarity made even stronger when the Platonic basis of Shakespeare's sonnets was recognized. Here were two supremely great artists sharing the same sexual and philosophical ideas. The esthetes could hold up their image of Shakespeare as the equal of the Shakespeare revered by straight men.

Still, however inspiriting it may have been to read Simpson and Symonds, those young men of poetic temperament had to proceed very cautiously in their subtle crusade. Symonds was careful to stress the essential spirituality of the Michelangelo sonnets, all the while hinting that there was more to be said. "Though his modern editor shrinks from putting a literal interpretation upon them, I am convinced that we must accept them simply as an expression of an artist's homage for the worth and beauty of an excellent young man." [163] He reserved his real thoughts for his study of Greek pederasty, *A Problem in Greek Ethics*, published in 1883 in a limited edition of ten copies.

Then in 1884-86 there appeared in *Blackwood's Edinburgh Magazine* a series of anonymous articles, " New Views of Shakespeare's Sonnets: the Other Poet Identified," which discussed the spiritual content of the sonnets and the influence of Dante.

These skirmishes in the field of forbidden love only made things worse for the esthetes. When they opened the door to Plato and Socrates, there also slipped in a whiff of something corrupt, fetid, sulfurous, certainly un-English. In the eyes of most Englishmen who knew anything at all about it, Socratic love was a cloak beneath which sinful acts were carried out. To them it was a pretense by which the esthetes could further their indecent cause. A straight-minded Englishman could not help but notice that the pure soul so adored by the esthetes somehow always found itself a place in a beautiful body or an adorable face. Why were there no paeans to plain-looking men with beautiful souls?

Further, the transcendental thoughts of the esthetes were expressed in such equivocal language that one was left to wonder what part physical sex played in their lives. Was their language only "idle chatter of a transcendental kind"? It was a question raised by W.S. Gilbert in the operetta *Patience*. Gilbert's esthete knows what the philistines are thinking about him. "If he's content with a vegetable love, which would certainly not suit me, / Why what a most particularly pure young man this pure young man must be!"

The popularity of Gilbert and Sullivan's 1881 operetta was an indication of how ideas about transcendental love had percolated down to a fairly wide public. The esthetes were making themselves known, so much so that they could be snickered at in popular theatre. There was bound to be a reaction. Many Englishmen were not to be taken in by the flowery talk, and they raised their voices against the invasion of an alien, extraterrestrial love into the lives of down-to-earth citizens. Satire was one way of combating it. Satire, however, tends to promote the thing satirized by making it

[143]

better known. More forceful methods were called for: denunciation and legal action.

Earlier in the century the eminent historian Thomas Babington Macaulay had warned his readers about Greek love. "The most immoral Restoration rake," he fulminated, "would have shuddered at the words that passed between Socrates and Phaedrus." (Little did this historian know about the mores of Restoration aristocrats.) More effective than this extravagant ranting was legal action. In 1885 Parliament strengthened the law against homosexual acts by passing the notorious Labouchère Amendment. This was the law under which Oscar Wilde was prosecuted.

Two years after this amendment became law, Wilde wrote a short story called "A Portrait of Mr. W.H." (published in 1889). It was the aforementioned article in *Blackwood's Edinburgh Magazine* (1884), dwelling on the Platonic aspects of the *Sonnets*, that prompted Wilde to compose this clever bit of fiction. His real inspiration, however, had a more intimate source. In May 1886, the thirty-one-year old Oscar had been seduced by the seventeen-year-old Robert Ross. Initiated into gay sex and liberated by it, Wilde saw the sonnets in a new light. "Indeed the story is half yours," he told Ross, "and but for you would not have been written." [164]

His story tells of a man who is convinced that the Fair Youth was a boy actor in Shakespeare's theatrical company – and thus the inspiration for several of the dramatist's female characters. Taking his cue from a pun in the crucial sonnet 20 ("a man in hue, all hues in his controlling") and from the dedication to Mr. W.H., Wilde's fictional protagonist persuades himself that the boy's name was Willie Hughes.

Wilde had done his homework. He had boned up on Simpson and Symonds and immersed himself in the scholarly commentary. He refers to the atmosphere of Platonic love, notes the comparison of Shakespeare with Michelangelo, and challenges the Pembroke and Southampton theories. Reading the sonnets, the narrator (Wilde is careful to keep himself at one remove from the sentiments expressed) felt as if he "had been initiated into the secret of that passionate friendship, that love of beauty and beauty of love, of which Marsilio Ficino tells us, and of which the Sonnets may be held to be the perfect expression."[165]

Wilde has a field day in disposing of both the earl of Pembroke and the earl of Southampton as possible Fair Youths. Southampton was not a handsome man, and Pembroke as he appears in the Wilton portraits was "a swarthy dark-haired man."[166] Therefore neither could be the fair-haired youth of the Sonnets. His own theory accounts for the "Mr." in the dedication. No publisher of the time, Wilde rightly points out, would have dreamed of addressing a lord of the realm as mister. These objections to the prevailing theories have never been rebutted.

Of course the main thrust of Wilde's tale is to bring out once for all that the Fair Youth was not a mature man but a boy, a teen-ager, a stripling, like Robert Ross. Wilde may have exaggerated when he claimed there was no fog in London until Whistler painted it, but it is fair to say that there was no boy in the sonnets until Wilde sketched him in. In all the writings on the *Sonnets* prior to Wilde's story, there is hardly a single reference to the Fair Youth as a boy, in spite of his being addressed as a "lovely boy" in sonnet 126 and explicitly and lovingly described as having a teen-age boy's physique in sonnet 20. "Boy" was the shibboleth that distinguished the gays from the straights. When the latter saw the word "boy" in the sonnets and tried to pronounce it, it always came out "friend." It is inconceivable that Shakespeare would have called a mature nobleman a boy. When Aufidius in Shakespeare's play calls Coriolanus "boy," Coriolanus is stung to the quick (5.6. 100-110). As usual, predilection and prejudice obscured the facts. The straights could not tolerate the thought that Shakespeare might be a pederast, while Oscar Wilde re-enacted his own seduction by a teen-age boy and ignored the aristocratic status of the Fair Youth. In both cases, wishful thinking trumped scholarship.[167]

As long as the Fair Youth was imagined to be a mature man and not a beardless adolescent, there could be no possibility of solving the great mystery. But in seeking to solve it, he embarked on a path that would lead in just a few years to his disgrace and imprisonment. After his release, he said of the sonnets, "I have loved them, as one should love all things, not wisely but too well."

Wilde neatly disposed of the old theories to make room for his own. Unfortunately, he fudged and distorted the evidence just as much as his predecessors had done. He made two fundamental errors: he accepted, as nearly everyone had, Mr. W.H. as the person who inspired the sonnets, and he ignored the clear indications that the young man was above the poet in the social scale. That the Fair Youth was a nobleman was the one solid fact on which the older theories were built. More than once Shakespeare draws attention to his own lowly status as an actor vis-à-vis the youth's position (e.g., 25, 111).

All along the stumbling block lay in the predispositions of those who took an interest in the problem, the straights seeking a heterosexual Shakespeare and the gays trying to steal Shakespeare from the straights. Both sides paid little attention to the Rival Poet, whose presence is felt behind the whole middle section of the Fair Youth sonnets. Apparently, both sides felt that knowing who the Rival Poet was would add nothing to the sexual debate. This was a serious mistake, and the consequence is that the controversy between the Southamptonites and the Pembrokists still remains stranded at the point it had reached in the middle of the nineteenth century.

CHAPTER 12

The Rose of the Sonnets

THE PLACE to look for the Fair Youth is not in the publisher's dedication to the 1609 Quarto, hiding behind the initials W. H., but in Chapman's works, and specifically in two works published at the time the sonnets were being composed: the epistle to his *Homer Prince of Poets: Translated according to the Greeke, in twelve Bookes of his* Iliads and his long poem *The Tears of Peace*. The name of his patron should appear there, praised with what Shakespeare called the "strained touches rhetoric can lend" (82). If this patron is the Fair Youth, all that we can know about him should match all that the sonnets tell us about him. The point at which Shakespeare's sonnets with their description of the Fair Youth overlap with Chapman's poetry is the place where we will find the Fair Youth. Once this is understood, the great mystery is transformed from one of Sherlock Holmes's three-pipe problems into a one-cigarette problem.

There is quite a lot of descriptive information that can be gleaned from the 1609 Quarto. First of all, the young man must be a teen-ager. He is called "boy" more than once, an epithet not suitable for anyone in his twenties. Boys became adolescents when they first produced semen, and they turned into men when they grew a beard.[168] This young man has started to masturbate (4) and still has a girl's face (20). Secondly, there are several physical characteristics that must be taken into account. He is of exceptional attractiveness, with a shapely body; the poet refers to "the composed wonder of [his] frame" (59). His hair is the color of marjoram, brownish or auburn (99). His good looks are an inheritance from his mother (3), whom he is said closely to resemble. Thirdly, he is unmarried, but under considerable pressure to find himself a wife. Young noblemen were expected to be engaged before they were twenty. Fourthly, he is of a taciturn nature, aloof and self-controlled (94). Fifthly, although a mere adolescent, he is already famous (80). Sixth: he occupies a superior social position. There is a vast chasm between the poet-actor and the young man. This is no stable boy that Shakespeare might have met while traveling on horseback, and no pubescent boy-actor in some theatrical company. Seventh: this paragon of young manhood is naturally and spontaneously compared by those who know him to a rose, the emblem of perfection. In sum, this youth is an extraordinarily personable, blondish teen-ager, who is resistant to marriage and admired by the public.

One thing more. In sonnet 125, Shakespeare implies that the Fair Youth is entitled to the honor of a canopy. "Were't aught to me I bore the canopy" is how the poem begins, suggesting that the canopy would not mean much to him but that the young man is entitled to it. This covering made of rich material was carried over the head of a royal person on state occasions, and those who carried it were members of the nobility. Only those of the highest rank were entitled to the honor of sitting under the canopy. Cotgrave's 1611 dictionary defined a baldachin as "the canopie that's carried over a prince." According to Leslie Hotson, "Anyone with a respectable knowledge of the Elizabethans is aware that no peer less than a viceregent or viceroy was permitted to walk abroad under a carried canopy or cloth of state."[169] In the royal entry through the streets of London in 1604, King James, as noted by the Venetian ambassador to England, "rode under a canopy borne over his head by four-and-twenty gentlemen, splendidly dressed."[170] The poet Michael Drayton in his versified description of the same triumphal procession also remarks on the canopy.

> When now approched glorious Majestie,
> Under a gold-wrought sumptuous Canopie.
> Before him went his goodly glittering traine,
> Which though as late wash'd in a golden raine.
> All so embraudered that to those behold,

> Horses as men, seem'd to be made of Gold:
> With the faire Prince, in whom appear'd in glory,
> As in th'abridgement of some famous story.[171]

As will become clear, Shakespeare was prompted to write sonnet 125 after seeing (probably in his mind's eye) the young man, sitting under a canopy as the witness to the proceedings in an important legal case.

This extraordinary young man was Shakespeare's idol and Chapman's patron. If we turn now to *The Tears of Peace* and the *Iliads*, we should find his name. A quick glance at the dedications reveals that we are on the right path. Embedded in these texts are phrases that caught Shakespeare's eye and were used by him in his quarrel with Chapman. "A prince's statue, or in Marble carv'd / Or steele or gold . . . Time into lowest ruines may depresse" prompted Shakespeare's retort: "Not marble nor the gilded monuments / Of princes shall outlive this powerful rhyme" (55) .

And there at the head of the dedication is the name of the Fair Youth: Prince Henry, "the high Born Prince of Men, *Henrie*, Thrice Royall Inheritor to the United Kingdoms of great Britanne."[172]

This "Great Prince," King James's eldest son, was one of the very few men in England who would be entitled to sit under the canopy of state; and this young man answers to all the particulars of the Fair Youth of the *Sonnets*.

His name was first put forward by Robert Palk in 1916.[173] Palk also understood that Chapman was the rival poet and that Prince Henry was his patron. Unfortunately, Palk, like all the interpreters of the sonnets, was misled about the date of sonnets 1-126. Unable to reconcile Chapman's Homer and Henry's patronage with the generally accepted early date of the sonnet sequence, Palk took a desperate and mad leap into absurdity by hypothesizing that the sonnets had been written not by Shakespeare but by Sir Walter Raleigh!

On July 2, 1603, not long after the death of Queen Elizabeth and the coronation of James as King of England, Henry (born 19 February 1594) was installed Knight of the Most Noble Order of the

Garter. At the ceremony, he was "much commended for his quick witty answers, princely carriage, and reverend performing his obeisance at the altar."[174] Although he was only nine years old, he was already being groomed to play an important part in affairs of state. Already he displayed a manner and attitude beyond his years. When he was ten years old, he was the center of attention at court. William Alexander Stirling, who was a gentleman extraordinary of Prince Henry's chamber, wrote of him in a poem called "Parænesis:"

> And O! how this (deare Prince) the people charmes,
> Who flock about Thee oft in ravish'd bands,
> To see thee yong, yet manage so thine Armes,
> Have a Mercuriall minde, and Martiale hands,
> This exercise thy tendor courage warmes:
> And still true Greatnesse but by Vertue stands.[175]

As the king's eldest son, Henry would succeed to the throne, and by the time he was twelve years old, he was being cultivated by foreign diplomats and agents, especially those from France and Spain. Both on the continent and in England it was understood that this young man was destined to be a leading force in both politics and religion. His countrymen viewed him as entrusted with a sacred mission, the destruction of Catholicism, and the Protestants turned him into a symbol of their cause. The Puritans acclaimed him: "Henry the 8. pulled down abbeys and cells, / But Henry the 9 shall pull down Bishops and bells."[176] One poet idolized him as

> World's richest Jewell, Nature's rarest Gemme,
> Mirrour of Princes, Miracle of Youth,
> All Vertues' Pattern, Patron of all Truth;
> Refuge of Armes, ample Reward of Arts,
> Worth's Comforter, milde Conqueror of Hearts:
> The Churche's Tower, the Terrour of the Pope,
> Heroick Henry, Atlas of our Hope.[177]

The philosophical poet and courtier Fulke Greville, a man not easily awed, said of the Prince, "Both for wisdom and strength of body there was not the like to be found among the English."[178]

In 1607, about the time Shakespeare wrote his first sonnets to the prince, the Venetian ambassador to the court of James wrote home that "the vivacity of the Prince grows apace, and every day he gives proof of wisdom and lofty thoughts far in advance of his years."[179]

This ambassador was an interested party and a close observer of the prince, whose anti-Catholic sympathies appealed to the Venetians. When he was only thirteen, he offered his services to them in their stand against the Pope if only he were old enough. The ambassador provided his government with a discerning sketch of the young man.

Henry is about twelve years old, of a noble wit and great promise. His every action is marked by a gravity most certainly beyond his years. He studies, not with much delight, and chiefly under his father's spur, not of his own desire, and for this he is often admonished and set down. Indeed one day the King, after giving him a lecture, said that if he did not attend more earnestly to his lessons, the crown would be left to his brother, the Duke of York, who was far quicker at learning and studied more earnestly. The Prince made no reply, out of respect for his father; but when he went to his room and his tutor continued in the same vein, he said, "I know what becomes a prince. It is not necessary for me to be a professor, but a soldier and a man of the world. If my brother is as learned as they say, we'll make him Archbishop of Canterbury." The King took this answer in no good part; nor is he overpleased to see his son so beloved and of such promise that his subjects place all their hopes in him; and it would almost seem, to speak quite frankly, that the King was growing jealous; and so the Prince has great need of a wise counsellor to guide his steps.[180]

Even as a mere child, Henry took an interest in manly exercises, in tilting and the martial arts. He had to live up to the image of young rulers on horseback. It was an age in which adolescents distinguished themselves as warriors. Ivan the Terrible as a child cultivated power and at age fourteen crowned himself czar. Charles XII of Sweden at age fifteen crowned himself king and set out to do battle with Peter the Great of Russia, another adolescent obsessed by the military. Richard II of England was only fourteen when he stood alone against Wat Tyler's rebels and quelled them. Prince Henry was cast in the same mold. When he sat to Nicholas Hilliard for his portrait, an exquisite miniature, about 1607 or 1608, Henry chose to wear armor. (See Figure 8: Prince Henry wearing the armor given him by the Prince de Joinville.)

His particular role model was Henri IV of France, who had been a soldier in the field when he was only fifteen, and who looked upon the English prince as his own son, so much alike were they in their opposition to Catholicism and their fascination with warfare. When Henri IV died, the young prince cried, "My second father is dead," and went to bed for days. In one of the finest portraits, Henry chose to wear the armor given him by the French king. (See Figure 9: Henry wearing armor given by King Henri of France.)

Equally as great as his love of weapons of the field was his interest in ships and the Royal Navy. The shipwright Phineas Pett (1570-1647) built a twenty-five-foot long pinnace for the ten-year-old prince. The boy, true to his nature, christened it *Disdain* and immediately in the cabin of the ship had Pett sworn in as his per-

FIGURE 8. Prince Henry, c. 1607, wearing the armor given him by the Prince de Joinville. Miniature by Nicholas Hilliard.

FIGURE 9. Prince Henry wearing the armor given him by Henri IV of France. Artist unknown.

sonal servant.[181] A few years later, in 1608, Pett laid the keel for one of the largest warships ever built, the *Prince Royal*, in which Henry took a proprietary interest.

The Groom of the Prince's Bedchamber, William Haydon, who had the opportunity to observe him on a day-to-day basis, gave a description of the young man as he was after the sonnets had been composed.

"He was tall and of an high stature, his body strong and well proportioned, his shoulders were broad, his eyes quicke and pleasant, his forehead broad, his nose bigg, his chinne broad and cloven, his haire inclining to bleeke, whereas before it had beene of a whitish colour, the colour of his face some what swarte and scorched with the sunne, his whole face and visage comely and beautifull, looking for the most part with a sweete, smyling, and amiable countenance, and withall full of gravity, and Princely majesty, resembling much in shape of his body, and divers actions the King of Dennemarke his Uncle."[182]

IN LOOKS he took more after his mother's side of the family than his father's. Queen Anne was the sister of the King of Denmark, and she passed on to her son her Danish complexion and her trim figure. Early in the sonnet sequence, Shakespeare remarks on this. "Thou art thy mother's glass, and she in thee / Calls back the lovely April of her prime" (3). Their similarity is evident in their portraits. (See Figure 10: Queen Anne, c. 1605, portrait attributed to Marcus Gheeraerts. Figure 10a: Henry, Prince of Wales, by Robert Peake the Elder.)

His delicate face and his blond complexion darkened by outdoor activities are mirrored in sonnet 20: "a woman's face" but "a man in hue." When Shakespeare wrote that beauty, birth, wealth, and wit "entitled in thy parts do crowned sit" (37), and when he praised "the composed wonder of your frame" (59), he was echoing the popular sentiment. The most complete description of the prince by a contemporary comes from Francis Bacon, the philosopher and statesman, who served as solicitor under James I. Bacon remarked that "in body" the prince was "strong and erect"

FIGURE 10. Queen Anne, about 1605. Attributed to Marcus Gheeraerts.

FIGURE 10a. Prince Henry, about 1609. Oil Painting by Robert Peake the Elder (detail).

and that "his limbs [were] gracefully put together," and that Henry's face "can be compared with that of a very beautiful girl." (Bacon's "Memorial of Henry Prince of Wales" is reprinted in Appendix A.) Because of the prince's position, all this beauty and grace was on constant display for the public. He was "the world's fresh ornament" of the first sonnet, "beauty's rose," the future king of England who was expected to usher in a new age even before he came to the throne. Ben Jonson in a masque honoring Prince Henry described him in terms as adulatory as Shakespeare's and employing the same imagery.

> He doth fill with grace,
> Every season, ev'ry place;
> Beautie dwels, but in his face:
> He is the height of all our race.
> . . . .
> He is lovelier, then in May
> Is the Spring, and there can stay,
> As little, as he can decay.[183]

The sonnets repeatedly refer to the young man as a rose, begin-

ning with the second line of the first sonnet, where the word is italicized to emphasize its significance. The image of the rose would
pass through several changes in the sequence, reflecting the vicissi-
tudes in the relationship of the boy and the poet (54, 67, 95, 98, 109).
That Prince Henry was the "Rose" of the sonnets would have been
obvious to those who knew him and were familiar with life at court.
As the rose was the perfect flower, so the prince was the ideal young
man. After his early death, he was usually personified as a rose. The
controller of the prince's household, Sir Charles Cornwallis, called
him "a scarce blown rose."[184] It was the poets' preferred epithet for
him. Hugh Holland invoked him: "O Rose! / of thousand Damsels
late desired, / Whose crimsin hew their snowie bosomes fired."[185]
Sir Arthur Gorges lauded him as "This Royall rose."

> Why fell he then amidst his floweringe race,
>   Whilst yet his bud was greene and fresh his rynde,
>   Whilst he exceld in every gifte and grace,
>   That is admired most in humane kinde.
>   Adorned with wisdom and such pieties
>   As made him mynion to the deities?[186]

Chapman, who of all the poets owed him most, proclaimed, after Henry's untimely death, that

> ... after ages
> Would be inflam'd, and put on holy rages
> With thy inspiring vertues; cursing those
> Whose breaths dare blast thus, in the bud, the Rose.
> But thou (woe's me) art blown up before blowne.[187]

Prince Henry quickly became an icon, the product of a concert-
ed effort by certain members of the court, especially those of the
Protestant faith, to rear and educate him as a true Renaissance
man, adept at the social graces, a student of classical learning, a patron of the arts, a soldier and statesman, someone who could lead
the nation as it took its place as a rival of France in all respects.
After having been up to the time of the defeat of the Spanish Armada a second-rate country, an island on the fringe of civilization, it
was now emerging as a pivotal force in European affairs. In the eyes

of many England needed what King James failed to be: a forceful sovereign, a man of power rather than a man of peace. Prince Henry was their man.

When the Fair Youth appears in the regalia of a prince of the realm, the admiration expressed in the sonnets becomes less personal and less physical. Without Prince Henry as their centerpiece, the sonnets easily take on a prurient tone of sexual abandonment. That is what has troubled many readers. But when the young man is identified as a prince royal, the most admired man of his time, Shakespeare's idolatrous verse turns out to be what everyone else was saying, only less poetically. In fact, some of the extraordinary passion that invests the sonnets begins to sound factitious and forced, once it is realized that Shakespeare was writing as a servant of the court. When he calls the boy his "sovereign" and himself "servant" and "slave," as he does in the sonnet (57) that Auden could not imagine ever having been sent, he was only slightly exaggerating their actual social positions. The following sonnet is even more groveling and sycophantic in tone: "Being your vassal bound to stay your leisure." In 1609 one could not only imagine it; one would expect it.

Like so many others, Shakespeare was affected by the charisma of the precocious prince, but it is also obvious that he was catering to the vanity of the young man and contributing to his self-promotion campaign. His task was not to make the heir to the throne famous, which he already was ("your fame" [80]), but to give him the immortality that the prince craved. "Your name from hence immortal life shall have"(81). The young man was fully aware of the role on the stage of history that had been assigned to him by birth and fortune, and he played it to the hilt. He wanted immortality, and he looked upon artists as the necessary instruments for achieving it. Unctuous flattery uttered to his face he disdained, but he was not averse to praise in print. That would last.

Astonishingly perceptive and self-aware (and surrounded by advisors), he told an historian what he expected of writers. "We make choise of the most skilfull workemen to draw or carve the portraiture of our faces, and shall every artlesse Pensell delineate the disposition of our minds? Our apparell must be wrought by the best Artificers, and no soile must be suffered to fall upon it: and shall our actions, shall our conditions be described by every bungling hand? Shall every filthie finger defile our reputation? Shall our Honour be basely buried in the drosse of rude and absurd writings? Wee are carefull to provide costly Sepulchers, to preserve our dead lives, to preserve some memorie that wee have bene: but there is no monument, either so durable, or so largely extending, or so lively and faire, as that which is framed by a fortunate penne."[188]

Certainly Shakespeare was happy at first to accommodate him and to provide the monument that the prince desired. In the art of self-exaltation and self-glamorization, Henry anticipated and surpassed the excesses of Hollywood. He was like a movie star cultivating his image, and he was backed by political forces forging a national icon more powerful than Hollywood agents "hyping" a teen-age idol.[189] No flattery, however extreme, could embarrass him. He lapped up what the best poets and painters could offer.

What would have raised eyebrows in 1609 was not the fawning and the obsequiousness of the sonnets, which would have been viewed as the expected homage and as proper deference; it was the critical tone of some of them. The poet often takes this spectacular youth and ideal prince to task. He writes of imperfections in this paragon, finds that the soldier has chinks in his armor, the athlete has feet of clay, the beautiful rose its cankers. Characteristic of the young prince was his haughtiness and his emotional detachment. It was said of him that "he knew well how to keep his Distance, which indeed he did to all, neither admitting a near or full Approach either to his Power or his Secrets."[190] Shakespeare summed up this personality trait in the prince in one of his finest sonnets, number 94.

> They that have the power to hurt and will do none,
> That do not do the thing they most do show,
> Who, moving others, are themselves as stone,
> Unmoved, cold, and to temptation slow;
> They rightly do inherit heaven's graces.

> And husband nature's riches from expense;
> They are the lords and owners of their faces,
> Others but stewards of their excellence.

So far this sounds like the expected high praise. But the second half of the sonnet undercuts the first half, turning "heaven's graces" and "nature's riches" into their opposites.

> The summer's flower is to the summer sweet,
> Though to itself it only live and die:
> But if that flower with base infection meet,
> The basest weed outbraves his dignity:
>> For sweetest things turn sourest by their deeds;
>> Lilies that fester smell far worse than weeds.

This sonnet and the ones leading up to it testify to a wounding act by the boy that hurt Shakespeare deeply, an act that the poet took as a betrayal. Coming immediately after the sonnets about the Rival Poet, it suggests that the boy had abandoned Shakespeare for Chapman.

Elsewhere, the poet accuses the youth of sensual faults (35), of deeds that give rise to "lascivious comments," and cautions against "a canker in the fragrant rose" that will "spot the beauty of thy budding name" (95). By far the harshest criticism is uttered in sonnet 69, perhaps the most jarring of all the sonnets, in which the boy's outward attractiveness is set against rumors that are spreading about his behavior. The slanderers

> To thy fair flower add the rank smell of weeds;
> . . . But why thy odor matcheth not thy show,
> The soil is this — that thou dost common grow.

This is strong stuff. Shakespeare could get away with it because there was a faction in King James's court much opposed to the power and glory that was accruing to the ambitious prince. Far and away the most remarkable aspect of Shakespeare's treatment of him is not the extravagant flattery, which other poets might emulate, but the occasional brutality and unsparing ruthlessness of his censure. However extravagant it might strike our ears, the adulation was in line with royal propaganda; the fault-finding, however, was not. Although there were observers at court who saw the imperfections in the golden boy, no one other than Shakespeare said such things in print. That is why the narrative behind the sonnet sequence had to be a roman à clef. That might be one reason, apart from their homoeroticism, why the sonnets were not reprinted in Shakespeare's lifetime.

Still, the question remains: why did Shakespeare take the risk of publishing this story of his troubled relationship to the prince? Picturing some of the unpleasant aspects of the nation's teen-age idol, it must have tarnished his image and furnished ammunition to the court faction that did not like him.

CHAPTER 13

The Master-Mistress
of His Passion

To JUDGE from the bewildering commentary it has pro-voked, of all the sonnets number 20 with its invocation to a "Master Mistress" is the most perplexing. The young man is depicted as an androgynous teen-ager who would appeal to the worshippers of Ganymede. Although he has a woman's face, he has a man's coloring and a man's commanding temperament. (In the line "A man in hue all hues in his controlling," hue means complexion, and in Shakespeare's time complexion could refer to both the color of the skin and the composition of the elements within the individual, that is, his inborn disposition.) In the narrative of the sonnet Nature, thought of as a woman, gave the stripling a pretty face, then fell in love with her own creation, and in order to enjoy his/her beauty outfitted him with a penis. This is Shakespeare's reworking of the myth about Salmacis and Hermaphroditus. The poet, unlike Mother Nature, loses out in this transformation. He is in love with a pretty face but the addition of a penis deprives him of the possibility of fully enjoying all the beauty that he sees. The youth will provide pleasure to women, and only by sharing a woman with him, as in sonnet 42, can the poet come close to embracing him physically.

This is one aspect of the sonnet. Added to it is a stereotype of male and female personalities. Partaking of the qualities of a woman, the fair youth has a gentle heart, while as the ideal man he has none of a woman's deceitfulness. This is typical of what Socratic lovers believed. Not typical is the statement that the young man's masculinity "steals men's eyes and women's souls amazeth." Ganymedeans professed that women, being the lustful sex, would be attracted by the male body, while they as Socratic lovers would be drawn to the male soul.

It might seem that Shakespeare slipped up here in allowing this inconsistency to stand, admitting in effect that the Ganymedean position was hypocritical. Perhaps he erred as Oscar Wilde did when he took the stand to testify in the case he brought against Lord Queensberry, who was charged with criminally libeling Wilde as a sodomite. Everything was going well for Wilde. He won over the jurors with his ease of manner, his affability, his fabulous charm, and his unstoppable wit. But the counsel to the defense was leading him on, waiting for the right moment to entrap an over-confident Wilde.

Asked if he kissed a certain boy at a party, Wilde replied, "Oh, dear no. He was a peculiarly plain boy. He was – unfortunately – extremely ugly. I pitied him for it."[191]

From that moment on, the charade was over. He had admitted that he would have kissed the boy if only he had been pretty. Eventually, in two more trials, the truth came out, and beauty and truth were one.

In Shakespeare's case there is another possibility. Perhaps he was deliberately confessing his real passion to the Fair Youth while protecting himself with a smokescreen behind which only the discerning reader could see the truth. Many of the sonnets are difficult to understand because they provide only one half of an exchange of thoughts. The dark matter here far outweighs what is visible. How the boy responded to the sonnets, what he might have said in a note or by word of mouth, has to be inferred from the sonnets themselves. Certainly there was a response of one kind or another, and it was important for Shakespeare to know what the young man might be thinking.

Sonnet 20 abruptly alters the course of thought in the sequence. After nineteen sonnets about preserving the boy's good looks either through his progeny or through the poet's verse, Shakespeare now chooses to dwell on the boy's peculiar sexuality. He addresses him more intimately than previously, calling him "the Master Mistress of my passion." Here "passion" means both a love poem and a very strong emotion.[192] Something must have happened after the composition of sonnet 19 that caused Shakespeare to write a frankly erotic poem, in which for the first time the boy's genitals are mentioned or even hinted at, and to declare the nature of his feelings for the young man. That strange and remarkable epithet "master-mistress" provides a clue as to what that something might have been.

SHAKESPEARE must have coined the term; it appears nowhere else in the literature of the time. The thought behind it, however, was not original with him and must have seemed less strange in 1609 than it does now. There is one possible source for the expression that the interpreters have overlooked, even though Shakespeare would certainly have known about it.

After the scuffles of the 1590s the disagreements between Shakespeare and Chapman became more profound, and the contention between them took on a new aspect when they came to deal with the crisis of belief that characterized the Renaissance. The revenge tragedy provided the perfect vehicle for dramatizing the troubled state of mankind, with a hero like Hamlet torn between his Christian conscience and family honor. These two poet-thinkers, who were so unalike in almost every respect, agreed on one essential issue: they both sensed that the human spirit had to progress beyond Christianity into some new, undefined area of belief and thought. Shakespeare may have unwittingly initiated the philosophical debate when he published his "newly . . . enlarged" version of *Hamlet* in 1604, a play too long for performance, very challenging in its dialectics, and intended mainly for readers. The play ends with Hamlet putting his fate in the hands of providence, leaving the reader with a sense of order being restored after a series of violent crimes and misdeeds.

Chapman, still smarting after Shakespeare's treatment of him in *Love's Labour's Lost* and *Troilus*, saw a weakness where others saw great insight and artistic brilliance. For him, Hamlet, neither the play nor the man, could serve as an instructive example of what was needed. "Chapman must have felt something like contempt for the character of Hamlet," says Thomas Marc Parrott. "The very qualities which humanize Hamlet and render him more sympathetic to our modern minds, his irresolution, his self-contempt, his excess of emotion, his incapacity for deliberate action, his sudden and spasmodic bursts of energy, must all have unfitted him in Chapman's mind for the high position of a tragic hero." [193]

So Chapman resolved to correct Shakespeare. His *Bussy D'Ambois*, which was performed in 1604 or 1605, presents a radically different picture of the human situation. Unlike Hamlet, all doubts and hesitations, Bussy is a man of action, valiant and arrogant, a hero in the mold of Achilles, involved in political and sexual intrigues as he seeks to rise in society. All those around him are driven by self-interest and lust; and to get ahead, he must emulate them. There is no higher cause, no providence. At the end there is no sense of order restored, only of energies exhausted.

Shakespeare's response came a year or so later. If Chapman argued that we cannot redeem the world until we see it for what it truly is, Shakespeare insisted on removing the last illusions. In *King Lear* Shakespeare's vision of human society is even bleaker than Chapman's. The dominant image in Bussy is of the heroine, Bussy's mistress, bound on a wheel of torture; in Shakespeare, Lear is "bound upon a wheel of fire." Neither dramatist offers the consolations of Christianity.

Prince Henry would have attended performances of these plays (apart from *Hamlet*, which he might have read): *Lear* as acted by Shakespeare's own company at court (1606) and *Bussy* as staged by Queen Anne's own players (1604). [194]

Bussy was printed in 1607, when the play was revived by the Children of Paul's. The renewed interest in the play encouraged Chapman to write a sequel, *The Revenge of Bussy d'Ambois*, staged at Blackfriar's in 1608 or 1609. [195] In the meantime, his thoughts had matured, and now as self-appointed instructor in the higher morality he hoped to present a less pessimistic view of the human universe. This meant creating a tragic hero who was neither a Hamlet nor a Bussy. The avenger in the sequel is Bussy's brother Clermont. Unlike Bussy, Clermont knows how to contain the fires that burn in him; he has his brother's valor, but not his temper. He possesses a gentle mind, a contempt for riches, and a scorn for all things servile and ignoble. Chapman could well have intended Clermont as a model for young Prince Henry, who would have been among the first to see it performed. Chapman had jut published his *Iliads*, dedicating it to Henry, and in a soliloquy Clermont admonishes readers of Homer not to take Achilles as a model.

> When Homer made Achilles passionate,
> Wrathful, revengeful, and insatiate
> In his affections, . . .
> He did compose it all of industry,
> To let men see, that men of most renown,
> Strong'st, noblest, fairest, if they set not down
> Decrees within them, for disposing these,
> Of judgment, resolution, uprightness,
> And certain knowledge of their use and ends,
> Mishap and misery no less extends
> To their destruction (Act 3).

Though he is deeply concerned about justice, this stoical man does not let a passion for vengeance govern his actions. He is described as the "Senecal man," one who "may with heaven's immortal powers compare, / To whom the day and fortune equal are; / Come fair or foul, whatever chance can fall, / Fix'd in himself, he still is one to all" (Act 4).

In a scene with his best friend the duke of Guise, Clermont reveals the paradoxical nature of the highest kind of love.

> *Guise.*
> How strangely thou art loved of both the sexes;
> Yet thou lovest neither but the good of both.
> *Clermont.*
> In love of women my affection first
> Takes fire out of the frail parts of my blood:
> Which till I have enjoy'd, is passionate,
> Like other lovers': but, fruition past,

I then love out of judgment; the desert
Of her I love still sticking in my heart,
Though the desire and delight be gone,
Which must chance still, since the comparison
Made upon the trial 'twixt what reason loves,
And what affection, makes in me the best
Ever preferr'd; what most love, valuing least.
Guise.

Thy love being judgment then, and of the mind,
Marry thy worthiest mistress now being blind.
Clermont.

If there were love in marriage, so I would:
But I deny that any man doth love,
Affecting wives, maids, widows, any women:
For neither flies love milk, although they drown
In greedy search thereof; nor doth the bee
Love honey, though the labor of her life
Is spent in gathering it; nor those that fat
On beasts, or fowls, do anything therein
For any love: for as when only nature
Moves men to meat, as far as her power rules,
She doth it with a temperate appetite,
The too much men devour, abhorring nature;
And in our most health, is our most disease;
So, when humanity rules men and women,
'Tis for society confined in reason.
But what excites the bed's desire in blood,
By no means justly can be construed love;
For when love kindles any knowing spirit,
It ends in virtue and effects divine,
And is in friendship chaste and masculine.

So far, Chapman's view of the two kinds of love, the love between man and woman, which is basically carnal, and the love between man and man, which partakes of the divine, pretty much agrees with Shakespeare's and probably with the opinion of many men at that time. Now what the duke of Guise says in reply to Clermont, astonishing and disconcerting to the modern reader, gave Shakespeare the opening he needed in writing to young Henry. In praising this ideal man, the duke thinks of him not as fully a man but as a man with feminine qualities. Although he regards him as his master because of his soldierly abilities, he addresses him as his mistress because of his moral virtues.

> *Guise.*
> Thou shalt my mistress be; methinks my blood
> Is taken up to all love with thy virtues.
> And howsoever other men despise
> These paradoxes strange, and too precise;
> Since they hold on the right way of our reason,
> I could attend them ever (Act 5).

Clermont's sympathetic disposition and his temperance lend him a feminine aura. His gentleness combined with his valor as a soldier, along with his dedication to justice, make him a paragon among men.

To the extent that perfection embodied both male and female qualities, Shakespeare agreed with Chapman. Both these philosopher-poets saw the ideal love as rising above concupiscence, and in that higher sphere the organs of generation vanish. The sexes merge into one. Shakespeare's boy is seen as "a man in hue" but with "a woman's gentle heart." And when Nature "pricks" him out, the poet relinquishes him to women for their pleasure while offering him his untainted love. (Victorian commentators, at least those who published their thoughts, were blithely unaware of Shakespeare's pun. An anonymous writer in 1886 gave the line a pious interpretation: a true Christian is "not proudly pricked up in the pomp of worldly vanity."[196]).

Shakespeare seizes upon Chapman's concept of a master-mistress and uses it as a rejoinder, continuing a quarrel over the Ganymede ideal that had begun in the 1590s. For Chapman loving a woman is a matter of passion. Reason and judgment are, or should be, embodied in men. It follows that true love is a "friendship chaste and masculine." Shakespeare agrees with Chapman that true love is chaste (hence the disavowal of interest in the male organ), but that does not mean that it is without passion. In Chapman's master-mistress, wisdom and masculine love are equated, and moderation and self-restraint are supreme virtues. Not so with Shakespeare, whose heart and mind are inflamed by his master-mistress. In spite of his protestations, his love is idolatrous and blinding and lost to reason. He may call the boy fair, kind, and true (105), yet he has his doubts (69). The poet behaves throughout like a man abandoned to love, ecstatic a good part of the time, but often jealous, hurt, feeling disregarded. Against "the right way of reason" Shakespeare sets "my passion." From the beginning, it is the boy's physical attractiveness, the Ganymede image, that enthralls the poet. Chapman's masculine love is philosophic and founded on mature judgment; Shakespeare's on beauty, and to that he surrenders himself abjectly. His sonnet 20 is not an evasive deception; it is an honest statement of how his ideal of Ganymedean love differs from Chapman's.

In sending this sonnet to the boy, Shakespeare opened a new stage in their relationship. Obviously, he hoped that Henry would find his passion, his song of love, his unreserved devotion, more compelling than Chapman's austere teachings.

In his worship of beauty, Shakespeare was like Michelangelo, who also wrote sonnets telling of his infatuation with a young man. There were significant differences, however. Like Shakespeare, Michelangelo felt subjugated and overpowered by his fair youth, Tommaso de'Cavalieri. Punning on the name, Michelangelo lamented, "If, to be happy, I must be conquered and chained, / it is no wonder that, naked and alone, / an armed cavalier's prisoner I remain." But the poet and the sculptor responded in markedly different ways when the boy was aloof and unkind. Shakespeare was a "slave" to his young man, subject to his whims. "I am to wait, though waiting so be hell, / Not blame your pleasure, be it ill or well" (58). Where Shakespeare was only hurt, Michelangelo was tormented. A sense of the sin involved in his love for a young man made Michelangelo blame himself. The boy's inconsiderateness and callousness were taken as condign punishment and omens of eventual damnation.

Great sin and cruel vengeance go together;
And it's only he who values himself the least
who runs most quickly to be hurt the most.
What would you put me through:
that my last day, which must needs be good,
should become one of injury and shame?

He tried to calm his fear of damnation by appealing to the Platonic doctrine, giving himself the wings of Jove, transporting himself and his Ganymede to heaven.

A violent burning for prodigious beauty
is not always a source of harsh and deadly sin, if then the
heart is left so melted by it
that a divine dart can penetrate it quickly.

Far from hindering empty passion from flying higher,
love stirs and wakes us, and feathers our wings;
and from that first step, with which it's not satisfied,
the soul can mount up and rise to its creator.

The love I speak of aspires to the heights;
woman is too different from that, and it's not worthy
of a wise and manly heart to burn for her.

One love draws toward heaven, the other draws
down to earth;
one dwells in the soul, the other in the senses,
and draws its bow at base and vile things.

For Michelangelo, ineffable beauty could not be accepted as an end in itself; in the tradition of Platonism it had to lead one on to the supreme being. It had to be religious.

I see in your beautiful face, my lord,
what can scarcely be related in this life:
my soul, although still clothed in its flesh,
has already risen often with it to God.[197]

What sets Shakespeare's boy sonnets apart from Michelangelo's is that Shakespeare's lack any sense of sin. His fantasies never carried him very far in the direction of the forbidden, and his disclaimer in sonnet 20 of any lustful intentions towards the boy should be accepted as a sincere statement, not as a camouflage for hidden desires. This in turn may signify that there was a difference between Michelangelo's Cavalieri and Shakespeare's Henry. For the poet, beauty becomes an end in itself. While Michelangelo prays that his infatuation with physical beauty will not imperil his soul, that it will instead lift him up spiritually, Shakespeare tries to preserve the beauty that transfixes him by reconstituting it in the beauty of his verse. As in Mallarmé's "*L'Après-midi d'un faune*," sexual longings are abjured and replaced by poetry. In a sense, Shakespeare becomes his own divinity, by his creative powers raising the young man to his level and offering immortality.

Unlike Michelangelo, Shakespeare became less religious as he grew older, and pagan imagery grew more prominent in the plays written in the latter half of his career. But the Italian's divinities, their un-Christian muscularity obscuring and sometimes obliterating their spirituality, exposed the conflict in his psyche, a conflict that drew him towards male hustlers rather than to someone like the young prince.

Shakespeare's position was between Chapman's and Michelangelo's, between the ethical man and the religious man. By the time he wrote *The Revenge of Bussy D'Ambois*, Chapman had replaced the Ganymede of his younger days with a master-mistress, a mature man instead of a boy. Wisdom, the power of the intellect and the control of one's passions combined with a woman's gentleness and emotional subtlety, defined his ideal. Michelangelo was forever torn between his longings and his consciousness of sin. Shakespeare took the path of the pure esthete, seeking perfection of form and endeavoring to preserve it in the amber of words. In the androgyne, the Ganymede, he found the ultimate artistic subject, the union of body and soul, of the passing moment and eternity, a fleeting glimpse of heaven on earth, whose transience must be overcome by the mysterious power of art. The beauty of the poet's verse, "whose action is no stronger than a flower" (65), would miraculously make time stand still.

The poet did not want the teen-age prince for himself; he urged

[169]

him to marry and reproduce himself in order to defeat time. Nor did he want to possess the boy physically. Instead he wanted to live within the ambience of the boy, "feasting" on the sight of him. The mere thought of him was "as food to life" (75).

For Michelangelo, the lovely boy was an angel come down from heaven, clothing itself in a human body, an angel full of compassion who would lead the artist up the *scala coeli*, the ladder to heaven. It was his way of justifying his passion for beauty and overcoming his fear of the sin he was committing, whether in reality or in his imagination. Chapman's conception of male bonding was more purely pagan, more Senecan than Christian. No ladder to heaven drew his eyes upward; his longing was for justice on earth, which would be achieved by wise, valiant, dispassionate men, not men enthralled by beauty but men who loved one another through their devotion to what Clermont calls "the high and general Cause" (Act 4).

Shakespeare's adulation of the androgyne took a third path, one that sets his sonnet sequence apart from other erotic poems. He looked at that heavenly ladder, with the beautiful boy posed on it, and came to realize that they both stood at the top of it, and that the steps they would eventually have to take could only carry them downwards. It is a curious but obvious fact that some of the most quoted and most famous love poems in the language are really about the unhappy process of falling out of love. Neither the boy nor the poet is to blame for what happens. They cannot contend against time and society. There will be the inevitable withering of beauty under the onslaught of time and the inevitable corrosion of the icon.

What gives the sonnet sequence much of its power is that it was not generated according to some preconceived scheme. It evolved without an end in view out of Shakespeare's experiences, and only afterwards was a pattern imposed on it. It developed mainly in response to actual events, many of which can be identified. The improvisational nature of the sequence, the obvious roughness of it, give the emotions expressed in it a feeling of authenticity, not the Wordsworthian authenticity of emotions recollected in tranquility but instead a hemorrhaging of the emotions, flooding the page. Miraculously, instead of the garbled phrases and prolix ramblings that a lesser writer would have set down, Shakespeare channeled his feelings into the strict and demanding form of the sonnet. What Shakespeare accomplishes here is what actors dream of (Shakespeare, let us not forget, was an actor) – the improvised performance that surpasses the rehearsed one, being more intensely and spontaneously felt, more contagiously exciting.

Auden thought that what he saw as the messiness of the sonnet sequence indicated that they were not planned for publication. This is certainly true of the first few sonnets. They were not written for the eyes of anyone other than the young boy and a few close and interested parties. However, when the poet begins to claim that his verse is immortal and perdurable, when in sonnet 55 he asserts that "not marble nor the gilded monuments / Of princes shall outlive this powerful rhyme," when he sets his own verse against that of the Rival Poet, it is obvious that Shakespeare realized that he was embarked on a reckless venture, unlike anything he had attempted before. In writing his plays, Shakespeare was the great improviser, as Wagner acutely characterized him. In them, however, he spoke through other characters. Here he came on stage alone and spoke in his own persona. He was performing a daring impromptu act, challenging the careful constructs of sonnet form by letting life dictate the scenario while he transformed it into a work of art. What life would do to the boy, erase his beauty and cloud his perfection, the poet would simultaneously undo. It had to be published because, as we shall see, Chapman was rushing his own proud verse into print.

The sonnet sequence begins with an image so perfectly suited to what was to follow that is hard to believe that it was actually the first poem written and sent to the boy. If real life always shaped itself so exquisitely, there would no reason to create art. The first words tell the reader that beauty is to be the subject of the sonnets. "From fairest creatures we desire increase / That thereby beauty's *Rose* might never die." The italicized word would signal to Shakespeare's more literate and insightful readers that it was the key to the ensuing sonnets. It would function as the emblem of love, as in the well-known French allegorical poem, *Roman de la Rose*, and equally as the rose of heaven, of paradise, as in the concluding cantos of Dante's *Divine Comedy*, earthly love and celestial love in one symbol. The nineteenth-century commentator Richard Simpson had it right. "The word 'rose' here is full of import. In the range of its associations it reaches from the meaning that must be given to it in much of the *Romaunt of the Rose* to the sublime conception of Dante in the 30th and 31st cantos of his *Paradiso*. The aspiration for the immortality of the 'rose of beauty' is the root of love."[198] But Simpson neglected to mention that the Rose was also an appellation for the young man who was being encouraged to produce an heir.

The reader of the 1609 *Sonnets* would certainly follow the poet's struggle against disillusionment, his valiant efforts to halt the flight of time, to preserve in verse the androgynous, adolescent beauty that in reality lasts for only two or three years. Auden saw it as "an agonized struggle . . . to preserve the glory of the vision he had been granted in a relationship, lasting at least three years, with a person who seemed intent by his actions upon covering the vision with dirt."[199] But a reader who belonged to the inner circle would know who the young boy was and would follow the narrative aware of the specific events that occasioned many of the sonnets. This knowledge would give insights into the meaning of the sonnets that is denied those who don't know exactly what inspired them. Shakespeare obviously did not want this self-exposure to be published to make money, since he was very wealthy in 1609, nor to spread his fame by acquiring more readers. He was a well-known, highly praised author with an extraordinary body of work behind him. He wanted his sonnets published because he wanted to go on record.

CHAPTER 14

Contemporaneous Events

A S MIGHT be imagined, Shakespeare often relied on events
or occurrences of the time to provide inspiration for a sonnet.
A few of the sonnets can be pegged to specific incidents and
firmly dated. In sonnet 107, as we have seen, he turned the treaty of
1609, with its assurance of twelve years of peace, into an occasion for
proclaiming his confidence in the lastingness of his poetry. Since
these events by their very nature involved prominent members of
the court, they would be noted in the annals or in someone's journals. From them, it should be possible to track down a number of the
topical references, to imagine oneself back in the court of King
James, and to learn what lies behind a particular sonnet.

Sonnet 25 ("Let those who are in favor with their stars, / Of
public honor and proud titles boast") is plain enough as it stands
and hardly needs much elucidation. But its reference to "great
princes' favorites" who "at a frown they in their glory die" becomes more pointed and caustic when the gentlemen are identified. They are the earl of Southampton (Henry Wriothesley) and
the earl of Pembroke (William Herbert), who were evicted from
their lodgings on orders from Prince Henry on December 17, 1608.

Henry had been living at Oatlands, some miles from London,
and wanted to be closer to the center of action. According to witnesses, "The Prince complaining to the King that his lodging was
too far distant, the King replied that he could take such course as
he would to remedy it. Hereupon the prince sent to the earls of
Southampton and Pembroke to move their households and horse
as he wished to occupy their lodging. When they refused, he sent
his own people to remove them perforce, at which these Lords

were in great indignation. This action is regarded as great proof of spirit in a Prince who though only fifteen years old gives the highest promise in all he does."[200] It was known that the king dreaded his son to the point that "he would not deny anything he plainly desired."[201] In this instance, however, the king may have been happy to oblige his son: in 1604 there had been rumors that Southampton would attempt a *coup d'état*.[202] Here was a moment that Shakespeare must have relished. For once, Shakespeare could rejoice in his inferior social position, not subject to the power ploys of the mighty. "Then happy I that love and am beloved / Where I may not remove nor be removed."

Sonnet 68 is Shakespeare's comment on the feminization of dress and manners under James's regime. The king encouraged his courtiers to dress elaborately and would reprimand or dismiss those who did not, while making an exception of his son, who was instructed to avoid "baytes for filthy Lecherie." The sonnet is another hymn to the youthful natural handsomeness of Henry, who represents the true beauty of a better time in contrast to the false beauty of the present age, when wigs and ornaments are the fashion and "the golden tresses of the dead [are] shorn away, / To live a second life on second head." While the king wanted the men around him to be richly adorned, Prince Henry set a different tone for his courtiers. He advocated moderation in dress as opposed to "extreame excess and pride of Apparell."[203] As Katherine Duncan-Jones has noted, this sonnet could hardly have been published when Elizabeth ruled.

In some of the most memorable and striking sonnets, Shakespeare condemns the prince for not living up to his reputation. In sonnet 69, the poet remarks that scandalmongers are spreading ugly rumors about the young man's behavior. To his "fair flower [they] add the rank smell of weeds." The final couplet is unusually severe and reproachful: "But why thy odor matcheth not thy show, / The soil is this – that thou dost common grow." (In the original "soil" appears as "solye," an obvious misprint for "soyle," an Elizabethan spelling of "soil.") Shakespeare piles three meanings on this word. First, it indicates the ground or basis of his censure. But it also suggests filth, and in Shakespeare's time, a special kind of filth: sexual copulation, especially of animals. The *Oxford English Dictionary* cites Florio for this meaning, and Shakespeare uses the word in this sense in *Measure for Measure* : "First hath the woman / Most wrongfully accus'd your substitute, / Who is as free from touch or soil with her / As she from one ungot" (5.1.141-44). In *King Lear*, "soiled" carries this same sense of animals copulating: "The fitchew [polecat] nor the soiled horse goes to't / With a more riotous appetite" (4.6.124-5). And in *Troilus and Cressida* Diomedes, telling Paris that Helen is a whore and a bawd, says, "Hee merits well to have her that doth seeke her, / Not making any scruple of her soyle" (4.1. 57, 1609 Quarto).

Some of Shakespeare's feelings about sexual intercourse with a woman are made abundantly clear in the Dark Lady sonnets. At times they sound like Lear's fulminations: "Down from the waist they are Centaurs, / Though women all above: / But to the girdle do the gods inherit, / Beneath is all the fiends: there's hell, there's darkness, / There is the sulphurous pit" (4.6.126-130). In sonnet 69 Shakespeare is appalled to find that his ideal boy has reduced himself to the level of common men, succumbing to the desires of the flesh and seducing a married woman. His attitude here differs from the way he had felt earlier in sonnets 40 and 41 when he had learned that he and Henry had shared the same mistress. In Shakespeare's sexual psychology, this sharing brought him and the boy closer together. The woman was probably an easily available courtesan, someone who kept company with the actors. The woman behind sonnet 69 was of a different station, a member of the nobility. Moreover, she was married, which made the prince guilty of furthering adultery.

Stories about a sexual affair involving Prince Henry were rife at the time this sonnet must have been written, early 1609. The woman in the case was Frances Howard, the daughter of the earl of Suffolk, King James's Lord Chamberlain, and born, according to the best evidence, in May 1590. In January 1606, when she was only fifteen, she was married off to Robert Devereux, 3rd earl of Essex, who was only fourteen at the time. Devereux had been educated with the prince, and for a while the two youngsters were close friends. The marriage was a practical arrangement, meant to unite two powerful families, rather than two loving youngsters. Although vows were sworn, the business of consummating the marriage was put off while Devereux broadened his horizons by going on a tour of the continent. About the time he returned from the Low Countries in November 1608, she left her country estate for the excitement of London and the court, where, it was later said of her, that she "ran at random and played her pranks as the toy took her in the head, sometimes publicly, sometimes privately, whereby she both disparaged her reputation and brought herself into the contempt of the world."[204] Her portrait, the one attributed to William Larkin, reveals a handsome woman confident of her powers, with a look more challenging than seductive. (See Figure 11: Frances Howard, Countess of Somerset.)

On the evening of 2 February 1609, she danced in Ben Jonson's *Masque of Queens*, with Henry in attendance. Soon the court was abuzz with rumors that he had taken her to bed. To judge from the sonnet, Shakespeare at first assumed that his idol had been the pursuer and had seduced the virgin wife of Henry's childhood friend, an act that was a double violation, both of friendship and marriage. Years later, when other incidents had made Frances, whether rightly or wrongly, appear to be the court strumpet, gossipmongers reported that it was she who had practiced her wiles on the rather innocent young man. Her father's uncle, earl of Northampton, had deliberately sent her out to catch the eye of the prince. She had "prostituted herself" to him, and he had "reaped the first fruits."[205]

FIGURE 11. Frances, Countess of Somerset, née Howard. Oil painting attributed to William Larkin, about 1615.

[176]

This version of the events reached Shakespeare's ears, and he realized he had been too quick to blame the young boy. Immediately in the following sonnet, he took back his condemnation, declaring that the Galahadean purity and handsomeness of the prince would inevitably attract malicious rumors. "Slander's mark was ever yet the fair." The sonnet reads like a sigh of relief. "Thou hast passed by the ambush of young days / Either not assailed, or victor being charged."

Prince Henry's subsequent attitude makes it probable that the second version of the story is the true one, and that Frances Howard was the aggressor who succeeded in overcoming his scruples. He was not attracted to women, and she was ambitious. Urged on by her conniving parents, she was more likely to take advantage of the youngster's sexual naiveté than to let it stand in her way. As one chronicler later noted, Prince Henry's "more heroic innate qualities . . . taught him to reject her following temptations with indignation and superciliousness."[206] According to court gossip, Frances Howard was sexually voracious and blatantly indiscreet. Henry "named her the *Bona Roba* of England," that is, a notable prostitute.[207] He certainly displayed hostility to her and her family, once remarking, "If ever he were king, he would not leave one of that family to piss against a wall."[208]

Not long after this episode, Frances Essex hitched her wagon to another star when she became the lover of Robert Carr, that blond favorite of King James. But that is another story, well told by Anne Somerset in *Unnatural Murder: Poison at the Court of James.*

Sonnet 124, which belongs among the more opaque sonnets, requires a considerable amount of background knowledge to be fully understood. Shakespeare contrasts his steadfast love for the prince with the equivocations of political men who are "subject to Time's love, or to Time's hate." His own kind of love "fears not Policy, that *heretic* / Which works on leases of short-numbered hours." All this is conventional and clear enough. The murkiness comes at the end where the reader expects a ray of light and a neat summing up. Instead Shakespeare writes that as witnesses to the truth of what he has said, he can "call the fools of Time, / Which die for goodness, who have lived for crime." There seems to be more thought crammed into these lines than they can hold. Here again, a difficulty arises because the poet expects his readers to be familiar with a contemporary event. The italicized "heretic" and the emphasis on politics point to a man who was much in the news in the spring of 1609.

James Elphinstone had been a judge in Scotland and a secretary to King James when Elizabeth still reigned as monarch. An ardent Catholic, he wrote a letter in 1599 to Pope Clement VIII as if from King James. When Queen Elizabeth learned of it, she questioned its supposed author, who denounced it as a forgery. Unfortunately, that did not put an end to the matter. James became king of England; Elphinstone followed him to London and was promoted Lord Balmerino. The troublesome letter resurfaced in 1607, when James, disputatious and proud of his skill in theological disputes, was carrying on a debate on the subject of the English oath of allegiance with Cardinal Bellarmine, the pope's point man in religious polemics. In reply to James's *"Triplici nodo triplex cuneus,"* the Cardinal produced the letter, in which it appeared that James had once written to Rome expressing his hope that some Scotsman might be appointed cardinal to represent England at the Vatican. James recalled the 1599 letter and summoned Lord Balmerino for questioning. Balmerino equivocated, saying that he had written to the pope only to ask for support in nominating a kinsman to the position of bishop and that James had signed it. This created a furor in the English court, and no one was more angry than James. He denied having signed the letter, and finally, in October 1608, Balmerino confessed his guilt, falling on his knees before the king to ask his pardon. A trial ensued, at which the accused allowed himself no extenuations, admitted the guilt was entirely his, and said that his purpose had not been to reform religion in Scotland and England, but that he had taken "merely a politic course." Further, he expressed "his desire to give the King satisfaction to the last drop of his blood."[209] In March 1609, he was sentenced to be drawn and quartered, a traitor's death. Shakespeare's sonnet touches on all the main points in the tale of Lord Balmerino, and the final line applauds the man for his most honest, least temporizing act.

[178]

In the last sonnets that Shakespeare wrote to Prince Henry the recurrent theme is the constancy of his devotion to the young man. But there is a somber undercurrent of meaning: the prince has not been equally devoted to him. The words resonate with a sense of disappointment and faithlessness. The poet fears that politics and conventional morality have meant more to the prince than friendship.

The penultimate sonnet is one of the most touching in the whole cycle, once the circumstances behind it are made known. What Shakespeare wanted above all from the prince is what the prince gave to someone else. The poet had to stand on the sideline, offering his "oblation, poor but free," while another person, a shipwright, was accepted into Henry's inner circle. As with the preceding sonnet about Balmerino's betrayal, Shakespeare found his inspiration in a trial that involved important members of the court.

During 1608 and 1609 Phineas Pett, the shipwright who in 1604 had built a small ship for the ten-year-old prince, was in charge of the design and construction of the *Prince Royal*, in which Henry took a personal interest. With its three decks and a keel measuring 115 feet, it was to be the largest ship in the English navy. (See Figure 12: Phineas Pett, and Figure 13: *The Prince Royal* under construction.)

However, for some time questions had been raised about Pett's

FIGURE 12. Phineas Pett, shipwright, c. 1612. Artist unknown.

FIGURE 13. *Prince Royal* under construction. Artist unknown.

skill as a builder of ships and about his probity as a supplier of material. A commission of inquiry had found huge cost overruns in work that Pett had done in repairing other ships, and the timber that was being used on the *Prince Royal* was found to be old and unsuitable. Furthermore, there was so much waste that the final cost would be half again as much as at first estimated. Although the board of inquiry had done a thorough job, the Lord High Admiral rejected its indictment without taking a close look at the evidence proffered. He himself had advanced Pett's career, and moreover Pett was the prince's favorite shipbuilder. But Lord Northingham, that thorn in Henry's side, had initiated the investigation, and he was angered at this quick dismissal of the charges. He took the matter to King James, who wisely decided to re-open the inquiry, over which he personally would preside.

The hearing took place on May 8 at Woolwich, where the ship lay. A lengthy and minutely detailed document listed Pett's errors and concluded that the ship "can never be made strong and fit for service, and least of all for our seas." This document had been drawn up by Northingham's informers, led by Captain George Weymouth, whose knowledge of ships matched that of Pett.

The court of inquiry was set up in rooms adjacent to the shipyard. As Pett in his autobiography described the scene, King James, after having surveyed the *Prince Royal*, "seated himself in the chair under the state [canopy], at a little table standing right before him; the Prince and Lords taking their stands on his Majesty's right hand." During the long questioning, Pett had to sit on his knees, "baited by the great Lord and his bandogs . . . and, which was worst, his Majesty's angry countenance still bent upon me, albeit the Prince's Highness, standing near me, from time to time encouraged me as far as he might without offence to his father, labouring to have me eased by standing up, but his Majesty would not permit it."

At one point, the commission went to the ship itself to confirm a measurement vital to the case for the prosecution. When it was found that the measurement supported Pett, "the whole multitude heaved up their hats, and gave a great and a loud shout and acclamation, and then the Prince's Highness called with a high voice these words: 'Where be now these perjured fellows that dare thus abuse his Majesty with these false informations, do they not worthily deserve hanging?'"

The hearing ended with Pett being cleared of all charges. Later he expressed his thanks to Henry. "I presented myself upon my knee to the most noble Prince my then master, who, taking me from the ground, did so affectionately express his joy for my clearing and the satisfaction his father had received that day, that he protested he would not only countenance and comfort me hereafter but care to provide for me and my posterity while he lived."[210]

The sonnet celebrates the victory of Pett, "a true soul," who defeated the suborned *informer* – the word is italicized – Captain Weymouth. Almost every line of the sonnet contains a reference to the inquiry and the evidence presented: "the canopy" under which King James and Prince Henry sat; "great bases for eternity" alluding to the ship's keel, the largest ever laid in England up to that time; "waste," "rent," "ruining," "compound," and "seconds" referring to the cost overruns, the money paid to informers, the general corruption, the compromised evidence and the unsuitable timber. They all evoke a world of fraud and corruption, bribery, subornation, overcharges, and second-rate goods.

Underneath it all lies Shakespeare's identification with Pett, who came from a poor family and had worked his way up from ordinary carpenter to master shipwright. In the process he had become a servant of the prince. Like Pett, Shakespeare was not one of the nobles who were entitled to carry the canopy for the prince; but, again like Pett, he was a true soul, not a corrupt courtier suborning witnesses. Like Pett, Shakespeare was now the victim of accusations attacking him as a man of bad character. The image of Pett, on his knees for hours while the accusations against him were examined, gave way in Shakespeare's mind to the image of the acquitted Pett being embraced and comforted by the happy prince.

It is conceivable but unlikely that Shakespeare was present. His company of actors was out of London, where the plague was raging, and on May 9 they performed in Ipswich, about seventy miles from Woolwich.[211]

"Let me be obsequious in thy heart," says the poet, hoping to be accepted as Pett was. His "oblation" or offering of love to the young prince is superior to Pett's in that it is "not mixed with seconds, knows no art," whereas the mutual devotion of the shipwright and the prince depends on self-interest and on material concerns. The two of them are in debt to each other because of the machination of politicians and moneymakers, while the poet's offering is "poor but free, . . . only me for thee."

CHAPTER 15

A Double Portrait

KNOWING who the principal characters are and being in possession of some of the background information, the extra-textual matter or what might be called the back-story, we can follow the narrative thread that connects the sonnets. To the reader of 1609, the Fair Youth, the Rival Poet, and William Shakespeare would not have been the shadowy figures they are to us. Although they bore no names, they might as well have; that early reader certainly recognized who they were. As he turned the pages, he would have fleshed out the boy and the poet and seen Prince Henry and William Shakespeare involved in a troubling relationship that had to end unhappily.

They were not star-crossed lovers. They were two strong personalities with high aspirations. Henry was the boy wonder intent on becoming a great king; Shakespeare was the master artist who hoped to play a part behind the scenes in that endeavor.

Is it purely coincidental that the portrait of Shakespeare generally considered the most authentic and most life-like, the so-called Chandos portrait, was painted at about the same time that Shakespeare was composing these sonnets? Is it merely fortuitous that this portrait, which is really the only one we have that might have been drawn from life, was painted when Shakespeare was offering posterity his most autobiographical work? Together the sonnets and the portrait reveal the man as no second-hand account could possibly do. Set the Chandos portrait against the portrait of Prince Henry in the armor given him by Henri IV of France, and the two main figures of the sonnets come vividly to life.

(See Figure 14: Shakespeare, the Chandos portrait, and Figure

FIGURE 14. Shakespeare at about the time the sonnets were published. The so-called Chandos portrait. Attributed to John Taylor.

15: Prince Henry about 1609.)

All the main themes are etched in those faces and accoutrements, the aristocrat in chivalric costume set against the strolling player, a ring in his ear, the teen-age boy against the middle-aged man, beauty against plainness, the ambitious warrior against the accomplished artist. Ironically, the precocious prince is all pose and costume, the aging actor is the man pure and simple.

The authenticity of the Chandos portrait has often been questioned, mainly because the sitter looks swarthy and his hair is dark. In the Shakespeare monument, the poet seems to have auburn hair. The apparent swarthiness of the visage may be due to the darkening of the varnish. The Chandos, attributed to John Taylor, has a good provenance, having belonged to the great actor Thomas Betterton (1635? –1710), who may have acquired it from the dramatist William Davenant (1606–1668). If the Chandos portrait pictures Shakespeare the actor, with his make-up on, it would explain why Davenant and Betterton treasured it.

The 1609 Quarto brought together in a remarkable union Eng-

FIGURE 15. Prince Henry, about 1609. Oil painting by Robert Peale the Elder.

land's most famous poet and its most admired young man. But the sonnets would have provided only a footnote in literary history if Shakespeare had written only the first nineteen. With sonnet 20, the master-mistress sonnet, the poet and the prince found a common cause and discovered a common bond. The cause was to celebrate Henry as England's destiny; the common bond was their sexual orientation. But both the cause and the bond would doom the relationship and bring about a rupture between them. Those first readers must have been enthralled by a narrative that brought to light a scandal-tinged relationship between two superstars and that went on to show step by step, week by week, how that relationship fell apart.

To begin at the beginning, we should remind ourselves once again of the boy who first caught Shakespeare's eye. His looks, his personality, his youth, his high station in society, his political and religious views combined to make him the most remarkable figure in England at the time. When Shakespeare composed his first sonnet to Henry, the teen-age boy was already a striking figure and a commanding presence, strong of body and forceful in his opinions.

A contemporary witness described his athletic activities in 1607, when he was only thirteen:

> For practice, hee used in a manner daily to ride and manage great horses, with which hee had his stables most excellently furnished, oftimes to runne at the Ring, and sometimes at Tilt, both which he so well performed and dexterously performed, and with so great a comelinesse, as in those his first yeares, he became second to no Prince in Christendome, and to many that practised with him much superiour.
>
> His other exercises were dancing, leaping, and in times of yeare fit for it learning to swimme, at sometimes walking fast and farre, to accustome and enable himselfe to make a long march when time should require it; but most of all at Tennis play, wherein, to speake the truth, which in all things I especially affect, hee neither observed moderation, nor what appertained to his dignity and person, continuing oftimes his play for the space of three or foure hours, and the same in his shirt, rather becoming an Artisan then a Prince, who in things of that nature are onely to affect comelinesse, or rather a kinde of carelessenesse in shew, to make their activities seeme the more naturall, then a laborious and toiling industry.[212]

From a very early age, Henry had a mind of his own. Perhaps in reaction against the general licentiousness of James's court, he quickly developed into a serious young man, averse to swearing and foul language, devoted to Protestantism, and despising hypocrisy. His noble nature combined with his physical appearance made him a prince of legend. James had set down in *Basilikon Dóron*, a text in Latin on the art of government, written in 1599 and intended for his son, a number of precepts for a sovereign, urging his son to follow them as faithfully as "Alexander did the Iliads of Homer." Henry did observe and follow them, while his father did not. In his writings, the king had warned his young heir to "employ every man as ye think him qualified, but use not one in all things, lest he was proud and be envied."[213] Yet the king stroked and patted in public that young, blond Scot, Robert Carr, who had more influence over the sovereign than any other individual during the time Shakespeare was penning his sonnets to the prince.

Carr was the power behind the throne. In December 1607, James knighted him and appointed him a gentleman of the bedchamber.

Naturally, the prince, only seven years younger, resented the attention given to Carr. To counteract his father's favorite, Henry built up his own sphere of influence. As one chronicler said, Carr was "drawn up by the Beams of Majesty, to shine in the highest Glory, grapling often with the *Prince* himself in his own *Sphear*, in divers *Contestations*. For the *Prince* being a high born *Spirit*, and meeting a young *Competitor* in his Fathers Affections, that was a *Mushroom* of yesterday, thought the *venom* would grow too near him, and therefore gave no *countenance*, but *opposition* to it."[214]

Young though he was, Henry soon had his own entourage, almost a second court, an alternative to the king's and often in direct opposition to it. (He would not have his own official court until he was promoted Prince of Wales in 1610.) He represented the hope of the Protestant reformers, who feared his mother's overt Catholicism. He was "saluted by the Puritans as one prefigured in the Apocalypse for Rome's destruction."[215] Half a dozen books written by churchmen were dedicated to him in 1606. By the time he was fourteen he had his own establishment at St. James's, which was, in the words of a contemporary, "more frequented than the King's, and by another sort of Men; so the King was heard to say, *will he bury me alive?*"[216] His household quickly swelled from seventy servants in 1603 to as many as three hundred in 1609.

IT IS DIFFICULT to imagine how a very young man, headed for political stardom, would read these sonnets. Because of their intimate tone, they may have meant more to him than one of his official portraits. This boy wonder entered Shakespeare's life at a time that was crucial to both of them. Henry was in his formative teens, while Shakespeare was in his retrospective years. In Henry's case, the ordinary difficulties of adolescence were compounded by the conflict between his homosexual predisposition and his historical destiny. The poet was an aging man, nostalgic about past loves and longing for the social recognition denied to professional actors. "The *stage* doth staine pure gentle *bloud*," said the poet John

Davies, probably with Shakespeare in mind.[217] The god-like youth, handsome and powerful, became the wonder-worker whose friendship might conceivably make the actor's dreams come true.

To the young man, pressed on all sides by moralists and policy-makers, Shakespeare's sonnets must have been as soothing as the balm of Gilead. Here was an older man loving him for what he was, not for what he was being groomed to be, a poet who unashamedly touched upon those feelings he had to repress. Just as the poet found the prince to be a source of comfort, so the prince found in the poet a mentor whom he could trust. Others treated Henry as a public figure, someone who had to be guided and educated to play a major part on the European stage. Shakespeare saw through the political façade and looked into the boy's heart. Where others were exhorting him to better himself, Shakespeare was urging him to be himself.

The trouble was that this prince was an adolescent who had yet to come to terms with his own nature. He wanted to be recognized as a militant soldier who would counteract his father's pacifism; yet he was father's son in his sexual inclinations. In Shakespeare he found someone who understood him as no one else did. Other poets panegyrized Prince Henry but not in language permeated with homoerotic sentiments. And Shakespeare was careful to define his admiration as purely Platonic. He never once in all the sonnets mentions being physically aroused by any part of the boy's anatomy. He desexualizes the boy, makes him an angel, enshrines him, and puts him out of reach. Nothing hurts him more than to see this idol defiled, to hear him slandered (70), or to learn that he might be deceitful (93) or lascivious (69). What psychologists term the halo effect, the tendency to view the adored one as perfect in all respects because he is perfect in one, is in full operation in these sonnets, which express a love that on its own terms could never be physically consummated. The divine spirit is an aura surrounding the loved one, generated by imaginings projected by the lover. In the case of Shakespeare, the longing was for the adolescent male, a youth still fairly innocent of the way of the world, on the verge of manhood but still untried sexually, and occupying a high place in society.

It is doubtful that anything like these sonnets in tone and feeling could ever have been written, circulated, and printed while Queen Elizabeth ruled the land. It was the prurient and hot-house atmosphere of the court of King James that made them possible. Shakespeare's stroking of the prince's ego was the verbal and chaste equivalent of the king kissing and caressing his male favorites in public.

In a fine study of the cult of Prince Henry, J. W. Williamson said, "It was consistently the case that the boy could not distinguish between the fiction of poetry or paint and the less exalted realities of the adult world. . . . He believed fervently that the symbols were made flesh in him, that in him the hand of God had made incarnate His truth and justice."[218]

Surrounded by advisors and admirers, by counselors and tutors, the teen-age prince was not so much the initiator of actions as the front man for those who yearned to see England emulate or even surpass the martial greatness of France and the artistic magnificence of the Italian courts. They made Henry the center of a personality cult, and Shakespeare and Chapman were there to contribute to the "hype." As servants to the royal court, they were aware of their role in the process and perhaps were even sought out and enlisted by the prince's supporters. Shakespeare's idolatry served their purpose up to a point.

Still, without the magnetism and extraordinary allure of the young boy, their efforts would have fallen flat. Given the impression that the prince made on others, Shakespeare's glorification of the boy seems less like hyperbole than genuine amazement. When he asks, "What is your substance, whereof are you made, / That millions of strange shadows on you tend?" (53), he unites an image of the hundreds of servants and advisors in the prince's establishment with a vision of his magical power, the substance of his being.

In the *Sonnets* of 1609 the playwright-poet exposes and displays his faults and virtues with a startling frankness. Yet these poems were not coerced from him, and they were not printed without his permission. Shakespeare clearly wanted this volume to serve as a testament as much as a confession. In part it was meant as his artistic credo. On the one side stood Chapman and the churchmen, the conventional moralizers; on the other side stood Shakespeare, the artist for whom beauty was an irresistible attraction. Between them stood Prince Henry, a statesman skilled beyond his years, preening himself as the next king, one who instinctively recognized the absolute need for the support of adherents and disciples and professional mythmakers. Now what he heard from them was different from what he read in Shakespeare's sonnets. These poems expressed a devotion that was free of political and religious cant. His love for the prince is not "subject to time's love or to time's hate. . . . No, it was builded far from accident; / It suffers not in smiling pomp, nor falls / Under the blow of thrilled discontent, / Whereto th'inviting time our fashion calls" (124). Everyone else wanted the prince to serve a purpose; only Shakespeare wanted him to be himself alone, a thing of beauty, a joy forever. The tragedy was that the thing did not last; the joy came from what the poet created.

In the sonnets, time and the flesh are the enemies of the poet. Without them, however, there would be no need for his craft. In one way or another, most of the sonnets deal with the onrush of time and the inexorable gravitational pull of the body. The great difference in ages between the two, some thirty years, was both an obstacle to their friendship and a bridge to mutual understanding. As the center of opposed forces within his family, the teen-age prince needed outside guidance. His father was envious of his success, while his increasingly giddy mother was unable – because others feared her Catholic beliefs would infect the child— to care for him properly. He disdained his father's pacifism but sided with his Protestantism; he fought against his mother's Catholicism but needed her warmth and support.

Chapman and Shakespeare were father substitutes (not the only ones), but here again Henry was torn between diametrically opposed views. These poet-tutors had contrary lessons to teach their charge. Chapman stayed strictly within the confines of his role, while Shakespeare wandered off on a deviant path. While Chapman inculcated ethical principles on the boy, Shakespeare espoused the cause of art and beauty. Both had their selfish reasons. Chapman desperately sought support for his vast Homer project, while Shakespeare wanted to rise in the ranks of society. Peerless in his own realm, he hoped to overcome his middle-class origins and his theatrical background and be welcomed among the upper reaches of the nobility. His entry into this charmed circle would be gained, he thought, by the sonnets. Plays, no matter how brilliant in style and profound in thought, could not win the respect of the royal circle any more than a string of fine movies can nowadays earn a Nobel Prize in Literature for a Hollywood screenwriter. Plays were fugitive vehicles not meant to last; they were almost as ephemeral as an actor's performance. When Chapman published his tragedy *The Revenge of Bussy D'Ambois*, he was careful in offering it to Sir Thomas Howard to say that in Italy and elsewhere on the continent plays could properly be dedicated to noblemen and great princes. They have not considered it "any least diminution to their greatness to have their names winged with these tragic plumes." Shakespeare seldom treated his plays, the Second Quarto of *Hamlet* being one exception, with the respect he gave to his non-dramatic poetry. He dedicated his early narrative poems to the earl of Southampton, but not one of his plays was dedicated to a nobleman. As an actor, he knew that they fully existed only in performance, not in print.

Writing sonnets was another matter. Even a nobleman might himself indulge in that prestigious literary exercise, as Sir Philip Sidney did in the 1580s, composing the long and largely autobiographical sonnet sequence *Astrophel and Stella*, which set a standard for others to equal. But Shakespeare went beyond what his predecessors had done. He took the extraordinarily bold step of addressing his sonnets to the prince and holding a mirror up to him. They were not dedicated to him as was common in this form; they pictured him. Shakespeare seemed bent on creating something strange and new: a detailed portrait or monument (his own word) of a living figure in the form of sonnets. It could not have been planned that way from the start, yet that was how it turned out. This portrait in words was also unusual in that the portraitist was painted into the picture. Sonnets 1 to 126 provide a double portrait of artist and subject.

CHAPTER 16

The Course of Tainted Love

ALTHOUGH much has been lost through the passage of time, something has been gained in our appreciation of the sonnets. What to the first readers was a scandal, certain to stir up strong personal feelings, is now primarily a work of art, not quite the monument Shakespeare at first intended, but something rarer and more excellent, an opportunity to peer into the mind of a supreme genius wrestling with his own emotions. With our knowledge of the background events alluded to and an awareness of the extent and nature of the rivalry between Shakespeare and Chapman, we can re-read the Fair Youth sequence as they were meant to be read. These sonnets, which occupy about eighty percent of the entire *Sonnets*, constitute a gripping epistolary love story of attraction, consummation, disillusionment, and rejection.

Shakespeare may have been first smitten by the young boy in 1606, in April, to judge by the commemorative tone of sonnet 104: "Three April perfumes in three hot Junes burned, / Since first I saw you fresh." The first few sonnets were probably written a year or so later, more likely at the suggestion of the queen than on Shakespeare's own initiative. Henry was then only thirteen and had just attained puberty. Sonnet 4 urges the boy to find sexual release in marriage rather than in masturbation. The poet reminds him that the latter means will not produce a replica of his beautiful self. "For having traffic with thyself alone / Thou of thyself thy sweet self dost deceive." As was customary at that time, plans for his marriage were already afoot, plans in which the queen wanted to be involved. In sonnet 3, Shakespeare flatters both mother and son for their attractiveness. "Thou art thy mother's glass, and she in thee/ Calls back the lovely April of her prime."

In sonnet 14 Shakespeare shifts the object of his praise from Henry's physical attractiveness to his soul. As an actor in the king's company, Shakespeare would have met and talked to Henry, and received thanks for those first sonnets. Now the poet looks into the young man's eyes and finds there that truth and beauty are one and the same. That moment, when he and the young man first exchanged glances that said more than words, would leave a lasting impression. He relives it in sonnet 104, the moment "when first your eye I eyed." The Hilliard miniature of Henry, painted at about this time (1607–1608), is probably a good likeness of the face that inspired these first sonnets. (See Figure 8: Prince Henry by Nicholas Hilliard, page 152 above.)

In the next few sonnets the poet harps on the boy's handsomeness, urging him to marry and produce a son in order that his good looks will be preserved. For a poet eulogizing the heir to the throne, this was an odd path to take. A conventional poet would remind the young man of his responsibilities and of the role that he was meant to play in European affairs. Everyone knew Henry wanted to be the leader of an aggressive England; everyone knew of his love of soldiery. Yet Shakespeare never once in these first sonnets touches on those subjects. He must have sensed from the beginning that behind Henry's consuming interest in the army and navy lay an indifference to women. It was hardly a secret in court circles. Commenting on the marriages of his friends, Henry remarked, "I would not be so soone married, and yet I wish to see my Father a grandfather."[219]

One of the minor mysteries of the sonnets is why a poet in love with a young man should insist on his getting married – "insist" seems to be the right word when the poet composes sixteen sonnets on the subject. The answer is that finding a bride for the future king was already a major political and religious concern. Vexing to the king makers, those powers behind the throne, was the teen-age prince's aversion to marriage and his lack of interest in the other sex. He preferred martial arrangements to marital ones. He liked to play war games with boys his own age and scorned the company of girls his own age. Given this situation, his mother,

[193]

who felt increasingly isolated from policy-making, thought that her son might prefer to listen to her when it came to affairs of the heart. Shakespeare would probably never have embarked on the sonnet sequence if the queen herself had not put him in the way of temptation, hinting that he should use his poetic gifts to flatter the boy into marriage, and a nod from the queen to a servant of the court was a virtual command.

The involvement of Queen Anne solves one of the minor mysteries of the sonnets. The literary critic C. S. Lewis was perplexed by the first group of sonnets and asked the sensible question, "What man in the whole world, except a father or a potential father-in-law, cares whether any other man gets married?"[220] The answer is: a servant poet who has been told to care.

In sonnet 14 Shakespeare shifts the object of his praise from Henry's physical attractiveness to his soul. As an actor in the king's company, Shakespeare would have met and talked to Henry, and received thanks for those first sonnets. When this Socrates and this Alcibiades first looked into each other's eyes, the 1609 *Sonnets* began life.

BY SONNET 15 Shakespeare is becoming more intimate with the boy, gently coming on to him by suggesting that the highest flights of the poetic muse can preserve the ideal that time will destroy. At first the boy's loveliness is treated rather abstractly, as if it were something that the poet could discuss coolly and unemotionally. But in sonnets 17 and 18 the tone changes abruptly. First, the poet, having fallen under the spell of the boy's charm, undertakes to preserve in verse "the beauty of your eyes" (17). In the next sonnet, the poet's muse takes wing. "Shall I compare thee to a summer's day? / Thou art more lovely and more temperate." With that single heartfelt sentence the poet unabashedly declared himself. He hardly would have done so if he had not suspected that the war-loving, girl-shy young man in a homoerotic court shared his own sexual proclivities.

(Havelock Ellis, sexual psychologist, writing as if in possession of some secret information, teasingly commented that "Chapman was the admiring disciple of a youthful master who is definitely associated with homosexual interests."²²¹ He coyly refrains from naming the youthful master.)

SONNET 20 MARKS a change in the relationship of poet and prince. Shakespeare now feels assured that he understands the young man better than anyone else. They are kindred souls. Responding to Chapman's picture of the ideal man as a compound of feminine gentleness and masculine valor, a compound that makes him so strangely "loved of both the sexes," Shakespeare portrays the teen-age, androgynous Henry as the ideal combination of man and woman. While Chapman's perfect man is an intellectual construct, Shakespeare's is a creature of physical perfection, with a woman's face and a man's temperament, the master-mistress of the poet's passion.

From this point on, the sonnets take an intimate and familiar tone. He regards the boy as friend and confidant, with whom he can share his most personal thoughts. He confesses how much the boy means to his happiness. If he feels depressed, despising himself for his "outcast state," his thoughts turn to the boy and "then my state, / Like to the lark at break of day arising, / From sullen earth sings hymns at heaven's gate" (29).

In the twinned sonnets 29 and 30, in lines of unforced and spontaneous feeling, he sings to the young boy. In sonnet 29 his concern is with his reputation.

> When in disgrace with fortune and men's eyes
> I all alone beweep my outcast state,
> . . .
> Haply I think on thee, and then my state,
> Like to the lark at break of day arising,
> From sullen earth sings hymns at heaven's gate;
> For thy sweet love remembered such wealth brings
> That then I scorn to change my state with kings.

In the next sonnet he laments the death of dear friends.

> When to the sessions of sweet silent thought
> I summon up remembrance of things past,
> I sigh the lack of many a thing I sought,

And with old woes new wail my dear time's waste;
Then can I drown an eye (unused to flow)
For precious friends hid in death's dateless night
And weep afresh love's long since cancelled woe.
. . .
But if the while I think on thee, dear friend,
All losses are restored, and sorrows end.

Now very quickly his genius was swept away by the overpowering attraction of the young boy, which challenged him as an artist to match the loveliness he saw before him with the allurement of his verse. What Shelley saw in a nineteen-year-old Italian girl, "an image of some bright Eternity," Shakespeare saw in the young English prince. He was like a painter or sculptor who comes upon an ideal subject that obsesses him until it has been metamorphosed into the artist's medium. But in this particular case, the artist came into competition with a philosopher who sought to change what the artist wanted to preserve.

At least this intimate approach was worth the gamble. And it paid off. He was not rebuffed, and his increasingly ardent sonnets were not returned. In sonnet 20, in which for the first time he like a true lover and not a paid poet mentions the physical qualities – a woman's face, a man's complexion, a bright eye – that make the boy so bewitching, he avows his passion and defines the Ganymedean creed. It was a step he had to take because by this time he was engaged in a struggle with Chapman for control of the image that the boy prince represented. In the next sonnet, Shakespeare designedly provoked a quarrel with Chapman, implying that he was the better poet and that Chapman's motives were mercenary. Confident of his powers, he offered the prince immediate monumentality, of the sort that a great portraitist could confer on a nobleman, whereas Chapman offered only second-hand immortality through Homer's imperishable epic.

But Chapman was up to the challenge. His pen could draw a portrait of the prince as the Renaissance man, future ruler of England, commander of its army and navy, supporter of the arts and humanities, a man whose forebears were Achilles and Alexander.

[196]

By championing Chapman's Homer, the prince would partake of the glory of the ancient Greeks.

Before 1607 the quarrel between Shakespeare and Chapman had been largely philosophical, a disagreement over principles. For Chapman, the love of Ganymede was the love of wisdom and reason. For Shakespeare, it was a love of beauty and a surrender to passion. After 1607 the conflict between them became more personal. From being an argument over ideas, it became a battle to capture the prince, with both poets "bound for the prize of all-too-precious you" (86). Chapman, maintaining a precarious existence as poet and playwright, desperately needed his patronage. Shakespeare ardently desired him as a companion. Chapman's advantage was that he occupied the moral high ground, and Prince Henry was the front man for a strict Protestantism. Shakespeare's was that he was the better poet, and the heir to the throne wanted to be glorified by the best artists. Shakespeare knew this, and the question was, could the artist prevail over the moralist?

In his philosophic poem *The Shadow of Night*, Chapman had defined Ganymede, "the bird of Jove," as beauty of the mind, not body. It soars nearest to the divine and "furthest is from spot of earths delight."

> If wisdome be the mindes true bewtie then,
> And that such bewtie shines in vertyous men,
> If those sweet Ganemedes shall onely finde,
> . . . .
> Love of Olimpius, are those wizerds wise,
> That nought but gold, and his dyjections prise?
> This bewtie hath a fire upon her brow,
> That dimmes the Sunne of base desires in you (lines 472-478).[222]

When Shakespeare in sonnet 20 praised the delicate, girl-like beauty of the boy and said little or nothing about beauty of mind, he flung down the gauntlet at Chapman, declaring that love of the physical object was the gateway to heaven and that the philosophic mind could not stand up to the passionate heart.

In the next sonnet, Shakespeare went even further in his efforts to provoke and challenge his rival. Chapman had completed the translation of another large section of the Iliad (*Homer, Prince of Poets, translated according to the Greeks in Twelve Books of his Iliads*), which added books 3, 4, 5, 6 and 12 to the six he had published in 1598. In November 14, 1608 he registered it for publication. The manuscript of this brave undertaking was circulated among the court literati, and Shakespeare paid particular attention to it, especially to the dedicatory epistle, "To the High Borne Prince of Men, Henrie," in which Chapman with characteristic effusiveness invoked Homer as the god of poetry and learning who above all others merited the good offices of the magnificent prince.

> For as the Sunne and Moone are figures given
> Of his refulgent Deitie in Heaven,
> So Learning and her Lightner, Poesie,
> In earth present his fierie Majestie.
> Nor are Kings like him since their Diademes
> Thunder and lighten and project brave beames,
> But since they his cleare vertues emulate —
> In Truth and Justice imaging his State,
> In bountie and Humanitie since they shine.
> Than which is nothing (like him) more divine —
> Not Fire, not Light, the Sunne's admired course,
> The Rise nor Set of Starres, nor all their force
> In us and all this Cope beneath the Skie,
> Nor great Existence, term'd his Treasurie –
>   Since not for being greatest he is blest,
>   But being Just, and in all vertues best (lines 76-91).[223]

At the end of this poem Chapman compared the highest poetry, poetry in the service of justice, to "violets in their beds."

As a rejoinder, Shakespeare (after having just co-opted Chapman's master-mistress ideal) composed sonnet 21, in which, like a brash and cocky athlete, he ran circles around his opponent. He could not declare that he was the better poet by far, but he could demonstrate that he was and let the reader decide for himself, backhandedly flattering Henry's taste. He played with Chapman's images, improving on them, showing Chapman how the thing should be done, all with the *sprezzatura* of an infinitely superior artist. Chapman's "all this Cope beneath the Skie" became the euphonically superior "this huge rondure." Chapman's insipid and colorless "Set of Starres" is transmuted and alchemized into "those gold candles fixed in heaven's air." The whole poem belittles Chapman for the triteness of his imagery, implying that its banality is a sign that his devotion to the prince is unfelt and insincere.

> So is it not with me as with that Muse,
> Stirred by a painted beauty to his verse,
> Who heaven itself for ornament doth use,
> And every fair with his fair doth rehearse,
> Making a couplement of proud compare
> With sun and moon, with earth and sea's rich gems,
> With April's first-born flowers, ["violets in their beds"] and all
>   things rare
> That heaven's air in this huge rondure hems.
> O, let me, true in love, but truly write,
> And then, believe me, my love is as fair
> As any mother's child, though not so bright
> As those gold candles fixed in heaven's air.
>   Let them say more that like of hearsay well:
>   I will not praise that purpose not to sell.

It was clever, and it was cruel. Shakespeare was doing more than toying with Chapman's poetry, and more than criticizing his philosophy; he was impugning his motives for dedicating his Homer to the prince. He uncharitably questioned Chapman's integrity and uprightness, declaring that his own purpose was "not to sell" and insinuating that Chapman's purpose was venal. He brutally restated the conflict between reason and passion as one between money and devotion.

It was the proper business of poets to seek patronage and to extol the virtues of their benefactors. In 1593 when the plague had brought about the closing of the theatres, Shakespeare had sought the financial support of the earl of Southampton and earned it by writing *Venus and Adonis*, prefacing it with the obligatory words of flattery. In 1608 he could afford to take a lofty tone. He was prosperous and famous, with an annual income that a grandee might enjoy, while Chapman was living from hand to mouth, lamenting in *Tears of Peace* his "poor and abject life."

Shakespeare's emotional involvement with the royal boy was most intense at the time he wrote sonnets 30 through 42. It was then that his desires, both conscious and subconscious, came closest to complete fulfillment. As in a Greek pederastic relationship, he was a tutor and advisor to the adolescent angel, while at the same time he made love to him, partaking of his divinity, through the intermediary of a woman. Ganymedean love could go no further without turning sordid and beastly.

In sonnet 30 – "When to the sessions of sweet silent thought, / I summon up remembrance of things past" – Shakespeare recognized that the young man had given new meaning to his life. He was a middle-aged man who was once again swept up by the power of love when he had least expected it. He calls to mind "precious friends hid in death's dateless night" and weeps "afresh love's long since cancelled woe." But now when he thinks of the boy "all losses are restored, and sorrows end."

With the poet in this state of mind and with the prince eager to listen to someone who was completely sympathetic and understanding, there were moments, private moments, when the social restraints slipped away, when the actor and the prince became intimates playing out a drama familiar to all lovers, in which accusations were blurted out, recriminations uttered, and reconciliations tearfully effected. At times Henry had to turn his back on Shakespeare. Between sonnets 32 and 33 something occurred or something was said that hurt Shakespeare deeply. He refers to it as the young man's "disgrace" and makes it the subject of sonnets 33 and 34. That the poet-actor could upbraid a prince of the realm in strong language was a measure of the trust they placed in each other. The young man quickly regrets his mistake and, with tears welling up in his eyes, apologizes to the poet, who finds it difficult to forgive him.

> Nor can thy shame give physic to my grief;
> Though thou repent, yet I have still the loss;
> Th'offender's sorrow lends but weak relief

To him that bears the strong offence's loss.
Ah, but those tears are pearl which thy love sheds,
And they are rich, and ransom all ill deeds (34).

For Shakespeare it must have been a poignant scene, one to which he would return when he could see it in a different light. Those tears in the young boy's eyes would only strengthen and reaffirm the bond between them. But while that understanding brought them closer together as soul mates, it threatened to separate them in the social world.

Inevitably, there were complications. In forgiving him, the poet colluded with the offender, sanctioning the misdeed. In sonnet 35 the poet "authorizes," that is, both writes about and approves, the boy's "trespass" by comparing it to the faults of others. What had the boy done? The only solid clue as to the nature of his offense is the mention in sonnet 35 of his "sensual fault." Although the poet was deeply hurt, he was determined to deal with the matter in a practical way: "to thy sensual fault I bring in sense." He would allow himself to be known as the Ganymedean lover in order to absolve the boy of any blame.

In the next two sonnets-as-letters, Shakespeare declared that he must make a lover's sacrifice. Realistically, the close bond between them had to be broken because society was frowning on their relationship. Shakespeare forgives the prince, knowing that political pressures force them to draw apart. The poet blames himself; it is his reputation as a man with a Socratic disposition that makes their relationship so fragile.

Let me confess that we two must be twain,
Although our undivided loves are one;
So shall those blots that do with me remain,
Without thy help, by me be borne alone.
. . .
I may not evermore acknowledge thee,
Lest my bewailed guilt should do thee shame,
Nor thou with public kindness honour me,
Unless thou take that honour from thy name (36).

If the prince publicly recognized Shakespeare as a trusted friend, he would stain his own reputation. The poet's "bewailed guilt" must refer to his homosexuality, not his profession as actor, since it must tie in with the boy's "sensual fault." It was something they shared. By taking all the guilt on himself, Shakespeare could clear the boy's reputation. "So shall those blots that do with me remain, / Without thy help, by me be borne alone." In the spirit of true devotion, he decided to give up the young man's company in order to quiet the unpleasant rumors. "Let us divided live . . . That by this separation I may give / That due to thee which thou deserv'st alone" (39).

Shakespeare's determination to put some distance between himself and the beloved youth only led to more convoluted psychological entanglements. If Shakespeare's purpose in removing himself from the scene was to preserve the manly reputation of Prince Henry, then the young man could do even better. To demonstrate to the court gossips and rumor mongers that he was not overly interested in other men, he took a woman to bed. Shakespeare took this as a spiteful act. The boy had disavowed the Socratic ideal by carrying his suggestion that they separate to the absurdity of copulating with the opposite sex.

The boy's thoughts ran something like this. "There can be no need for us to separate unless there is some truth to the whisperings about our mutual devotion. And if you can stand to be separated from me, you don't really love me as much as your sonnets say you do. Well, I can break with you as easily as you can break with me, and breaking with you means an end to that high-minded, untainted Ganymedean love that brought us together."

The next sonnet (40) tells us that the woman the young man turned to was, not surprisingly, someone whom Shakespeare knew and whom he used to satisfy his own carnal needs. The tone of the sonnet and Shakespeare's judgment of the young man is expressed in two striking words that come in the concluding couplet: "lascivious grace" – a perfect example of what Wallace Stevens called "the clashed edges of two words that kill." Those two words say it all: the boy's position as a noble, his charm as an adolescent, as well as his sexual misbehavior.

Take all my loves, my love, yea take them all;
What hast thou then more than thou hadst before?
No love, my love, that thou mayst true love call;
All mine was thine, before thou hadst this more.

(Take my mistresses, dear boy, what have you gained? Nothing. All I loved was already yours.)

Then if for my love, thou my love receivest,
I cannot blame thee, for my love thou usest.

(I cannot blame you for trying – by taking my mistress – to replace my kind of manly love with conventional heterosexual love.)

But yet be blamed, if thou this self deceivest,
By willful taste of what thyself refusest.

(Nevertheless, you are deceiving your true homoerotic self by resorting to a woman, driven by carnal appetite. For that you are to blame.)

I do forgive thy robb'ry, gentle thief,
Although thou steal thee all my poverty.

(You aren't really taking anything from me; the woman means nothing to me.)

And yet love knows it is a greater grief
To bear love's wrong than hate's known injury.

(It is much more painful to be inadvertently hurt by a loved one than to be deliberately hurt by someone else.)

Lascivious grace, in whom all ill well shows,
Kill me with spites, yet we must not be foes.

(You are a lusty, charming, handsome prince, and even when you do something cruel, it seems all right – "ill well shows." Your motive for what you've done is apparent – "well shows." You've made your point; you're trying to spite me. But surely we can still be friends.)

In the next few sonnets, a reconciliation was worked out. Taking the first step, the poet forgave the prince, whose rank and good looks and innocence put him in the way of temptation. "Gentle thou art, and therefore to be won, / Beauteous thou art, therefore to be assailed." But the forgiveness came with a reservation.

Ay me, but yet thou mightst my seat forbear,

[203]

> And chide thy beauty, and thy straying youth,
> Who lead thee in their riot even there
> Where thou art forced to break a twofold truth:
> Hers, by thy beauty tempting her to thee,
> Thine, by thy beauty being false to me (41).

By taking on the poet's mistress, the boy was violating two codes of behavior: the mistress should be true to one man (at a time); and the boy should be true to the Ganymedean ideal. He should have spurned the woman as Adonis spurned Venus.

The final step in bringing the poet and the boy together again took place in the poet's mind. In sonnet 42 he began by lamenting the triangular love situation, and he ended by finding joy in it.

> Loving offenders, thus I will excuse ye:
> Thou dost love her, because thou knowst I love her.
> . . .
> If I lose thee [to her], my loss is my love's gain,
> And losing her, my friend hath found that loss.
> Both find each other, and I lose both twain,
> And both for my sake lay on me this cross.

The ambiguity of "my love's gain" points to the happy resolution. The surface meaning is: my love (the boy) has taken my mistress, and my loss is his gain. The deeper meaning is: my particular kind of love for the boy finds an inexpressible pleasure in the arrangement. The poet's "seat" is occupied by the boy; the physical barrier between the poet and the boy is broken; by penetrating the woman's vagina the poet makes love to the boy. "Here's the joy, my friend and I are one." (See pages 103–106 above.)

Even if Shakespeare saw Prince Henry in his mind's eye as he embraced the woman, he could hardly have said so. He went as far as delicacy – or his subconscious — allowed. And this kind of copulation at a distance was the most that the middle-aged actor could hope for.

As private correspondence, this group of sonnets forms an extraordinary confession. As published poems, they must be unique in the literature of the time: the equivalent of modern tabloid sensationalism about the famous raised to the level of great art.

CHAPTER 17

No Holds Barred

JUST WHEN Shakespeare had established a close bond with the young prince, Chapman intruded. Both poets wooed Henry but for different purposes. Chapman needed his backing in order to accomplish his task; Shakespeare wanted the young prince's affection and company as the fulfillment of a deep desire. He wanted to rise in the ranks of society, winning a place there by virtue of his genius, just as the shipwright Phineas Pett had. In exchange for what they desired, Chapman and Shakespeare both promised the prince immortality. Both believed that for the vaulting ambitions of the prince no monument was so durable "as that which is framed by a fortunate penne." Knowing Henry's Martian inclinations, Chapman tied his fame to Homer, the chronicler of the soldierly virtues. Shakespeare made a different and daring pitch, saying that Henry would be memorialized directly in the poet's verse, not indirectly through Homer.

In the dedicatory epistle to his Homer, Chapman warned:

> A Prince's statue, or in Marble carv'd
> Or steele or gold, and shrin'd (to be preserv'd)
> Aloft on Pillars or Pyramides,
> Time into lowest ruines may depresse;
> But, drawne with all his vertues in learn'd verse,
> Fame shall resound them on Oblivion's herse
> Till graves gaspe with her blasts and dead men rise.
> No gold can follow where true Poesie flies.[224]

Shakespeare replied with what endures as one of his finest sonnets, fulfilling what its final lines promised. He collided head-on with Chapman, picking up on his phrases and assailing the military mentality.

> Not marble nor the gilded monuments
> Of princes shall outlive this powerful rhyme,
> But you shall shine more bright in these contents
> Than unswept stone, besmeared with sluttish time.
> When wasteful war shall statues overturn,
> And broils root out the work of masonry,
> Nor Mars his sword nor war's quick fire shall burn
> The living record of your memory.
> 'Gainst death and all oblivious enmity
> Shall you pace forth; your praise shall still find room
> Even in the eyes of all posterity
> That wear this world out to the ending doom.
>   So, till the judgment that your self arise,
>   You live in this, and dwell in lovers' eyes (55).

Shakespeare felt intimidated by Chapman's erudition, a sore point he obsessively returns to in the sonnets. Knowing "small Latin and less Greek," in Ben Jonson's perhaps untrustworthy phrase, he could not compete with his rival in familiarity with classical literature. He could, however, set his artistry against Chapman's learning, as he does in sonnet 78, in which he describes the effect the boy's influence has had on the two poets. He claims that it has been greater on him than on his rival. Chapman was already a savant and scholar, and the prince could do no more than inspire him to improve his style by adding a few feathers to the poet's wings, that is, help him write better by supporting him monetarily — an effective dig at Chapman's most sensitive point. But, says Shakespeare, his case is different. The prince has taught him to fly, to lift him out of ignorance and up to the level of Chapman's scholarship.

> Thine eyes, that taught the dumb on high to sing
> And heavy ignorance aloft to fly.
> Have added feathers to the learned's wing,
> And given grace a double majesty.
> Yet be most proud of that which I compile,
> Whose influence is thine, and born of thee:

In other's works thou dost but mend the style,
And arts with thy sweet graces graced be.
But thou art all my art, and dost advance
As high as learning my rude ignorance (78).

The repeated phrase – "Thy sweet graces graced be" and "given grace a double majesty" – are also glances at Chapman's dedicatory epistle to Henry. Chapman says that the prince by benefiting the art of poetry will raise it above the scandalous. "Clear'd by your faire Grace, / Your Grace may shine the clearer."[225]

While the two poets were sparring with each other, Chapman received some welcome news. For some years he had held an ill-paid sinecure in the prince's household and had labored unselfishly on his Homer translations in the hope that their worth would be recognized and that he would be given the financial support which would enable him to complete the work. Early in 1609 the prince came through with a grant of £300 to encourage him to finish his translation.[226] At about the same time, Henry submitted to his father a composition in Latin in which he argued that kings and princes are more in need of learning than men of lesser station.[227]

After having struggled for years as a poor scholar and eked out a living as a playwright, Chapman had at last secured for himself a measure of financial security. Invigorated by the prospect of a daily and uninterrupted companionship with his beloved Homer, he took advantage of the peace treaty negotiated by James I to compose, with extraordinary speed, *The Tears of Peace*, in which he both celebrated the king's accomplishment and instructed his son on the value of learning and reason.

Four years earlier Chapman had found himself in prison for ridiculing King James. In *Eastward Ho*, a play that he co-authored with Ben Jonson and John Marston, the king is mocked for selling knighthoods to anyone who would pay thirty pounds. Now Chapman hoped to find himself in James's good graces by celebrating his diplomatic triumph. Here Chapman himself was faced with a diplomatic challenge. His muse had to guide him between the Sylla of a pacifistic king and the Carybdis of a bellicose prince. How could he appeal to both at once? He began by dedicating the work to "the High Born Prince of Men Henrie" and then invoking "the great King of Peace" in the first line of the poem. His next task was to convince Henry that the king was pursuing the right course. He did this by appealing to the religious side of the prince, while bizarrely comparing him to Achilles.

> And thou, great Prince of men; let thy sweet graces
> Shine on these teares; and drie, at length, the faces
> Of Peace, and all her heaven-allyed brood;
> From whose Doves eyes, is shed the precious blood
> Of heavens deare Lamb, that freshly bleeds in them.
> Make these no toyes then, gird the Diadem
> Of thrice great Britaine, with their Palm and Bayes:
> And with thy Eagles feathers, daigne
> The reach of Mortalls, and their earthly love;
>   To that high honour, his *Achilles* wonne,
>   And make thy glory farre out-shine the Sunne (lines 242-255).

It was at this point that the spirit of Homer opportunely arose before him to conduct him to the goddess of Peace. The poem is a lengthy disquisition setting the false peace made by political maneuvering against true peace of mind, a peace governed by man's soul. Peace sheds tears of grief at the state of the world in which love has died.

At the end of *Tears of Peace* in the *"Corollarium ad principem,"* Chapman thanks Henry, "great Prince of men," for his sponsorship of the Homer translations. The poem was a shrewd presentation, lauding both the king and his son, whose growing popularity with the religious right the father viewed with alarm. Artistically and intellectually, it was a prodigious achievement, 1232 lines set down in about four weeks' time, a solemn treatise on the causes of war, in which Chapman vows to wage war against those who seek only to satisfy their senses, to enjoy earthly delights, and who thereby encroach on the wishes of others, with war inevitably resulting. Chapman swears, in lines filled with contempt for the world and disgust with the body his soul inhabits, to devote his life to the cause of peace, now that he has the support of the prince.

Shakespeare was impressed — and worried. Sonnets 79 and 80 attest to this. His muse is sick at the thought that "a worthier pen" has taken his place. His "saucy bark" is inferior to Chapman's ship "of tall building and of goodly pride." In sonnet 86 he returns to the naval metaphor, this time with the implication that Chapman is a pirate plundering the prince. "Was it the proud full sail of his great verse, / Bound for the prize of all-too-precious you, / That did my ripe thoughts in my brain in-hearse, / Making their tomb the womb wherein they grew?" If he wanted to stay on the good side of Henry, it would have been untactful of him to disparage the poet on whom the prince had bestowed a handsome benefaction. That would have been a reflection on the young nobleman's taste and acumen. But Shakespeare's lines ring with the shock of the unexpected.

> O, how I faint when I of you do write,
> Knowing a better spirit doth use your name,
> And in praise thereof spends all his might,
> To make me tongue-tied, speaking of your fame (80).

In the next few sonnets, manifestly written within the span of a few days, he vacillates between bouts of depression and bursts of bravado. A day or two later, however, writing sonnets 81 and 82, he has gathered himself together, regaining confidence in his powers as a poet, asserting that the prince's lasting "monument shall be my gentle verse," belittling Chapman's rhetoric as "strained," and contrasting his own "true plain words" with Chapman's "gross painting." He even jibes at Chapman for burying the prince, rather than giving him eternal life. *Tears of Peace* ends with a funeral oration. Shakespeare replies, "For I impair not beauty, being mute, / When others would give life and bring a tomb" (83).

A day or two later, his mood has changed again. His growing awareness that Chapman has won the attention of Henry and that stoicism and Christian contempt for the flesh have prevailed over his own insistence on physical beauty as the incarnation of the higher wisdom brings him to the point of lashing out even at the prince himself. He accuses the boy of being too fond of praise, implies that Chapman took advantage of that fault, and says that the boy's love of self, a curse on his "beauteous blessings," taints the praise he receives (84). Blinded by his infatuation, Shakespeare cannot see how guilty he himself has been in catering to the youth's craving for adulation. Sonnet 87, with its legalistic language and references to a charter, a "fair gift," and a patent, must have been written with Henry's grant to Chapman in mind. He says, self-deprecatingly, that he himself is not worthy of such a bestowal, that "the cause of this fair gift in me is wanting," but in spite of that he had lived in the belief that they shared a bond of mutual affection and high regard for each other.

All that now seemed suddenly to vanish. What a less impassioned man would take as a mere disappointment and a momentary loss, Shakespeare takes as a breach of faith. His attachment to the boy is far greater than the boy's to him, and the deep emotions are felt on one side only. So at first he neurotically tries to hold on to the image of the glorious youth by fighting against himself to "prove thee virtuous" (88). Since he has been cast out, he must somehow be at fault, though what the fault is he cannot bring himself to say. Gradually, through sonnets 92 to 96, he shifts the blame from himself to the boy. He lives "like a deceived husband," "supposing thou art true" (93), facing the possibility that the boy's sweet looks and his virtues are things apart. Then comes the devastating recognition in sonnet 94 ("They that have power to hurt and will do none") that the very impassiveness of the young man, his remoteness, his lack of a need to love anyone is the very source of his magnetism. Love in this relationship flows only one way. The prince lives on a lofty plane; the poet lives only by adoring him.

Still, even the god-like aloofness of this paragon, his serene independence sheathed in his physical attractiveness, cannot make virtues of his faults, though "beauty's veil doth cover every blot" (95). Those defects of character appear all the greater when set against his angelic looks. The poet rounds out this sequence by reminding the boy prince that he possesses a dangerous power that must not be used for the wrong ends. With his charismatic appeal and high position, he could be a young lion among a flock of sheep.

The poet has dropped the charge of betrayal, put aside the favoritism shown to Chapman, and reverted to the main theme of the sonnets: his own infatuation with a delusory image of perfection, marred by a "canker in the fragrant rose" (95). Alas, this prince did not embody the soul of man meant to soar upwards into the empyrean. He was not an English Ganymede; he was merely an adolescent compelled to sink downwards under the weight of physical desires and earthly ambitions.

In the meantime, George Chapman had not been idle. Within the confines of the court circle, the war of words would have been a lively topic of conversation, with malicious tongues eager to keep each poet informed of the other's slurs and innuendoes. His translation of Homer, now enlarged to include twelve books of the *Iliad*, was in the press. He had composed the dedicatory poem "To the High Borne Prince of Men, Henrie" and added fourteen sonnets addressed to other patrons and well- wishers.

Chapman had read Shakespeare as carefully as Shakespeare had read Chapman. And if Shakespeare wanted to play the game of snide allusions and stabbing thrusts, Chapman could play it too. As his *Iliads* was being set in type, he sent to the printer a "Preface to the Reader," in which he strikes out at those who "whisper behind me vilifyings of my translation." He had in mind those who had accused him of not knowing Greek as well as he protested and of having translated Homer from a French version, his *Iliads* being only a loose paraphrase of the original.[228] In fact, he had made good use of a Greek and Latin parallel text prepared by Jean de Sponde, printed in Basle in 1583.[229] Chapman left himself wide open to some of these charges. His 1598 version of parts of the *Iliad* was carefully slanted to glorify Achilles as much as possible. At that time Chapman was seeking the patronage of the earl of Essex, the swashbuckling soldier whom he pictured as a modern Achilles. By 1608, Essex had been executed, and Chapman revised his translation to bring it closer to the original.[230]

Chapman's most stinging remarks are directed at one particular individual among his critics: Shakespeare. To appreciate their effectiveness, it is necessary to keep in mind certain facts that would be known to those who followed the controversy. First: Shakespeare's coat of arms, acquired in 1596, bore as its crest a falcon with its wings spread. (See Figure 16.)

FIGURE 16. Shakespeare's Coat of Arms.

Although Shakespeare had secured the coat of arms for his father, his main purpose had been to gain for himself the title of gentleman. Ben Jonson in *Every Man out of his Humour* (1599) had in the character of Sogliardo satirized Shakespeare the social climber as a man "so enamored of the name of Gentleman, that he will have it, though he buys it." Shakespeare proudly chose as his motto, "Non sanz droict;" Sogliardo's is "Not without mustard." Secondly, he boasted of the immortality of his verse, and in sonnet 107 he set the power of his poetry against that of Chapman, writing as if he were in the position of bestowing immortality on whom he wished. Toward the end of his preface, Chapman gave vent to the rage he felt at being unfairly treated.

> But there is a certaine envious Windfucker [a kind of falcon], that hovers up and downe, laboriously engrossing al the aire with his luxurious ambition and buzzing into every eare my detraction – affirming I turne Homer out of the Latine only, &c – that sets all his associates and the whole rabble of my maligners on their wings with him to beare about my empaire and poyson my reputation. One that, as he thinkes, whatsoever he gives to others he takes from himselfe, so whatsoever he takes from others he addes to himself. One that in this kind of robberie doth like Mercurie, that stole good and supplied it with counterfeit bad still. One like the two gluttons, Philoxenus and Gnatho, that would still emptie their noses in the dishes they loved that no man might eate but themselves. For this Castrill [kestrel, a *small* falcon, a neat jibe], with too hote a liver and lust after his owne glorie, and to devour all himselfe, discourageth all appetites to the fame of another. I have stricken: single him [out] as you can.

[212]

The gist of this outburst is that Shakespeare is so avid for fame and social prestige that he will stop at nothing to put down his rival for the prince's attention. Shakespeare has chosen the right emblem for his coat of arms. He is a bird of prey, ruthlessly attacking Chapman in order to add to his own reputation.[231]

Shakespeare's desire to insinuate himself between Chapman and Prince Henry explains a minor mystery in sonnet 20, the master-mistress sonnet. Shakespeare describes the prince as "A man in hue all *Hews* in his controlling." It makes sense to take the italicized Hews as a pun on a proper name, and Oscar Wilde built his theory on the conjecture that Hughes was the name of a boy actor. Actually, Hews was a scholar, a friend and supporter of Chapman, who defended the poet against those who sought to tarnish his reputation as a translator. Chapman thanks him in the preface to his *Iliads*: the "right learned, honest and entirely loved friend of mine, M. Robert Hews, I must needs put into my confest conference touching Homer."[232] Shakespeare makes the prince the final arbiter, the controller, ranking above the scholar.

With both his Homer and his *Tears of Peace* about to be published, and with the boon of a £300 gift from the young prince, Chapman felt secure enough to strike back at Shakespeare. The philosophical quarrel between Shakespeare and Chapman became more personal and rancorous because of the stakes involved. Chapman now felt he had won the battle of the poets. But, as he well knew, it was neither the power of his verse nor his erudition that had gained him the victory. He had won because he stood for reason against passion, for the soul against the body, for heavenly against earthly wisdom, for philosophical thought against bewitching poetry.

"As the contemplative life is most worthily and divinely preferred by Plato to the active," he wrote in the "Preface to the Reader," "as much as . . . reason to sence, the soule to the bodie, the end it selfe to all things directed to the end, . . . so much preferre I divine Poesie to all wordly wisdome." Then he added another dig at Shakespeare, saying he felt nothing but contempt for "the bold rimes of everie Apish and impudent Braggart (though he dares assume anything); such I turne over to the weaving of Cobwebs, and shall but chatter on molehils (farre under the hill of the Muses) when their fortunat'st selflove and ambition hath advanced them highest."[233]

This was not his final thrust. His most damaging attempt to discredit Shakespeare lurked behind the words. Taking the position of moral tutor to the heir to the throne, he dared allude in print to what others were whispering about Shakespeare. Phrases such as "beastly ends," "luxurious ambition" ("luxurious" usually meant "lascivious"), and "too hote a liver" when applied to Shakespeare all hinted at sexual deviancy, if not perversion. In retaliation against Shakespeare's ridicule of him, Chapman "outed" Shakespeare. Perhaps "outed" is inaccurate, since Shakespeare's sexual orientation was hardly a secret. But Chapman wanted to make certain that the prince knew how others might interpret the sonnets. He exposed the evasiveness of sonnet 20, with its denial that the boy's "prick" was part of his attractiveness, as a diversionary tactic, directing attention away from the poet's "beastly" desires.

THE RIVAL POETS were now clawing at each other, abandoning civilized discourse. Chapman had struck at Shakespeare's most vulnerable point: his "licentious love" for the young prince. Shakespeare retaliated by reviving his Troilus drama in which he had satirized Chapman's interpretation of Homer.

Oddly, *Troilus and Cressida* as issued in 1609 exists in two states, the only difference between them being a change of phrase on the title page and the addition in the second state of an epistle to the reader. The first copies issued announced that here was the play "as it was acted by the King's Majestie's Servants at the Globe." This accords with an entry in the Stationers' Register, 7 February 1603, for *Troilus and Cressida* as "acted" by Shakespeare's company. In the succeeding copies this statement was deleted, and the reader was informed that "you have here a new play, never staled with the stage, never clapper-clawed with the palms of the vulgar, and yet passing full of the palm comical."

These contradictory statements require an explanation. It has been argued that the play was performed for a special, private audience, probably at the Inns of Court for an audience of barristers, who presumably were more sophisticated in their tastes than the public at the Globe Theatre and more likely to enjoy the salacious banter and acerbic humor in the play. With a slight equivocation the printer could claim that the play had never been applauded by an audience of common people. This explanation for the printer's epistle to the reader has been widely accepted, even though, as Alfred Harbage noted, it is hard to imagine that the epilogue to the play, which is directed at the panders in the audience, common enough at the public theaters, would have pleased a group of lawyers.[234] Furthermore, there is little evidence that new plays by professional dramatists were staged at the Inns of Court in Shakespeare's time.

There is a much more credible explanation that not only accounts for the change of title page but also explains why the play was published years after it was acted. In November 1608 Chapman had announced that he intended to publish an expanded version of his Homer (entered in the Stationers' Register, November 14, 1608), and ten weeks later, on January 28, 1609, Shakespeare declared his intention of bringing out his Greek play. This meant that the earlier battles would be fought again. Chapman had his troops in place; now Shakespeare marshaled his.

Chapman had twelve books of the *Iliad* nearly ready for the printer. In response, Shakespeare rewrote large parts of *Troilus*, with the reader, not the playgoer in mind. The muted satire of the original play, written to please the multitudes, the crowd attending the Globe, was sharpened, the characters made more disreputable, the sex more lewd. Pandarus, the procurer of sexual favors, and Thersites, the scurrilous, envious despiser of all that he sees, set the sardonic, anti-heroic tone of the play. Shakespeare did not pull his punches. Chapman's valorous Achilles – valorous in Chapman's eyes in spite of his atrocious behavior toward Hector – is depicted as cruel, loutish, arrogant, and cowardly. Shakespeare saved his most stinging blows for the fifth act. Contrary to what occurs in Chapman's sublime Homer, Shakespeare's Achilles does not kill Hector: he tells his Myrmidons to attack the unarmed Trojan and then orders his soldiers to cry out, "Achilles hath the mighty Hector slain" (5.8.14).

In rewriting *Troilus* Shakespeare threw caution to the winds. In *Tears of Peace*, Chapman had extolled Henry as England's Achilles and promised through Homer's spirit to raise Henry's fame above "the reach of Mortalls, and their Earthly love; / To that high honour, his Achilles wonne, / And make thy glory farre out-shine the Sunne."

Whether or not Shakespeare read these words when revising *Troilus*, he certainly knew Chapman's sentiments, and he knew that Henry had given Chapman's Homer his imprimatur. Defiling Achilles and trashing Homer, Shakespeare set himself in direct opposition to the noble ideals espoused by Chapman.

In discrediting and defaming Achilles as Henry's exemplar, Shakespeare drew a line in the sand between himself on one side and Henry and Chapman on the other. But asserting the differences between himself and warriors was not enough for Shakespeare. He had to retaliate against Chapman for the insinuations of sodomy. So he went out of his way to label Achilles' close friend and fellow warrior Patroclus as "his masculine whore" and "his male varlet" (5.1.14-16). This must have been acutely offensive to Chapman, who exalted male friendship and who regarded Achilles and Patroclus as forming a comradeship made in heaven.[35] More to the point, what did it say about Henry? If Achilles was the model for the prince, and Achilles was a sodomite . . . ?

The rewriting of the play meant that the title page had to be changed. This was no longer the play that had been "clapper-clawed by the vulgar." That play, which dated from the last years of Queen Elizabeth's reign, was acted before Prince Henry came on the scene. It was now a play aimed at the initiated readers at the court of King James, readers who knew of the contention between Chapman and Shakespeare and followed it avidly.

The play is without precedent among all Shakespeare's works in being prefaced by a letter to the reader praising the author. For once in his life Shakespeare sought publicity and advertised himself.

"This author's comedies . . . are so framed to the life that they serve for the most common commentaries of all the actions of our lives, that the most displeased with plays are pleased with his comedies. . . . So much and such savored salt of wit is in his comedies that they seem (for their height of pleasure) to be born in that sea that brought forth Venus. . . . And believe this, that when he is gone, and his comedies out of sale, you will scramble for them and set up a new English Inquisition."

Shakespeare himself would not have written this, but there can be no doubt that he wanted it said as a Parthian shot in his battle with Chapman.

CHAPTER 18

The End of the Affair

L IVING in the steamy atmosphere of King James's court, where the sovereign's male favorite, Robert Carr, ruled the roost, the handsome Prince Henry, the subject of many roving eyes, was hardly innocent and unknowing about erotic bonding between men. He clearly understood the difference between Chapman's kind of praise and Shakespeare's. Both served to promote him as herald of a new age. But the innuendoes about Shakespeare's predatory intentions would have produced a crisis in the relationship of the poet and the prince.

The ugly rumors persisted, and Shakespeare had to defend himself against them. In sonnet 121, he accuses the gossips of harboring vile thoughts, while at the same time he admits that his own tastes and preferences are not normal. Like a typical Ganymedean, he knows that his passion for the androgynous teen-age ideal must strike the ordinary person as strange; yet he also knows that his peculiar kind of love is of a higher order, that his grasping for beauty through the master-mistress is as legitimate a striving for the divine as Chapman's, and far superior to the adulteries committed by most men.

> For why should others' false adulterate eyes
> Give salutation to my sportive blood?
> Or on my frailties why are frailer spies,
> Which in their wills [lusts] count bad what I think good?
> No, I am that I am, and they that level
> At my abuses reckon up their own;
> I may be straight though they themselves be bevel.

By the time Shakespeare set down these self-defensive but bold lines, he must have determined that his worth and reputation as a poet required him to publish a substantial work that could be compared with *Tears of Peace*. He had to come up with something equally impressive not only as poetry but as philosophy, if only to bolster his belief in his own powers and the rightness of his position.

THE THOUGHT of gathering together the sonnets addressed to the prince may not have occurred to Shakespeare until he learned of Chapman's *The Tears of Peace*. Although his philosophical disagreement with Chapman was of long standing and was kept simmering in the plays they both wrote, it did not come to a full boil until Chapman opportunistically laid claim to the mind of Henry just at the time that Shakespeare had fallen in love with his face and figure and been awed by his rank. Challenged by *The Tears of Peace*, Shakespeare seized the opportunity to express a view of life quite the opposite of Chapman's. To be effective it had to have the scope of a major work, and all he had to begin with were a handful of sonnets. Chapman's impressive poem had 1232 lines in it, and it had been turned out in a remarkably short time. To be doubly impressive, Shakespeare would have to produce about as many lines in the more difficult and restrictive form of the sonnet in a comparable period of time. He more than succeeded, putting to shame Chapman's accomplishment.

On May 4, 1609, Chapman's lengthy poem was registered for publication. Substantial parts of it may have been circulating in manuscript from shortly after the peace treaty was announced in early April. On May 20 "Shakespeares sonnettes" was listed in the Stationers' Register. Thus *Tears of Peace* and the Quarto may have appeared in print within two or three weeks of each other in the summer of 1609.

A glance at the time line of the sonnets reveals the tremendous pressure under which Shakespeare wrote the last batch of them. Sonnet 86 strikes at the first pages of *Tears of Peace*, in which Chapman had warmed up to his subject by recording his conversation with the ghost of Homer. This cannot have been written before the first week in April, when news of the peace treaty between Spain and the Low Countries reached London. In sonnet 107

Shakespeare again alludes to *Tears of Peace* in the line "drops of this most balmy time." Sonnet 125, next to last in the Fair Youth sequence, refers to the trial of shipwright Pett on May 8. Putting all this together (and assuming here, as throughout this study, that sonnets 1 to 126 are roughly in chronological order of composition), it appears that sonnets 86 to 125 were written in about one month. Moreover, given the evidence presented earlier, Shakespeare must have composed nearly the whole young man sequence in an extended sonnet-writing binge, one hundred of them being set down in less than half a year, between December 1608 and the end of May 1609. Other sonneteers wrote at most fifty or sixty a year. Shakespeare turned out these sonnets at a faster rate, on the average, four a week, than Bach composed church cantatas. Moreover, many of these poems are miracles of craftsmanship.

There was, however, a price to be paid for this rush to create an impressive sonnet sequence. The hasty production accounts in part for the rickety structure of the 1609 Quarto. Some of his early, pre-1598 sonnets, which had never been printed before, could properly be incorporated to bulk up the volume because they fitted in with the over-all theme, the overarching design.[236] The main sequence of sonnets, however, could not have the firm organization of material that *Tears of Peace* had. Chapman's point of reference throughout was a system of thought, logical enough given certain premises. Everything was seen with heaven's eye. Shakespeare's sonnets to the prince had to be improvised to capture the eruptions of the heart and the flux of time. The spontaneity of composition harmonized with the poet's view of life as ungoverned by a divine system. The poems had to reflect the fits and starts, the joys and pains, of a relationship that changed almost from day to day, following a course whose twists and turns he could not predict. The surface formlessness of life was only spasmodically given shape by the rigidity of the fourteen-line stanza, each with its concluding couplet that reined in each outburst of feeling.

From the very beginning the source of the contention between the two poets was not poetry but philosophy. While Chapman tutored the prince in statesmanship and heroism, Shakespeare hoped to ad-

vise and counsel him in human relations. The rival poets were not rival lovers, each hoping to possess the boy physically. They were
competing for the mind of the prince while it was still in its formative
stage. The victor could claim that his beliefs were justified.

In the political arena, however, the odds were heavily against
Shakespeare. What chance did the actor-playwright stand against
the soldier-poet who as a young man had fought in Leicester's campaign against the Spanish armies in the Netherlands. How could
the sweet music of the *Sonnets* prevail against rugged rhythms of
the *Iliad*? What hope was there for beauty, "whose action is no
stronger than a flower" (65), when confronted by moral rectitude
and a philosophical system?

Chapman wanted to win the prince over to the humanitarian
position in which learning and reason would control men's sensuality. In the induction to *The Tears of Peace*, Chapman blames all
wars on "self-love, inflaming so, mens sensuall bloud, / That all
good, publique, drowns in private good; / And that sinks under,
his own over-freight; / Mens Reasons, and their Learnings, ship-
wrackt quite." The prince, however, was fond of military exercises and saw himself as a hero on the battlefield. As self-appointed tutor, Chapman recommended the study of Homer and likened the
prince to Achilles. But the comparison was cautionary as well as
laudatory. Achilles was not Chapman's idea of the perfect man; he
is too irrational, too much the prey of his own emotions. He lacks
true wisdom. What Chapman wanted to teach Henry is what he
got directly from the ghost of Homer. "Homer told me that there
are / Passions, in which corruption hath no share; / There is a joy
of soule." That particular joy springs from grief, which has its
source in man's conscience. The tears of peace are a necessary expression of humanity's sorrow at the terrible loss of life in wars.[237]

This was a shrewd and sagacious argument. Seeking patronage
from the court and careful not to offend its highest ranking members, Chapman tactfully extolled King James's peace initiatives
while at the same time holding up Achilles as a negative exemplar
for the soldier prince. (In the dedicatory poem that prefaces his
translation of Homer, Chapman set up Alexander the Great as role

model for Henry, saying that the great conqueror affirmed "that Homer's poesie/ Did more advance his Asian victorie / Than all his Armies."[238]

Shakespeare offers a complete contrast to all this. He strips the boy prince of the trappings of war and sees him as the incarnation of beauty. Chapman's master-mistress combines valor and tenderness, self-assertion and Christian humility. Shakespeare's master-mistress is true of heart as a man should be, and lovely to look at as young women should be. Chapman is an ascetic who condemns sensual pleasures and for whom the only legitimate passions are those of the mind, passions that elevate the soul, ascetic passions that degrade the body. Self-denial and sacrifice open the gates to the second life, for which life on earth is only a preparation. It was a firmly held conviction, and in life-loathing words of macabre intensity his poetic genius soared to one of its highest points, where revulsion from the flesh becomes the strongest of all passions. To find his way to heaven, he must

> . . . . cast this Serpent's skale;
> This loade of life, in life; this fleshie stone;
> This bond, and bundle of corruption;
> This breathing Sepulcher; this spundge of griefe;
> This smiling Enemie; this household-thiefe;
> This glass of ayre; broken with lesse then breath;
> This Slave, bound face to face, to death, till death (lines 1014-1020).[239]

This was an image that Chapman was fond of. He had used it earlier at the end of his double drama, *The Conspiracy and Tragedy of Byron* (Act 5, scene 4), which demonstrated the dangers of seeking earthly fame and glory. It was staged by the Children of Blackfriars early in 1608. As a recent editor of the Byron plays remarks, they were probably intended as "a mirror for princes," with Prince Henry particularly in mind. In the company of his royal parents, the young prince saw the plays as staged by the Children of Blackfriars early in 1608.[240]

There is in these lines a passion and a depth of sincerity that might well make Shakespeare cower, precisely because these thoughts are so alien to his own esthetic view. Contemplating death, Shakespeare takes an entirely different path. With him the body becomes Chapman's contemptible bundle of corruption only when it ceases to breathe. And there is no second life, except in the memory of those still living.

> The earth can have but earth, which is his due;
> My spirit is thine, the better part of me.
> So then thou hast but lost the dregs of life,
> The prey of worms, my body being dead,
> The coward conquest of a wretch's knife,
> Too base of thee to be remembered.
> > The worth of that is that which it contains,
> > And that is this, and this with thee remains (74).

Nowhere in the sonnets does the Christian God make an appearance. All the epiphanies are terrestrial ones, revelations of sensual beauty. Unlike Michelangelo, who could not overcome the guilt he felt in loving the face and body of a young man, Shakespeare exults in his passion. The only negative feelings he has about his love concern loss and disaffection. He is judged by himself and society, never by some omnipotent deity or universal cause. For him, as for Socrates, the madness of love is the greatest of heaven's blessings. His heaven lies in the face of an adolescent; his hell in a woman's sexual parts. Lust is a fault only because it distorts the face of beauty. As a pagan poet, he out-Marlowes Marlowe, the active, practicing homosexual who, like his Doctor Faustus, longed to be reborn as an ancient Greek. Shakespeare does not look to the past. His view is new and radical. He bears the future in him. As the bestower of immortality and the second life, the poet puts himself in place of god.

Naturally, his learned contemporaries held to the established ideas, a mixture of the pagan and the Christian, perfectly exemplified in the stoic and "Senecal" Chapman. In his quarrel with Shakespeare, the philosopher and moralist would inevitably win out over the impassioned poet, the monkish apologist over the prophet of a brave new world. But who reads Chapman now without being bored by the banality of his wisdom? And who reads Shakespeare now without being stirred, troubled, and perturbed? Between the two was the difference between learning and life.

The tenor of the sonnets becomes less erotic after the poet has achieved a kind of sexual union with Henry by sharing a woman with him (sonnet 42). Shakespeare now hopes to meet with the prince on the social level. Unlike Chapman, he does not have to lower himself by seeking patronage, and he knows that he is an aristocrat in the realm of poetry. He is, however, an actor, who has made himself "a motley to the view" (110). What he wants from the young nobleman is a friendship that would break down the social barrier. "Thy love is better than high birth to me, / Richer than wealth" (91).

He hopes that the prince can somehow intercede with Fortune, that "guilty goddess . . . That did not better for my life provide / Than public means" (111). And the young man does offer words of understanding to the older man who knows him so well. The words are like a blessing and make up for the opprobrium attached to his name.

> Your love and pity doth th'impression fill
> Which vulgar scandal stamped upon my brow:
> For what care I who calls me well or ill
> So you o'er-green my bad, my good allow? (112).

Yet he knows that the prince is slipping away from him. He sees "sweet love" in the prince's face, but senses that the boy's heart is in another place (93). He falls back to the thought that changes in their relationship are only a test of their love. "Let me not to the marriage of true minds / Admit impediments; love is not love / Which alters when it alteration finds" (116). In spite of such protestations, they both know that their relationship must end. The final rupture is delayed only because each is trying to resolve an inner conflict. On the one hand, Henry wants to preserve the admiration of a father-figure who sees into his soul; on the other hand, he knows that the Ganymedean love that Shakespeare bears for him is a political embarrassment. Shakespeare's impetuosity, boldness, and openheartedness could only implicate the soldier prince in a questionable friendship. Shakespeare, for his part, realizes that the prince can never adopt him as a friend and counselor. Yet, knowing his love is hopeless, he still cannot shake himself free from the spell cast by the aristocratic, aloof boy, a "ne-er cloying sweetness" (118), a "madding fever" (119), a "ruined love" that has to be built anew after each slight. "Drugs poison him that so fell sick of you" (118).

His disillusionment was as unmitigated and intense as his infatuation had been, and almost as precipitate. He had offered Henry a unique gift, something that no one else could possibly give. Better than anyone else he knew what he had accomplished in these sonnets: an intense concentration of thought united with a verbal intricacy of sound that far surpassed what his predecessors had been capable of. His exultation brought with it hybris. "Not marble nor the gilded monuments / Of princes shall outlive this powerful rhyme" (55). And with hybris came nemesis.

His reward for this supreme gift was a reminder that he could never sit at the prince's table. A few tears shed as a reminder of what could never be – that was the most he could expect.

What he was getting from the young man was not love but something more like pity, a condescending sympathy for the actor-playwright who could never enter the inner circle of the court, the homoerotic poet whom the prince of the realm could not embrace as warmly and as publicly as he could a tradesman, a shipbuilder like Pett. When Pett was charged with corruption by some of the highest and most powerful men in the country, the young prince stood by him and enthusiastically certified his innocence. An actor was a different sort of person, mistrusted by the ordinary citizen, condemned by city authorities, reviled by the Puritans. Shakespeare and his friends knew that while his genius earned him a place in the aristocracy, his profession denied him that place. Writing in 1603, a fellow poet, John Davies, wrote of the player "W.S.", "[Some] say fell *Fortune* cannot be excus'd, / That hath for better *uses* you refus'd." And in 1610, a year after the publication of the sonnets, in a poem "To our English Terence, Mr. Will. Shakespeare," the same writer lamented that the actor who could play royalty on stage could never be the real thing. "Some say (good Will) which I, in sport, do sing, / Had'st thou not plaid some Kingly parts in sport, / Thou hadst bin a companion for a King."[241]

Unlike Pett, Shakespeare could not even be companion to the high-born youth. He belonged to the actor's tribe and was, according to the law of the land, little more than a vagrant.

> O, for my sake do you with Fortune chide,
> The guilty goddess of my harmful deeds,
> That did not better for my life provide
> Than public means which public manners breeds.
> Thence comes it that my name receives a brand,
> And almost thence my nature is subdued
> To what it works in, like the dyer's hand.
> Pity me then, and wish I were renewed,
> Whilst, like a willing patient, I will drink
> Potions of eisel 'gainst my strong infection;
> No bitterness that I will not bitter think,
> Nor double penance to correct correction.
>   Pity me then, dear friend, and I assure ye
>   Even that your pity is enough to cure me (111).

At one point, when the poet had been away from London briefly, the prince had doubted the poet's loyalty. Upon his return, Shakespeare wrote to him, "O, never say that I was false of heart, / Though absence seemed my flame to qualify," and assured him that "my rose" meant all the world to him (109). Now, after receiving the young man's love and pity, the happy poet became presumptuous and overstepped his lowly station by treating the prince as his equal in the sphere of emotions. "For if you were by my unkindness shaken, / As I by yours, y'have passed a hell of time" (120). The implication that the poet's unkindness to the prince could possibly be viewed as comparable to the young nobleman's patronizing the poet must have set the egotistical boy's teeth on edge. It was a miscalculation on Shakespeare's part. Not that the tactless error made any difference in the long run.

Once the former cordiality was strained by small infractions of decorum, politics began to play a part. The love that pervaded the sonnets reeked of the same sexual dalliances that put the court of James I in bad odor in some circles. Encouraged by his puritanical supporters, Henry distanced himself from his father's life style. With each passing month, he became more independent of his father's court, which was intent on promoting peace on the continent and was disposed to deal with the Catholic forces at the conference table rather than on the battlefield. In keeping with its religious tolerance, the king's party did not discourage those public displays of homoerotic affection, with the king himself petting his favorites, which the supporters of Henry found disgusting. Given the political climate at court and his own ambitions, young Henry could not continue to encourage Shakespeare's attentions. However much he may have luxuriated in the poet's adulatory sonnets, in which he saw himself more glowingly depicted at times than in any of the portraits for which he sat, he could not act as an individual. He had to remain "unmoved, cold, and to temptation slow" (94).

Chapman also offered love but love of a proper sort, the kind that could be generously and properly acknowledged with a poet's stipend. He supplied the young prince with fatherly guidance and appealed to the lad's soldierly aspirations. In his political plays set in France, he called up visions of proud and rash Renaissance adventurers, those men of *virtù* that the young prince fantasized about. In his Homer he made the prince akin to Achilles, the great warrior. Shakespeare did the opposite. He turned the prince into Adonis, visualized him as the epitome of beauty, and called Achilles a pederast.

Those who were promoting the heir to the throne as another Henry V spread rumors about Shakespeare's sexual preferences, imputing to his sonnets a "beastly" desire, and Shakespeare responded to that charge. In those last few sonnets written in the spring of 1609, the poet says less and less about conferring immortality on the young man. The poet senses that Henry is growing cooler. When the prince sends him a gift, a book of tables, a memorandum book (the poet must have sent the prince one to accompany sonnet 77), the poet is affronted, probably more so than his reply suggests. To suppose that he would need some memento to be forever reminded of the young man was to diminish what the poet had experienced. "Thy record can never be missed, . . . nor need I tallies thy dear love to score" (122).

Shakespeare could detect in the gesture more than a hint that the relationship was coming to an end. In spite of protestations to the contrary, the friendship, or rather the alliance, had always been one-sided. Given the difference in their social positions, it had to be. But what galled Shakespeare was that it had never risen to the level of intimacy, to the kind of companionship, that the prince and the shipwright enjoyed. Shakespeare rightly understood that the memorandum book was a parting gift, given in kindness but deeply hurtful to the poet. He promptly gave it away, a gesture more temerarious than sending it back would have been, and boldly told the prince he had done so (122), a clear declaration that the parting was mutual.

As early as sonnet 36 — "Let me confess that we two must be twain" — he had foreseen the end of the affair, which, given the social chasm between the prince and the player, could only end in their permanent separation. Between their private loves and their public lives there would always be an unbridgeable gap. "In our two loves there is but one respect, / Though in our lives a separable spite." The poet knew that the love he bore the noble adolescent was pure, Socratic and Ganymedean, but his standing as an actor and his reputation as sexually suspect made a fraternal relationship with a prince of the realm impossible. "I may not evermore acknowledge thee, / Lest my bewailed guilt should do thee shame, / Nor thou with public kindness honor me, / Unless thou take that honor from thy name" (36). The time would come when Henry, advised by his counselors, would "frown on [the poet's] defects" (49) and shut him out. Balancing love and friendship against politics and discretion, the prince would be called to "audit" his relationship.

There was little more to be said on either side. Using the instances of Balmerino and Pett to make his point, Shakespeare reaffirmed the purity of his devotion, unadulterated by politics or career interests, and then sent one last sonnet to the "lovely Boy," in which he balanced the books. He has aged and withered, while the boy has grown more mature, becoming even more attractive physically. The poet utters a veiled warning and hints at the judgment that nature will pass on the young man. "Her *Audit* (though delayed) answer'd must be, / And her *Quietus* is to render thee." The italicized words threaten a settling of debts. By italicizing *Audit* Shakespeare ties together the beginning and end of the story. In sonnet 4 he had asked, "When nature calls thee to be gone, / What acceptable *Audit* can'st thou leave?"

The boy is blessed with an abundance of natural gifts that must, in the nature of things, be paid for in some manner or other. In the light of what was to happen to young Henry, the words were more chillingly true than Shakespeare could possibly have imagined.

CHAPTER 19

The Player's Revenge

Actually, those two lines were not the last ones addressed to the boy. There were two more verses, the concluding couplet. They are indicated by two sets of parentheses enclosing two white spaces. What Shakespeare said in those two lines, his parting shot at the golden boy, we shall probably never know. They seem to have fallen irretrievably into oblivion. Only a select few people in 1609 – Shakespeare's knot —would have been privileged to learn their contents. The sting in the tail of this bobbed sonnet imparted such a strong rebuke to the prince that either the poet himself or the printer struck it out. The blue-penciled lines were too indelicate, too accusatory, and too personal to be broadcast. Readers knew that empty parentheses indicated censored material.[242] In Ben Jonson's *Poetaster* "their ( ) Courts" signified "their damned Courts."

Creative genius, however, always finds ways of expressing subversive thoughts. If princes are concerned about their posthumous reputations, they should not tangle with poets. Those who write will have the last word. Shakespeare's method was to compose a 329-line poem in rhyme royal, "A Lover's Complaint," which he appended to the sonnets. The result was the strange amalgam of the 1609 Quarto, the two parts being of different genera and providing another mystery.[243] How does the "Complaint" connect with the sonnets?

This poem is so unlike the sonnets in tone, diction, and style that until about forty years ago the scholarly consensus was that it could not have come from Shakespeare's pen. Awkward for the Bardolaters was the apparent badness of the poem; equally awkward was the fact that Shakespeare's name appeared not only on the title page of the volume but also on the first page of the poem, as if to make assurance of authorship doubly sure. When the volume was reprinted in 1640 with the title and attribution *Poems: Written by Wil. Shake-speare, Gent.*, it was again included. Recently detailed studies of the text's vocabulary have pretty much confirmed Shakespeare's authorship.²⁴⁴ Not that that kind of verification is necessary. All one has to do is to ask why the "Complaint" was added to the sonnets, a question that the first readers would have been quick to ask and equally quick to answer.

During the nineteenth and twentieth centuries most editions of the *Sonnets* were printed without the "Complaint." During the last thirty or forty years, however, editors have come to recognize Shakespeare's authorship of the poem and its connection with the sonnet sequence. It provides, as one of them says, "a carefully designed complement of the whole . . . a carefully balanced thematic counterpart to them."²⁴⁵ As a complement, the "Complaint," with its wry tone and awkward verse, undercuts the passion and poetry of the sonnets. What Shakespeare gives so extravagantly in the main sequence, he uncharitably takes back in the "Complaint." The link between the two is formed by the last two sonnets, 153 and 154, inferior in quality, which are dedicated to Cupid and tell of his invincible power and the impossibility of suppressing sexual desire. The "Complaint" serves as a flippant epilogue, the poet, all passion spent, putting himself in the position of a jilted woman and seeing his sexual infatuation with the wondrous boy from her point of view. Taken as a whole, the 1609 Quarto relates the story of a man falling madly in love and then falling painfully out of it.

The young man of the "Complaint" treats the adoring older woman as the Fair Youth of the sonnets treated the idolatrous poet. Seen from the woman's angle, the spectacular boy appears less than perfect, vain, fully cognizant of his powers to inflame hearts, making full use of them while being untouched himself, and withal still irresistible. He has "kept hearts in liveries, but my own was free" (line 195), as he says of himself, echoing sonnet 94, in which the boy is one of those "who, moving others, are themselves as stone, / Unmoved, cold, and to temptation slow."

Although "A Lover's Complaint" follows the Dark Lady sonnets in the Quarto, it has nothing to do with her and everything to do with the Fair Youth. It tells the story of an aging woman who was once in love with a young teen-age boy, who is sketched in realistic, recognizable detail. It is a cool and acerb portrait of a spoiled boy by an artist who is no longer moved by his charms. The strong emotions that the poet once felt are now invested in the woman, who recalls them long after she has been cast aside.

In his attributes, the boy of the "Complaint" is the youth of the sonnets all over again, a virtual carbon copy, a physical doublet.[246] "His browny locks. . . hang in crooked curls" (line 85); he is just beginning to grow a beard (92-95); he is an expert horseman (106-12), physically attractive (99), often painted (134), and liked by all, enchanting both young and old, men and women (127-130). He is also the recipient from his admirers of "deep-brained sonnets" (209).

Henry would surely have thanked Shakespeare for the sonnets, sending him brief notes. In retrospect, these letters would have filled him with mixed emotions, recalling how much they once meant to him. His alter ego in the "Complaint" says:

> Of folded schedules [short notes] had she many a one,
> Which she perused, sighed, tore, and gave the flood;
> . . .
> These often bathed she in her fluxive eyes,
> And often kissed, and often gave to tear:
> Cried, "O false blood, thou register of lies,
> What unapproved witness dost thou bear!
> Ink would have seemed more black and damned here!
> This said, in top of rage the lines she rents,
> Big discontent so breaking their contents (43-55).

Outwardly, this downy-cheeked boy and the Fair Youth of the sonnets are exactly alike. Moreover, they have the same distant and chilly personality. The boy is proud of being untouchable.

Among the many that mine eyes have seen,
Not one whose flame my heart so much as warmed,
Or my affection put to th'smallest teen,
Or any of my leisures ever charmed.
Harm have I done to them, but ne'er was harmed;
Kept hearts in liveries, but mine own was free,
And reigned commanding in his monarchy (190-6).

Shakespeare in one of his "deep-brained" sonnets sensed that beneath the stern self-control of the boy there lurked destructive dangers. "Unmoved, cold, and to temptation slow," he may be, as well as the inheritor of heaven's graces; but ultimately his character must be measured by his actions, and "sweetest things turn sourest by their deeds" (94).

The gist of the "Complaint" is an indictment of a proud youth who ravishes by his gracious demeanor and his seraphic appearance and who uses his "innocence" deliberately to get his way. What the enamored poet of the sonnets could not bring himself to say and could only hint at is made evident in the "Complaint." When not completely blinded by the boy's charms, the poet could see that the rose might be blighted. Now, disguising himself as an older woman badly treated by a very young man, Shakespeare is able to recount his dead relationship with Prince Henry in the harsh light of a post-mortem.[247] He gives us the other side of the irresistible charmer. The sonnets and the "Complaint" form a three-dimensional portrait. Truly amazing is the way in which the youth of the sonnets, who more often than not appears with a nimbus over him, comes to life as a temperamental, overindulged teenager. This very young man – "Small show of man was yet upon his chin" (92) – who is well aware that his parts have "power to charm a sacred nun" (260), is a deceitful hypocrite, a seducer who preaches a stern morality, praises "cold chastity" (315), and "blush[es] at speeches rank" (307). His passion is "but an art of craft" (295). When Henry apologized for some affront or snub, there were tears in his eyes, and the infatuated poet could write to him, "[T]hose tears are pearl which thy love sheds, / And they are rich and ransom all ill deeds" (34). But now he sees that those tears – "that infected moisture of his eye" (323), along with his blushes – "that false fire which in his cheek so glowed" (324) – were feigned, clever dissimulations. The sealed notes that Henry sent to Shakespeare become the "register of lies" that the woman tears up, bathes in tears, and throws into the mud (43-57).

While there may have been a strong feminine component in Shakespeare's nature that made it convenient for him to write the "Complaint" from a woman's point of view, there may also have been a certain amount of self-recrimination in his giving himself such an unflattering persona to speak through, knowing that he had made such a fool of himself.

The other side of the prince did not come to the poet as a sudden, blinding revelation. In sonnet 96 he had perceived the youth's faults and had been tolerant of them and understanding.

> Some say thy fault is youth, some wantonness,
> Some say thy grace is youth and gentle sport;
> Both grace and faults are loved of more and less;
> Thou mak'st faults graces that to thee resort.
> As on the finger of a thronèd queen
> The basest jewel will be well esteemed,
> So are those errors that in thee are seen
> To truths translated and for true things deemed.

This forgiving language changes to accusatory sarcasm in the "Complaint." While the poet in love will not impeach the boy, the poet out of love sees this angelic creature as an evil tempter who uses his gifts to inveigle and betray. The "sweet graces" that inspired sonnet 78 are now seen as disingenuous and deceptive.

> Thus merely with the garment of a grace
> The naked and concealed fiend he covered,
> That th'unexperient [the innocent] gave the tempter place,
> Which, like a cherubin, above them hovered (316-19).

The boy of the "Complaint" has captured the woman's affections by telling her not to fear holy vows, and he makes himself blameless by claiming that he was never the one who initiated a love affair. "For feasts of love I have been called unto, / Till now did ne'er invite nor never woo" (181-2). This chimes in with the story behind sonnets 69 and 70 in which Prince Henry is first accused of having seduced a married woman and then excused because his attractiveness, both physical and societal, would inevitably make him the prey of amative and predatory women.

In the final couplet of sonnet 126 Shakespeare must have said in a few mordant words what the "Complaint" says in many. The de-infatuated lover composed a cynical recantation, a palinode in which he could provide the threatened *audite*, the settling of accounts.

One thing more remained to be done: he had to settle his score with Chapman. Henry had rejected Shakespeare and taken on Chapman. So to make his farewell to the prince doubly satisfying, in writing the "Complaint" Shakespeare mocked and parodied Chapman's poetic style. The clunky rhythms and turgid language were intended to make it appear that Chapman had written this damaging assessment of the prince. Words like "unexperient" and "spongy lungs" on the last page have a distinctly Chapmanesque sound to them and are typical of the writing throughout.

Shakespeare's readers must have relished the joke, while modern scholars were often taken in by it, rejecting the poem as Shakespeare's and sometimes astutely but wrongly attributing it to Chapman. One Shakespeare amateur, J. M. Robertson, member of Parliament, found time during the First World War to write an eighty-nine page essay demonstrating on the basis of vocabulary and syntax that the author of "A Lover's Complaint" was unquestionably – George Chapman![248] His careful analysis of the poem led him to conclude that it was as like Chapman as it was unlike Shakespeare. "The number of actual clues to him, the many coincidences of thought and phrase, the identities of theme and machinery, the general prevalence of his eccentric diction in the *Complaint*, the constant suggestion of his involved and forced construction, with the occasional emergence of vigorous lines and once of real elevation – all this constitutes, I think, a culminating proof that the poem is Chapman's."[249]

It never occurred to Robertson to consider the poem as parody, in spite of the fact that Shakespeare's name is on the first page. Putting his name there was Shakespeare's way of saying, "You may think that this is not by me, but it is!" His mimetic skills were never better displayed.[250] The poem was the actor's revenge on both the scholar Chapman and the princeling Henry. He got rid of the poison that had infected him by sending up Chapman and exposing Henry, simultaneously dispatching the conceited boy and the inferior poet. The final confrontation between Shakespeare and Chapman came over the education of the prince, and Chapman won. But Shakespeare had the last word. Playing the ventriloquist and using Chapman as his dummy, he exposed the young prince as a vainglorious, insincere youth puffed up with the praises of his sycophants.

CHAPTER 20

Mr. W. H.

B ECAUSE of the highly personal and intimate nature of the
sonnets, most of the early commentators chose to believe
that the 1609 Quarto was printed without Shakespeare's
permission. There was, however, little evidence to support this
belief, and now the 1609 Quarto is generally accepted as Shakespeare's throughout. The overall plan is his; the arrangement of
the sonnets is his; the "Complaint" is his.[251]

Those first readers would not have felt that they were reading
some poetry stolen from Shakespeare's desk. They would have
read the slim volume as a shocking exposé. The tone of the sonnets
is that of a man who wants to be heard, first as an admirer of the
prince and then as his disappointed devotee. Rejected by the
prince, denied the laureation that went to Chapman, he had to set
the record straight and reveal the dark side of the poster boy's
magnetism. He had to get him out of his system and de-glamorize
him. Equally important to Shakespeare was the need to assert his
poetic genius. If the actor-playwright could not occupy a place in
the prince's coterie, the poet could still astonish them with a work
that re-invented the sonnet. He knew that the sonnet sequence offered a profound exploration of sexuality, unique in its immediacy,
unmatched in its richness of language, and astonishing in the speed
of composition. If nothing else, the publication of the sonnets was
a way of hinting to the once idolized prince of the realm what
might have been and now could never be.

The question is not why Shakespeare would want to publish
this book, but who would risk the possible repercussions. Not only did the sonnets dwell on manly love as no other published poet-

ry had, they also bordered on lèse majesté. Henry's faction would have been incensed, although James, we may suppose, would not have been entirely displeased.

On the other hand, Shakespeare's name alone was a guarantee of intense public interest. To the literati of the time the prospect of a volume of sonnets by Shakespeare would have been exciting news. A further guarantee of success was the court gossip about the content of the sonnets. These poems were not secret epistles; many of them had the expressed aim of registering the prince among the immortals. In spite of their private nature, they were meant to be a public monument. Those few who had access to the sonnets would have marveled at their beauty or deprecated their sensuality. Others would eagerly have awaited the opportunity to make up their own minds.

Still, these sonnets could not be expected to sell like those erotic narrative poems, *Venus and Adonis* and *Lucrece*. Because a full appreciation of the sonnets required a good deal of inside knowledge, they could not have a wide readership. *Shake-speares Sonnets* was intended for a special initiated audience, a coterie of insiders, and there was small prospect of a second printing being called for.

THOMAS THORPE, who published the sonnets, had already acquired works by Jonson, Chapman, and Marlowe. There was nothing piratical or surreptitious about his publication of *Shake-speares Sonnets*. But the epistolary nature of the sonnets, delivered over a considerable period of time, raises a question about how Thorpe acquired them. The peculiar nature of the poems, personal and intimate in tone and feeling, yet patently intended to publicize and glamorize their recipient, glowingly laudatory yet at the end insinuatingly censorious, makes one wonder who put them into Thorpe's hands.

Shakespeare began composing them in a casual fashion and some time must have passed before he saw them as forming a substantial chronicle and an enduring artistic achievement. By that time the task of collecting and arranging them in the proper order may have become quite complicated, especially so if Shakespeare did not date them as he sent them off. The person who could be most helpful in putting the sonnets in order was the man who served as aide or secretary to Prince Henry.

Scholars with keen eyes for such things have noticed that in the 1609 Quarto the word "thy" is misprinted as "their" fifteen times. There are many such anomalies both in the sonnets and in the plays, attributable mainly to the fact that Shakespeare, unlike Ben Jonson, did not proofread copy before it went to the press. Sloppy handwriting could account for many errors, but the "thy"-"their" confusion in the sonnets occurs so often that something besides an indecipherable hand seems to be at work. One explanation is that the person who prepared the manuscript used in the printing house wrote "thy" in such a way that it was easily read as "their." This particular confusion is not found elsewhere in Shakespeare, so it is "reasonable to suppose that [the printer's] manuscript was a transcript made by someone other than the author."[252]

NOW THIS is evidence suggesting that someone other than Shakespeare turned the sonnets over to Thomas Thorpe. Who might that someone have been? Certainly not a professional scribe, who was paid for his legible hand.

The best clue to his identity is found in the dedication to the 1609 Quarto. It is unusual, if not unique, in two respects: it is written by the publisher and not by the author, and it lacks the customary epistle to the reader or some introductory words. But what could Shakespeare himself say to his readers without overstepping the limits of social decorum or being hypocritically sycophantic? It was left to the publisher to throw dust in the reader's eyes and to sidestep the delicate problems raised in the Fair Youth sonnets by dedicating the volume to a Mr. W. H. and promising *him* eternal happiness.

"To the only begetter of these ensuing sonnets, Mr. W. H., all happiness and that eternity promised by our ever-living poet wisheth the well-wishing adventurer in setting forth."

This deliberately cryptic note has occasioned as much discussion as any one of the sonnets. Not only the words themselves but their arrangement in thirteen lines and their punctuation (see the facsimile) have been studied as if they were as potentially revealing as the writing on Belshazzar's wall. Unfortunately, most of the scholarly Daniels who have pored over Thorpe's words have only muddied what once was clear. Before the Southamptonites and the Pembrokists began quarreling with each other over the identity of the Fair Youth, it was commonly understood that Mr. W. H. was the person mainly responsible for the procurement of the sonnets. Since then, those who puzzled over the mysteries of the sonnets have been misled by that word "begetter" into thinking that Mr. W. H. must be the Fair Youth. Who else would merit the "eternity" promised by the poet? They have foisted a new meaning on the word, taking it to mean "inspire," disregarding the accepted sense of the word.[253] Beget means either procreate or acquire. Hamlet uses the word in the latter sense when he tells the strolling players, "You must acquire and beget a temperance that may give it [your passion] smoothness" (3.2.7). The basic meaning of the word, ever since the time of King Alfred, has been "obtain."[254]

It was not until the middle of the nineteenth century that "begetter" acquired a meaning it had never had before, a meaning given to it by the Southamptonites and the Pembrokists and not by lexicographers. In 1817 Nathan Drake sensibly explained that Mr. W. H. obtained the manuscript of the sonnets and "lodged it in Thorpe's hands for the purpose of publication, a favour which the bookseller returned, by wishing him 'all happiness and that eternity' which had been 'promised' by the bard, in such glowing colours, to another, namely, to one of the immediate subjects of his sonnets."[255]

Rephrased and with the clauses disentangled, the inscription says that Thorpe, the risk-taker, in publishing (setting forth) these sonnets, thanks Mr. W. H., the person who gathered them together, and wishes him happiness and that eternal life promised by the immortal poet who says his sonnets will live forever. (As long as the poems live, so does the fame of W. H.) It was a bit arch and very cunning but quite accurate. The immortality that the poet had offered the prince was now withdrawn and fell to the man who collected them.

It may reasonably be assumed that "A Lover's Complaint," the last poem in the volume and the last to be penned, was submitted by

Shakespeare himself. Sure enough, the confusion of "thy" and "their" that characterizes the sonnets is not to be found in the "Complaint." The sonnets devoted to the Dark Lady would have been lying around for some years, probably since 1598, and must have been arranged and submitted by the poet himself to complete the design of the full sequence, the descent of Eros from heaven to hell.[256]

The begetter must have been a member of the entourage of the prince, someone physically close to him, and someone who preferred the semi-anonymity of the initials W. H. This shadowy figure was probably the same W. H. who authored a brief anecdotal account of the prince entitled *The True Picture and Relation of Prince Henry*, published in Leiden in 1634. He was also the author of a detailed account of Prince Henry's death, *The Relation of the Sicknes and Death of the most Illustrious Henry, Prince of Wales*. This W. H., who was obviously an intimate companion to the prince, has been identified as William Haydon, the senior groom of the prince's bedchamber.[257] He described himself as having "the honour to bee one of the most illustrious Prince Henry his servants." (We have encountered him in the chapter "Rose of the Sonnets" as Groom of the Prince's Bedchamber). The budgets for the prince's establishment list Haydon as one of several grooms of the bedchamber and as receiving £13. 16s. 8d for board, wages, and living,[258] a considerable sum, befitting a person of good family, refined in manners, and well educated. Addressing him as Master would have been quite appropriate. Haydon would have helped the prince dress, supervised his meals, announced callers, and undertaken such menial tasks as making the bed and changing the sheets. In almost continual attendance on his master, he would have slept on a pallet in the same room with him. What little is known about him suggests that he was close to Henry in age. Until a better candidate comes along, this modest and self-effacing young man must be the Mr. W. H. who collected, held on to, and perhaps dated the sonnets, and who by a confusion of "he who begets" with "he who inspires" would gather as much posthumous notoriety as his master, thus fulfilling Thorpe's expressed wishes.

CHAPTER 21

The Aftermath

WHILE Shakespeare the sonneteer was building a monument to Henry, the soon-to-be Prince of Wales, Shakespeare the dramatist was not unemployed. Because of the plague, which was especially deadly in London from July 1608 to December 1609, the theaters were closed much of the time, and the playwright-actor could concentrate on some new works for the stage.

In the conventional and generally accepted dating of his plays, *Antony and Cleopatra* and *Coriolanus* are assigned to 1608 and 1609, the very years in which he was composing the love-mad poems to Henry. In fact, the playwright found inspiration in his association with the young man. How could he not? It is hardly surprising that the actor-dramatist would seize on a subject that would allow him to exploit to the fullest his own emotional turmoil. What Antony was to Cleopatra, Shakespeare was to Henry. The forty-four-year-old dramatist, married but seldom home, could incarnate himself in the Roman soldier, roughly the same age, married but separated from his wife. In the poet's imagination Prince Henry, the master-mistress of his passion, became Queen Cleopatra. The gap in ages, nearly thirty years, between the poet and the prince was a vital factor in their relationship, as it was with Antony and Cleopatra. Only about fourteen years separated the aging Antony from Cleopatra, but as Shakespeare sat at his desk visualizing the scenes on stage, Cleopatra was a thirteen-or-fourteen-year-old boy actor, while he was the poet of sonnet 2, with forty winters besieging his brow. Imparting his own erotic intoxication to Antony, Shakespeare conjured up a military leader who would abandon his own

fleet for the sake of a woman, a display of "folly gone mad erotical-
ly," as Bernard Shaw rightly described the play.[259]

Many phrases in *Antony and Cleopatra* are strikingly similar to
those in sonnet 107. "The mortal moon hath her eclipsed endured," "not mine own fears, nor the prophetic soul . . . ," "the sad
augurs mock their own presage," "peace proclaims olives of endless age, and "death to me subscribes" all are echoed or para-
phrased in *Antony*. "No such close affinities exist between the sonnet and any other play in the canon," writes J. M. Nosworthy,
"and this must be in some way significant."[260] What these affinities may signify is that Shakespeare was hard at work on *Antony* in
April 1609, the date of sonnet 107.

Editors of the tragedy argue that it was written in 1608 or earlier, adducing as evidence an entry in the Stationers' Register for a
book called "Anthony and Cleopatra." They ignore what Nosworthy says about close affinities between the play and the sonnets,
and they brush aside what C. Knight wrote early in the nineteenth
century. Taking a sharper look at the Stationers' Register, Knight
argued:

"In 1623 Blount and Jaggard, the publishers of the folio, enter [in
the Register] 'Mr. William Shakspere's Comedies, Histories, and
Tragedies, so many of the said copies as are not formerly entered
to other men.' Amongst these is *Antony and Cleopatra*. All the plays
thus entered in 1623 were unpublished; and not one of them, with
the exception of *Antony and Cleopatra*, had been 'formerly entered'
by name. It is therefore more than probable that the *Antony and
Cleopatra* entered in 1608 was not Shakespere's tragedy; and we
therefore reject this entry as any evidence that Shakespere's
Antony and Cleopatra was written as early as 1608."[261]

H.H. FURNESS, editor of the 1907 Variorum edition of the play,
cautiously observed that when Knight rejects the date of 1608,
"even-handed justice must acknowledge that there is colour for his
rejection, and, furthermore, all who, confiding on this date, erect
their scheme of the chronology of these [late] plays, do so on a
foundation which, in respect to the present play, is not flawless."[262]

Yet recent editors have ignored Knight's well-reasoned argument.

There is another piece of evidence connecting *Antony and Cleopatra* with the year 1609. The word "pelleted," referring to tears, occurs only two times in Shakespeare's works: in *Antony* (3.13.165) and in "A Lover's Complaint" (line 18). Because it is dependent on the sonnets, the "Complaint" must have been composed after Shakespeare finished writing them and immediately before their publication.[263]

(*Antony and Cleopatra* may not have been staged during Shakespeare's lifetime. The Folio version contains stage directions that seem to have readers in mind, not the stage prompter or bookkeeper.[264])

BY THE TIME he came to write his next play, Shakespeare was no longer under the spell of the charismatic prince. *The Tragedy of Coriolanus* , also based on Roman history, reflects the detachment and impudence of "A Lover's Complaint." The hero of the play is a very young soldier, not much more than a child when he first went eagerly off to war, valorous but insufferably arrogant and self-willed. In the first scene of the play, he is described as being as virtuous as he is proud. His besetting sin is pride, pride in his class matched by contempt for the plebeians, accompanied by an insistence on being admired because of his high birth. The Coriolanus delineated in Plutarch's *Lives*, on which Shakespeare drew heavily, is the near identical twin of Prince Henry as described by his contemporaries and by Shakespeare in the sonnets. Plutarch's valiant young warrior has a "natural wit and a great heart," is "never overcome with pleasure nor money," and can "endure easily all manner of pains and travails." He was "more inclined to the wars than any other gentleman of his time," and he "began from childhood to give himself to handle weapons and daily did exercise himself therein. . . . Moreover he did so exercise his body to hardness and all kind of activity that he was very swift in running, strong in wrestling, and mighty in griping [grappling], so that no man could ever cast him. . . . [He] never yielded to any pain or toil he took upon him."[265] All this accords perfectly with the character and person of the armor-loving, hard-bodied, athletically trained Prince Henry, who from the age of seven was instructed in the use of arms. A contemporary remarked that the teen-age boy showed "a *Noble and Heroick Spirit*, no musick being so pleasant in his eares, as the sounding of the Trumpet, the beating of the Drumme, the roaring of the Canon, no sight so acceptable as that of Pieces, Pistols, or any sort of Armour."[266]

On the negative side, Coriolanus displayed a bad temper, a haughtiness and an emotional detachment that were also characteristic of Henry. The Roman soldier had "a certain insolent and stern manner, . . . which, because it was too lordly, was disliked." He was "insolent, / O'ercome with pride, ambitious past all thinking, / Self-loving" (4.6.30-2). In sonnets 94 and 95, the boy is described as cold and resistant to temptation, but he is also suspected of certain unspecified sins, the "canker in the fragrant rose." Coriolanus was at times so "choleric and impatient that he would yield to no living creature."[267] Shakespeare knew how headstrong and temperamental Henry could be, recalling the occasion celebrated in sonnet 25, when the fifteen-year-old stripling, exercising his princely right of eminent domain, forcibly removed the earls of Southampton and Pembroke from their lodgings simply because he wanted the space for his own use.

The young Roman and English patricians were alike in yet another respect. Each was attached emotionally to his mother and not to his father. Nothing made Coriolanus "so happy and honourable as that his mother might hear everybody praise and commend him."[268] Coriolanus's mother Volumnia exerted a greater influence on his life than anyone else. She tells him, "My praises made thee first a soldier" (3.2.108) and "Thy valiantness was mine, thou suck'st it from me" (3.2. 129). What Volumnia was to Coriolanus, Queen Anne was to Prince Henry. She was determined to make a man of Henry, as unlike his father as possible, the man who kissed young men in public, feared fighting, and swooned when swords were brandished in his presence.[269] She sided with the pro-war faction and hoped that one day Prince Henry would overrun France as Henry V had.[270] Under her watchful eye, he became increasingly alienated from his father, disagreeing with him on both religious and political matters, so much so that the king, as we have seen, regarded Henry as a threat to his own sovereignty and authority. The result was an emotionally stunted young man, a mother's boy. "There's no man in the world / More bound to's mother" (5.3.158-9). The most powerful scene in the play occurs near the end when the hero succumbs to his mother's pleadings not to destroy Rome, even though he knows he is sealing his own doom.

Taking his mother by the hand, and after a moment's silence, he says:

> "O mother, mother!
> What have you done? Behold, the heavens do ope,
> The gods look down, and this unnatural scene
> They laugh at. O my mother, mother! O!
> You have won a happy victory to Rome;
> But for your son, believe it, O, believe it,
> Most dangerously you have with him prevail'd,
> If not most mortal to him" (5. 3. 183-189).

Of all the ancient heroes of history none was more like Henry than Coriolanus. It was a nearly perfect match of English idol and Roman hero. Using the English prince as his model, Shakespeare could draw Coriolanus to the life. And if rumors are admitted into evidence, then even their tragic fates are similar, though Shakespeare could not have known just how similar when he wrote the scene in which Coriolanus is murdered by those who are envious of his popularity.

What most strongly attracted Shakespeare to Coriolanus was the class conflict, the plebs against the patricians, which is the central concern of the historical account. Coriolanus despises the commoners and cannot tolerate their opposition to his dictatorial commands. Similarly, the difference in social rank between the prince and the poet is one of the main motifs in the sonnets, particularly prominent toward the end of the main sequence, in which it is made apparent that the severance of their friendship is due ultimately to the poet's inferior station in society, both through birth and profession. Shakespeare stood to the prince as the plebs (who were citizens enjoying a certain number of political rights) stood to Coriolanus.

One remarkable scene in the play revives the atmosphere of male bonding that permeates the sonnets. Whereas intercourse with women is an inconvenient necessity for the physical business of maintaining the family from generation to generation, the embrace of a man by a man is what is longed for and dreamt of. When Coriolanus's uncontrollable temper and hatred of the plebs get him banished from Rome, he goes to the house of his former enemy Aufidius, with whom he has often fought on the field of battle. Aufidius clasps him to his breast, and, in a speech that Shakespeare invents (it is not in Plutarch), unabashedly reveals sadomasochistic desires in which the thrusting of male bodies at war with each other replaces normal sexual activity. The sexual excitement of the marriage night cannot compete with the thrill of battle in which the subconscious longings of the dream life break to the surface.

> . . . Let me twine
> Mine arms about that body, where against
> My grained ash an hundred times hathe broke,
> And scarr'd the moon with splinters. Here I clip
> The anvil of my sword, and do contest
> As hotly and as nobly with thy love
> As ever in ambitious strength I did
> Contend against thy valour. Know thou first,
> I lov'd the maid I married; never man
> Sigh'd truer breath; but that I see thee here,
> Thou noble thing, more dances my rapt heart
> Than when I first my wedded mistress saw
> Bestride my threshold. Why, thou Mars! I tell thee
> We have a power on foot; and I had purpose
> Once more to hew thy target from thy brawn,
> Or lose mine arm for't. Thou hast beat me out
> Twelve several times, and I have nightly since
> Dreamt of encounters 'twixt thyself and me —
> We have been down together in my sleep,
> Unbuckling helms, fisting each other's throat —
> And wak'd half dead with nothing (4. 5. 107-127).

[247]

This is the kind of warrior kinship that Coriolanus understands, cutting across political lines. Nothing like this appears elsewhere in Shakespeare's writings, not even in the English history plays. Nor does the speech move the plot forward. It is there because the dramatist, with his keen insight into character, knew his man and wanted him known to others. He had had opportunities enough to observe Prince Henry, and he had plumbed the submerged desires that motivated this self-controlled teen-ager, cold, remote, self-absorbed. The warrior prince, this disciple of Mars, was an image of Chapman's Achilles, not of Shakespeare's gentle Ganymede. No longer bedazzled, Shakespeare saw that the young man, the adolescent who steeled his body in athletics and disciplined his emotions through stoicism, who poured his energies into athletic contests and war games, who saw himself as leading the English troops against Catholic armies, preferred a kind of homoerotic union that was at the other end of the spectrum from the poet's tender affections.

Coriolanus, like "A Lover's Complaint," provided a harsh postludium to the sweet music of the sonnets. Seeing the boy with a lover's eyes, dazzled by his looks, "where beauty's veil doth cover every blot" (95), Shakespeare allowed himself only a few glimpses of Henry's imperfections. Everything changed when the spell was broken; things were no longer what they had appeared to be. The radiance of the boy wonder, the refulgent light that shone on all that came within his ambience, suddenly vanished. Reality caught up with the poet's fantasies.

The collapse of the ethereal world painted in the sonnets was more far-reaching than Shakespeare could have imagined. Even the subsidiary figures were transformed and reduced to rather shabby creatures. Men like Pett and Balmerino, who had served, respectively, as the type of good men falsely accused and political men turned honest, proved in reality to be poor representatives of what Shakespeare had had in mind. Balmerino, in the poet's eyes a kind of political martyr, one who confessing his crime would willingly die for the sake of truth, suffered a different fate. King James commuted his death sentence. In October 1609 he was given the liberty of free ward in Falkland, Scotland, and he died of natural causes in 1612.

There were rumors that King James had known about the letter ever since it was first written and that he had let it go forth in 1599 in order to win support from the Catholics when he had hopes of becoming Queen Elizabeth's successor. In this version of the events, Balmerino was the willing scapegoat of the duplicitous king.

Phineas Pett, the shipwright whom Prince Henry zealously defended against charges of corruption and embezzlement, actually lined his own pockets and was guilty as charged. By spending as much on the repair of old ships as it would cost to build new ones, he was able to use his ill-gotten gains to build himself an elegant house in town. Prince Henry triumphantly lifted up the man who knelt before his accusers, but all their accusations were true. Some time after his trial, Pett was charged with collusion. Assigned to ferret out misuse of material, he had teamed up with the wrongdoers. The investigating committee concluded that "having found the thief, he ran with him," joining the "filchers and abusers."[271] So much for the "true soul" who inspired sonnet 125.

What happened to Prince Henry himself was still more ironic, only here the poet had foreseen and intimated a change of fortune. In the last of the sonnets to him, Shakespeare had warned the admirable boy that nature herself, having endowed him with a fine figure, a handsome face, physical grace, and athletic talents, having in the poet's telling phrase made him the "minion of her pleasure," would eventually expect to be repaid in some way. As the recipient of gifts in such abundance, the youth was always in debt to nature. "Her *Audit* (though delayed) answered must be, / And her *Quietus* is to render thee" (126).

The final reckoning came when the young prince had reached the apogee of good fortune, at a time when his popularity was at its peak, his prospects as ruler of England and a Protestant Europe brighter than ever, and when he had physically matured into an image of ideal manliness. (See Figure 16: Henry, Prince of Wales, by Isaac Oliver, about 1612.)

In January 1610, he was created Prince of Wales. He set up his own regal court, issuing strict rules of behavior to his extensive retinue, emphasizing religious and moral values. A clean mind was to be

FIGURE 17. Henry, Prince of Wales, about 1612. Miniature by Isaac Oliver.

joined with a sound body. He promoted sporting activities, especially wrestling, tennis, and tossing the pike. It was all too virtuous to be good for all. Inevitably, this poster boy for a resurgent England aroused the resentment of those who were less gifted or less demanding, those who wanted more cakes and ale and fewer strenuous exercises, physical and moral. The high reverence and piety demonstrated by the demanding prince, the rigor and strictness with which he governed his house, was looked on by some as too presumptuous a challenge to King James's manners and customs, or, as one observer put it, "as a too great Upbraiding the contrary Proceedings of his Father's." The rivalry between the courts of the king and the prince grew until, as rumor had it, the father felt "a Malignity in his Heart against the Splendor of his Son's Retinue."[272]

BEHIND THE FAMILY QUARREL, the seething enmity between an envious father and a too fortunate son, lay the clash of national and international politics. The difference in temperament between the gentle, peace-loving father, whose motto was *"Beatifi Pacifica,"* and his martially inclined son, whose motto was *Fax mentis honestae Gloria* (Glory is the torch that leads the honorable mind), led to their estrangement, especially after Henry became Prince of Wales. Arrayed behind the king were the cautious maintainers of peace and the status quo; behind the prince were the warmongers, who wanted to see English armies on European soil. The king knew that the Puritans regarded his son "as one prefigured in the Apocalypse for Rome's destruction."[273]

But for the existence of a strong anti-Henry faction, it is doubtful that Shakespeare could have published the sonnets in 1609. As it was, there were many who would have welcomed any publication that weakened the seemingly irresistible rise of the paragon prince. One may surmise that when Shakespeare sensed Henry's aloofness, he asked for the return of the sonnets with the intention of publishing them.

The dissension between King James and his son came to an end when Henry contracted a fever in October 1612. The sturdy young man, who had trained himself to withstand the hardships of a soldier in the field, had to undergo something far worse: the debilitating efforts of the doctors to treat the symptoms of his illness. He insisted upon going about his daily routines as best he could – attending services in his private chapel, writing letters, training his body. On October 24, he played a game of tennis, dressed in his shirt as if it were summertime. He developed a fever, his lips turned black, he suffered convulsions, and was subjected to enemas and bleedings. To ease the convulsions, the doctors shaved his head and applied the still warm bodies of pigeons and roosters newly killed.[274] Two weeks later, on November 6, he died, only eighteen years old.

Foul play was suspected, for everyone knew that the ambitious prince had enemies at court. How could such a well disciplined boy, the picture of health, have wasted away and died so quickly? There were whispers that the king himself was implicated, that he sought to put a stop to his son's enormous, ever-growing influence. Feeding this rumor was another one: that Henry could not tolerate the influence that Robert Carr exerted over the king and that action was taken to forestall the prince's vengeance. "The Prince, having entertained a mortal Prejudice to the Favorite Car, he was *taken off* to prevent the Effects of it."[275] So went the rumors. Imaginative gossip hinted that he died a Hamlet-like death, tasting poisoned grapes as he played at tennis.[276] The fact that the King did not attend his son's funeral lent credence to even the most outrageous speculation.

The detailed reports of Henry's illness made it clear when perused by a later, more knowledgeable generation of doctors, that he had died of typhoid fever, an illness that medical men did not isolate and diagnose until the nineteenth century. There was no foul play. It was as Shakespeare had said: nature, which had given him so much, took back what it had given. He suffered the fate of those young men of Housman's poems, "the lads that will die in their glory and never be old."

The outpouring of grief at the news of his death was unparalleled, one observer claiming that it had "perhaps never been exceeded on any similar occasion."[277] The funeral procession, which wended its way from St. James's to Westminster Abbey, was over a mile long, included two thousand mourners in black, and took four hours to marshal. Six baronets carried the black velvet canopy over the hearse. A young man, stark naked, marched up to the Privy Chamber to announce that he was the prince's soul come from heaven.[278]

The sounds of a nation in grief and mourning were accompanied by the lamentations of the poets. John Webster, Cyril Tourneur, John Heywood, and John Davies of Hereford wrote elegies, as did John Donne, who wailed the inexplicable death of the "incomparable" prince whose "reputation was an ecstasy." William Basse called his elegy "Great Brittaines Sunnes-Set Bewailed, with a Shower of Teares" (printed 1613). Nothing came from Ben Jonson, but he was in Italy at the time.

Tourneur's elegy, "A Grief on the Death of Prince Henrie," was unusual in criticizing Henry's bellicosity. Death took Henry away, said Tourneur, "in feare that he would War prefer" over peace.[279] Chapman, as might be expected, contributed the most impressive of the elegies, "An Epicede or Funeral Song," in 656 lines, recounting the virtues of Prince Henry, describing his heroic bearing during the last weeks of his life, attributing the fever, in learned Chapmanesque fashion, to Rhamnusia, the hideous goddess of revenge, in envy of the prince, and ending with the funeral procession and in a fanciful reconciliation of father and son. It was a sincere gesture of gratitude by the poet to the young man who had supported him and who on his deathbed had remembered to assign him a life pension. It was a pledge that King James failed to honor; Chapman even lost his place as sewer.[280]

Webster was perhaps the only writer to allude to Shakespeare's ill treatment of Henry. In a 328 line elegy "A Monumental Column Erected to the living Memory of the ever-glorious Henry, late Prince of Wales," Webster refers to slanderous writings about the prince and says, "Silence should have hid their ignorance: / For hee's a reverend subject to be penn'd / Onely by his sweet *Homer* and my friend."[281] Webster may have had in mind Shakespeare's sonnets and Chapman's "Epicede."

Chapman completed his Homer translations in 1624 and died ten years later.

The schoolmaster Henry Peacham, who had warned young Henry about the dangers of Ganymedean sex, memorialized him in a poem "The Period of Mourning" in 1613. Years later in his *The Compleat Gentleman*, printed in 1622, a cultural handbook containing what a member of polite society needed to know, he listed all the important poets of the Elizabethan era. Shakespeare was not among them.

And Shakespeare was not among those who wrote elegies for Henry. At about the time copies of the *Sonnets* were coming off the press, he turned his back on London and the courts of King James and Prince Henry. After 1609 and to the end of his life, no new plays or poems by Shakespeare came into print. There may have been many reasons for this, but the most parsimonious explanation is that the name of Shakespeare had lost some of its magic. He was now a scandalmonger, and a plebeian one, who had unmasked the most idolized man in England. During the last years of his professional career, he lived in Stratford where he owned the largest house and over one hundred acres of land, settling there more or less permanently and spending, according to rumors, £1000 a year, a nice round figure, undoubtedly much exaggerated, that conveyed what it was meant to convey: that Shakespeare was a very rich man,[282] He was certainly better off financially than King James himself, who was bankrupt and had to sell titles to keep himself afloat.

Henry, Prince of Wales, is all but forgotten now. The poet who could have given him immortal fame reneged on his promise to do so. In the midst of his infatuation, he had assured the boy prince that "your monument shall be my gentle verse" (81).

> Or I shall live your epitaph to make,
> Or you survive when I in earth am rotten,
> From hence your memory death cannot take,
> Although in me each part will be forgotten.
> Your name from hence immortal life shall have,
> Though I, once gone, to all the world must die.
> The earth can yield me but a common grave
> When you entombed in men's eyes shall lie.
> Your monument shall be my gentle verse,
> Which eyes not yet created shall o'er-read,
> And tongues to be your being shall rehearse
> When all the breathers of this world are dead.
>   You still shall live – such virtue hath my pen —
>   Where breath most breathes, even in the mouths of men.

Seen in retrospect every line is deeply ironic. Shakespeare out-lived the boy but wrote no epitaph. No part of the poet is forgotten; his grave in Stratford is a tourist attraction, while the prince is remembered only by historians, his tomb ignored by passers-by. There is no monument over Henry's grave in Westminster Abbey. If Shakespeare had dedicated the sonnets to Prince Henry, as he must have intended at one time, they would undoubtedly have provided a monument in timeless verse. But Shakespeare de-sanctified the sonnets, and the promised monument became the tomb of an unknown. Instead, Shakespeare bestowed immortality on himself, letting his name appear in big, bold letters.

The publication of the sonnets in 1609 was an act of requital. He knew he had lost the chance of being friend to a prince. He had as-pired to be a kind of tutor to Henry in keeping with the Socratic ideal. But the rival poet had won. Chapman dedicated his Homer to the prince in order to instill the manly virtues in him. Shake-speare transmuted the blond boy's fugitive physical attractiveness into lasting poetry. But the hard body and tense muscles of the trained soldier and athlete was less to his liking than the soft curves of budding youth, which matched the lambent flow of his "gentle verse," just as the gnarled and strained verse of Chapman suited the values he stood for.

Ineluctably, and in spite of nature's gifts, time would bring a change in the lovely boy. The poet's business was to capture that ephemeral beauty in verse that would endure. He knew that as the young man passed from pubescence into early manhood, much of the charm would vanish. The "cherubin" of sonnet 114 would go the way of all flesh and descend into the world of selfish desires, of lusts and infidelities. Nothing could change that, certainly not beauty itself. The boy's beauty attracted women, who would draw him down to the level of the Dark Lady of the last sonnets.

These were the facts of life as he saw them, and nothing could be done to change them. What vexed the poet as he wrote the last of the boy sonnets was not these philosophical and esthetic concerns but social ones. Having envisioned himself as a member of the prince's inner circle, he found himself instead courteously but undeniably rebuffed. As he dashed off one sonnet after another, he believed that poetry would defeat time, forgive estrangements, and overcome social differences. What he found was that the unparalleled literary brilliance that put him far above ordinary mortals was no patent of nobility. No amount of genius could surmount the barrier of class.

He had offered the prince the greatest series of sonnets in the English language, poems at once intimate and philosophical, unrivaled in their technical facility, poems that matched Petrarch's lyrics to Laura as an expression of a transcendent love. But Prince Henry was no Laura. He was much more real. The final disillusionment was his lack of appreciation for what the poet had created. For William Shakespeare there was to be no freemasonry of kindred spirits such as Phineas Pett shared with Prince Henry. He had believed in that possibility. "Thy love is better than high birth to me," he had said, and to have that love taken away would make him "most wretched" (91). When the rival poet appeared on the scene, Shakespeare had sensed increasingly the disaffection of the young man, which he took to be a kind of breach of faith. Distracted by his love, "this madding fever," he could not fully accept the reality of the prince's growing coolness. "Still losing when I saw myself to win" (119), still hoping to win a place close to the prince, he plied him with songs about loyalty.

Although Shakespeare must have known all along what the final outcome would be, his coming to his senses is apparent in those last sonnets. Unlike the first in the series, there is no talk of saving the boy prince from the ravages of time, no promises of lasting monuments. Instead, he threatens the gifted boy with nature's audit, that cruel accounting that will place him in a common grave with the poet (81). In those concluding sonnets, probably written in May 1609, he vows, despite the boy's indifference, to be true to him, desperately offering oblations (125), not falling "under the blow of thralled discontent" (124), rising above intrigues and expediency. But he wasn't true to him. In "A Lover's Complaint," when he had sobered up, he gave his final assessment. Abandoned by the prince, rid of the poison that had infected him, he saw Henry as he really was. The publication of the *Sonnets* was first of all an exposé, a revelation of the reality behind the façade, but it was also an act of bravado by which Shakespeare the poet and actor triumphed over the nobleman, creating a lasting monument in art while consigning the prince to obscurity. Or perhaps to oblivion, if we accept Kierkegaard's subtle view of it. "If we consign something to oblivion," the Danish philosopher observed, "we suggest that it is simultaneously forgotten yet preserved."

Actually, Shakespeare had no choice. He could not name Prince Henry out of fear of severe reprisals.

Yet this cannot be the last word, as the self-reflective "Complaint" makes clear. In this epilogue the poet settles accounts not only with the young man but with himself. What makes this epilogue so essential to the full story is not only that it recapitulates the narrative of the Fair Youth sonnets but that it tells us what loving that young man meant to Shakespeare.

The "Complaint" begins with the woman, the poet's other self, in tears, as she shreds the letters that the young man had sent her, and ends with a recollection of the young man in tears. Framed by tearful scenes, the "Complaint" centers on that crucial time, recounted in sonnets 33 to 36, when for reasons of state, Prince Henry had to distance himself from the importunate, all-too-devoted poet. Although there is no record of what words were passed between them, the moment when they recognized "that we two must be twain" (36) probably constituted the emotional climax of their relationship. When the poet first senses Henry's coolness, he compares him to the sun slipping behind the clouds.

> Even so my sun one early morn did shine
> With all triumphant splendor on my brow;
> But out, alack, he was but one hour mine,
> The region cloud hath masked him from me now.
>   Yet him for this my love no whit disdaineth;
>   Suns of the world may stain when heaven's sun staineth (33).

Shortly after this, Henry met Shakespeare to explain and to apologize for his action. This moment when they separated may have been their most intimate moment. Both the teen-age adolescent and the middle-aged poet were reduced to tears. Continuing the weather imagery, Shakespeare describes the scene.

> 'Tis not enough that through the cloud thou break
> To dry the rain on my storm-beaten face,
> For no man well of such a salve can speak
> That heals the wound and cures not the disgrace.
> Nor can thy shame give physic to my grief;
> Though thou repent, yet I have still the loss.
> Th'offender's sorrow lends but weak relief
> To him that bears the strong offence's cross.

Then, in the final couplet, comes the moment that the poet will always cherish.

> Ah, but those tears are pearl which thy love sheeds,
> And they are rich and ransom all ill deeds (34).

At the end of the "Complaint," the poet returns to this scene, only now viewing it with a dispassionate eye. The tears are no longer like pearl.

> Each cheek a river running from a fount

> With brinish current downward flowed apace.
> O, how the channel to the stream gave grace.
>   . . .
> O father, what a hell of witchcraft lies
> In the small orb of one particular tear.
> But with the inundation of the eyes
> What rocky heart to water will not wear?
>   . . .
> For lo, his passion, but an art of craft,
> Even there resolved my reason into tears;
> There my white stole of chastity I daffed,
> Shook off my sober guards and civil fears,
> Appear to him as he to me appears –
> All melting; though our drops this diff'rence bore:
> His poisoned me, and mine did him restore (281-301).

Looking back, the poet realizes he was seduced by the prince's youth, charm, and social status, made use of and then cast aside. Yet he has no regrets. Given the opportunity, he would willingly repeat the experience.

> O, that infected moisture of his eye,
> O, that false fire which in his cheek so glowed,
> O, that forced thunder from his heart did fly,
> O, that sad breath his spongy lungs bestowed,
> O, all that motion, seeming owed [inherent],
> Would yet again betray the fore-betrayed,
> And new pervert a reconciled maid (323-329).

And why not, when the experience inspired some of the greatest poetry in the language, a sonnet sequence innovative in technique, psychologically profound, and unrivaled in its realism and emotional intensity?

APPENDIX A

MEMORIAL OF HENRY, PRINCE OF WALES,
By Francis Bacon

HENRY, eldest son of the King of Great Britain, late of blessed hope, now of happy memory, died on the 6th of November, 1612. He died to the great grief and regret of the whole kingdom, as being a youth who had neither offended men's minds nor satiated them. The goodness of his disposition had awakened manifold hopes among numbers of all ranks, nor had he lived long enough to disappoint them. Moreover, as among the people generally he had the reputation of being firm in the cause of religion; so the wiser sort were deeply impressed with the feeling that he had been to his father as a guard and shield against the machinations of conspirators, — a mischief for which our age has hardly found a remedy; so that the love of the people both for religion and for the King overflowed upon him, and was rightly taken into account in estimating his loss.

In body he was strong and erect, of middle height, his limbs gracefully put together, his gait kinglike, his face long and somewhat lean, his habit rather full, his countenance composed, and the motion of his eyes rather sedate than powerful. His forehead bore marks of severity, his mouth had a touch of pride. And yet when one penetrated beyond those outworks, and soothed him with due attention and seasonable discourse, one found him gentle and easy to deal with; so that he seemed quite another man in conversation than his aspect promised; and altogether he was one who might easily get himself a reputation at variance with his manners. Of praise and glory he was doubtless covetous; and was stirred with every show of good and every breath of honour; which in a young man goes for virtues. For both arms and military men were in honour with him; nor was he himself without something of a warlike spirit; he was given also to magnificence of works, though otherwise frugal enough of money; he was fond of antiquity and arts: and a favourer of learning, though rather in the honour he paid it than the time he spent upon it. In his morals there was nothing more to be praised than that in every kind of duty he seemed to be well trained and conformable. He was a wonderfully obedient son to the King his father, very attentive also to the Queen, kind to his brother; but his sister he especially loved; whom also he resembled in countenance, as far as a man's face can be compared with that of a very beautiful girl. The masters and tutors of his youth also (which rarely happens) continued in great favour with him. In discourse, as he exacted respect from others, so he observed it himself. And finally in his daily way of life, and the assignation of several hours for its several duties, he was constant and regular above the habit of his years. His passions were not over vehement, and rather equable than great. For of love matters there was wonderfully little talk, considering his age: insomuch that he passed that extremely slippery time of his early manhood, in so great a fortune and in very good health, without being particularly noted for any affairs of that kind. There was no one in his court that had great power with him, or that possessed a strong hold on his mind. The very pursuits in which he took most delight had rather their times than their excesses; and were repeated each in its turn, rather than some one allowed to take the lead and overrule the rest; whether that were moderation and self-restraint, or that in a nature not very precocious, but ripening slowly, it did not appear which would ultimately prevail. In understanding he was certainly strong, and did not want either curiosity or capacity. But in speech he was somewhat slow, and as it were embarrassed; and yet if you observed diligently the things he said, whether in asking questions or expressing opinions, they were ever to the point, and argued no ordinary capacity; so that his slow and seldom speaking seemed to come rather from suspense and solicitude than weakness or dulness of judgment. In the meantime he was a wonderfully patient listener, even in affairs which grew to length, and that attentively, and without growing weary; so that he seldom let his thoughts wander or his mind lose its power of attention, but kept it still fixed and applied to that which was saying or doing: a habit which promised great wisdom in him if he had lived. Many points there were indeed in this prince's nature which were obscure, and could not be discovered by any man's judgment, but only by time, which was not allowed him. Those however which appeared were excellent; which is enough for fame. He died in the nineteenth year of his age of a malignant fever, which – springing from the great heats and droughts, greater than islanders are accustomed to, – was very general among the people during the summer, though few died of it; but became towards autumn more fatal. Rumour, ever more malignant (as Tacitus says) upon the deaths of princes, suggested poison. But as no symptoms of such a thing appeared, especially in the stomach which is commonly most affected by poison, that report soon died away.

NOTES

[1] *Shakespeare's Sonnets*, ed. Katherine Duncan-Jones, Arden Shakespeare, 1997, p. 34.

[2] Vendler, *The Art of Shakespeare's Sonnets*, Cambridge, MA, 1997, p. 17.

[3] Ibid., p. 13.

[4] Colin Burrow, ed., *The Complete Sonnets and Poems*, Oxford, 2002, pp. 124-131. John Kerrigan, ed., *The Sonnets and A Lover's Complaint*, New York (New Penguin Shakespeare), 1995, pp. 46-55.

[5] Duncan-Jones, *Sonnets*, p.xv.

[6] A note by the actor Edward Alleyn saying he bought a copy of the *Sonnets* in June is "almost certainly a forgery by John Payne Collier." Duncan-Jones, *Sonnets*, p. 7.

[7] E.K. Chambers, *William Shakespeare*, 2 vols., Oxford, 1930, vol. 2, p. 215.

[8] Paul Hammond, *Figuring Sex between Men from Shakespeare to Rochester*, Oxford, 2002, pp. 101-104.

[9] *The Sonnets of Shakespeare*, ed. Raymond Macdonald Alden, Boston and New York, 1916, p. 382.

[10] Bradley, *Oxford Lectures on Poetry*, London, 1909, p. 331.

[11] *Transactions of the New Shakespere Society*, 1887-92, p. 197.

[12] Donald W. Foster, *Elegy by W.S. : A Study in Attribution*, Newark, 1989, pp. 226-231. Duncan-Jones, *Sonnets*, pp.36-41. John Kerrigan, *Sonnets*, pp. 7-8. G. Blakemore Evans, editor of the New Cambridge Shakespeare edition of the sonnets, is more guarded in his findings, but he does not argue against authorial approval, and he accepts the published arrangement of the sonnets. See also Katherine Duncan-Jones, "Was the 1609 *Shake-speare's Sonnets* really unauthorized," *Review of English Studies*, n.s., 34, 1983, pp. 151-71.

[13] *The Works of Christopher Marlowe*, ed. C. F. Tucker Brooke, Oxford, 1910.

[14] Chambers, *Shakespeare*, vol. 2, p. 266.

[15] *New Shakspere Society's Transactions*, 1875-76, p. 150.

[16] Chambers, *Shakespeare*, vol. 2, pp. 199-201.

[17] On the sexual psychology that connects *Venus and Adonis* with the sonnets, see Leslie A. Fiedler, "Some Contexts of Shakespeare's Sonnets, in *The Riddle of Shakespeare's Sonnets*, by Edward Hubler *et al.*, New York, 1962, pp. 55-90. Also, Fiedler, *The Stranger in Shakespeare*, New York, 1972, pp. 15-39.

[18] Chambers, *Shakespeare*, vol. 2, p. 177. For a balanced view of the evidence, see Ian Wilson, *Shakespeare: The Evidence*, New York, 1993, pp. 389-390; and Katherine Duncan-Jones, *Ungentle Shakespeare: Scenes from his Life* (Arden Shakespeare), 2002, p. 272.

[19] Kerrigan, *Sonnets*, p. 47. For an excellent discussion of homoeroticism in Renaissance England, see pp. 46-55.

[20] Duncan-Jones, *Ungentle Shakespeare*, pp. 86-87.

[21] A.L. Rowse, *Shakespeare's Southampton*, New York, 1965, pp. 123-4.

[22] Katherine Duncan-Jones, "Much Ado With Red and White: The Earliest Readers of William Shakespeare's 'Venus and Adonis (1593)," *Review of English Studies*, vol. 44, 1993; and Alan Bray, *The Friend*, Chicago, 2003, p. 187.

[23] Hammond, *Figuring Sex*, p. 49.

[24] Ibid., p. 50.

[25] See Stephen Orgel, *Imagining Shakespeare*, New York, 2003, pp. 90-94.

[26] Rowse, *Shakespeare's Southampton*, p. 182.

[27] Alan Stewart, *The Cradle King: The Life of James VI and I, the First Monarch of a United Great Britain*, New York, 2003, p. 222.

[28] Ibid., p. III.

[29] Alvin Kernan, *Shakespeare, the King's Playwright: Theater in the Stuart Court 1603-1613*, New Haven, 1995, p. 116.

[30] David M. Bergeron, *Royal Family, Royal Lovers: King James of England and Scotland*, Columbia, MO, 1991, p. 87.

[31] Ibid., p. 87.

[32] Anne Somerset, *Unnatural Murder: Poison at the Court of James I*, London, 1997, p. 59.

[33] Anonymous, *Haec-Vir, or the Womanish Man*, 1620, quoted in Sasha Roberts, *Reading Shakespeare's Poems in Early Modern England*, New York, 2003, pp. 40-41.

[34] Sir Thomas Howard in Sir John Harrington, *Nugae Antiquae*, quoted by Raymond S. Burns, ed., John Day's *The Isle of Gulls*, New York and London, 1980, p. 22.

[35] Roy Strong, *Henry, Prince of Wales, and England's Lost Renaissance*, New York, 1986, p. 16.

[36] Quoted in Lucy Monroe, *Children of the Queen's Revels*, Cambridge, 2005, p. 33.

[37] G.P.V. Akrigg, *Jacobean Pageant or The Court of King James I*, Cambridge, MA., 1962, p. 13.

[38] Nathan Drake, *Shakspeare [sic]and His Times*, vol. 2. London, 1817, p. 476.

[39] Stewart, *Cradle King*, p. 184.

[40] *Ben Jonson*, ed. C.H. Herford, Percy and Evelyn Simpson, 11 vols, Oxford, 1925-1952, vol. 8, p. 131.

[41] *Ben Jonson*, vol. 7, p. 331 ("The Speeches at Prince Henries Barriers").

[42] "A Monumental Columne," *The Complete Works of John Webster*, ed. F.L. Lucas, reprint, New York, 1966, vol. 3, p. 276

[43] Strong, *Henry Prince of Wales*, p. 51.

[44] *William Shakespeare: A Documentary Volume*, ed. Catherine Loomis (Dictionary Of Literary Biography, vol. 263), Gale Group, 2002, p. 147.

[45] See Hammond, *Figuring Sex*, p. 131.

[46] Louis Crompton, *Homosexuality and Civilization*, Cambridge, MA, 2003, p. 381.

[47] *The Basilicon Dóron of King James VI*, ed. James Craigie, vol. 1, Edinburgh and London, 1944, p. 174.

[48] For a full account of King James and his favorites, see Hammond, *Figuring Sex*, pp. 128-150.

[49] Bray, *The Friend*, p. 186.

[50] *The true Tragicomedy*, ed. John Pitcher and Lois Potter, New York, 1983, Act 5, scene 3.

[51] *Christianity, Social Tolerance, and Homosexuality*, Chicago, 1980, pp. 245, 251-253.

[52] K.J.Dover, *Greek Homosexuality*, Cambridge, MA, 1978, pp. 98-99; William Armstrong III, *Pederasty and Pedagogy in Archaic Greece*, Urbana and Chicago, 1996, pp. 6-11.

[53] See the discussion in Boswell, *Christianity*, pp. 92-96.

[54] John Addington Symonds, *Renaissance in Italy*, 2 vols., New York, 1935, vol. 2, p. 324.

[55] Hammond, *Figuring Sex*, p. 230.

[56] Mark D. Jordan, *The Invention of Sodomy in Christian Theology*, Chicago, 1997, pp. 45-47.

[57] This passage has been misinterpreted by Dante commentators who make nonsense out of it by taking hermaphrodite to mean bisexual, that is, one who loves both sexes equally. But clearly hermaphrodite means androgynous, two sexes in one. For a correct understanding, see Martha C. Nussbaum, *Upheavals of Thought: The Intelligence of the Emotions*, Cambridge , 2001, pp. 562, 569; and Richard Halpern, *Shakespeare's Perfume: Sodomy and Sublimity in the Sonnets, Wilde, Freud, and Lacan* , Philadelphia, 2002, p. 87.

[58] *Renaissance in Italy*, vol. 1, pp. 876-877.

[59] Thomas W. Laqueur, *Solitary Sex: A Cultural History of Masturbation*, New York, 2003, p. 148.

[60] Crompton, *Homosexuality*, p. 155.

[61] Boswell, *Christianity*, pp. 180-183, 205-206.

[62] Aristotle, *Problems*, book IV, section 26, translated by E.S. Forster, in *The Complete Works of Aristotle*, ed. Jonathan Barnes, Princeton, 1984, p. 1357. See the discussion of Aristotle as read by university students in David Riggs, *The World of Christopher Marlowe*, New York, 2004, pp. 73-77.

[63] See Theo van der Meer, "The Persecution of Sodomites in Eighteenth-Century Amsterdam: Changing Perceptions of Sodomy," in *The Pursuit of Sodomy: Male Homosexuality in Renaissance and Enlightenment Europe*, eds. Kent Gerard and Gert Hekma, New York and London, 1989, pp. 263-210; Randolph Trumbach, "Sodomitical Assaults, Gender Role, and Sexual Development in Eighteenth-Century London," in *The Pursuit of Sodomy*, 407-32; and Michael B. Young, *King James and the History of Homosexuality*, New York, 2000, pp. 135-55.

[64] B. R. Burg, *Sodomy and the Perception of Evil: English Sea Rovers in the Seventeenth-Century Caribbean*, New York, 1983, pp. 136-7. The reliability of Burg's findings has

been questioned by Theo van der Meer, op. cit., pp. 291 and 306.

[65] J.Z. Eglinton, *Greek Love*, New York, 1964, pp. 152-154, 481.

[66] Michael Rocke, *Forbidden Friendships: Homosexuality and Male Culture in Renaissance Florence*, Oxford, 1996; Joseph Cady, "The 'Masculine Love' of the 'Princes of Sodom:' Practising the Art of Ganymede at Henri III's Court: The Homosexuality of Henri III and his *Mignons* in Pierre de L'Estoile's *Memoires-Journeaux*," in *Desire and Discipline: Sex and Sexuality in the Premodern West*, eds. Jacqueline Murray and Konrad Eisenblicher, Toronto, 1996, pp. 123-54. The extent of Henri's homosexuality may well have been exaggerated by his enemies. See Michael Sibalis, "Homosexuality in Early Modern France," in *Queer Masculinities*, ed. Katherine O'Donnell and Michael O'Rourke, Hampshire, 2006, pp. 214-5.

[67] On "sodomitical sins" as a pervasive feature of Elizabethan urban culture, see Duncan-Jones, *Ungentle Shakespeare*, pp. 79-81.

[68] Magnus Hirschfeld, *Die Homosexualität des Mannes und des Weibes*, Berlin, 1914, p. 5.

[69] Joseph Pequiney, *Such Is My Love: A Study of Shakespeare's Sonnets*, Chicago, 1985, pp. 43-6.

[70] See O. L. Jiriczek, "Die erste englische Theokritübersetzung," *Jahrbuch der deutschen Shakespeare-Gesellschaft*, v. 55 (1919), pp. 30-34.

[71] Bruce R. Smith, *Homosexual Desire in Shakespeare's England*, 2d ed., Chicago, 1994, p. 50.

[72] G. B. Harrison, *Elizabethan Plays and Players*, Ann Arbor, 1956, p. 120.

[73] George Sandys in his commentary on Ovid's *Metamorphoses*, 1632, quoted in Smith, *Homosexual Desire*, p. 95.

[74] E. K.'s gloss on Edmund Spenser's *The Shepheardes Calender*. See the discussion in Gregory W. Bredbeck, *Sodomy and Interpretation: Marlowe to Milton*, Ithaca, 1991, p. 203-204.

[75] *The Art-Work of the Future* in *Richard Wagner's Prose Works*, translated by William Ashton Ellis, vol. 1, Lincoln, Nebraska, reprint 1993, pp. 167-8.

[76] Dover, *Greek Homosexuality*, p. 144, and William Armstrong Percy III, *Pederasty and Pedagogy*, pp. 39, 88.

[77] The German commentator Hermann Conrad said in 1879 that Shakespeare conceived of friendship with an ideality "of which the literature of the world has perhaps but a *single* other example: the second discourse of Socrates in *Phaedrus*." Quoted in *The Sonnets*, ed. Hyder Edward Rollins (*A New Variorum Edition of Shakespeare*) vol. 2, 1944, p. 233.

[78] *De Re Publica*, translated by Clinton Walker Keyes, London, 1928 (Loeb Classical Library), IV, 4.

[79] Marcel Proust, *The Guermantes Way. Cities of the Plain*, translated by C. K. Scott Moncrieff and Terence Kilmartin, New York, 1981, p. 639.

[80] Thomas Mann, *Stories of Three Decades*, translated by H. T. Lowe-Porter, New York, 1948, pp. 396, 412, 413.

[81] Marsilio Ficino, *Commentary on Plato's Symposium on Love*, translated by Sears

Jayne, Dallas, 1985, pp. 40-41, 115, 126, 135.

[82] See John Charles Nelson, *Renaissance Theory of Love*, New York and London, 1958, pp. 68-72.

[83] *Tusculan Disputations* IV, 33. J.E.King translation.

[84] Peacham, *Minerva Britanna* , London, 1612, p. 48.

[85] Barnfield, *Poems 1595-1598*, ed. Edward Arber, Westminster, 1896, pp. 5, 11, 8, spelling modernized. Barnfield, a life-long bachelor, may have paid a price for his homosexuality. He was disinherited in favor of his younger brother. See Andrew Worrall, "Richard Barnfield: A New Biography," *Notes and Queries*, September 1992, pp. 170-171.

[86] *Basilikon Dóron*, 1596, quoted in Bray, *The Friend*, 167.

[87] David M. Bergeron, *King James & Letters of Homoerotic Desire*, Iowa City, 1999, pp. 138-139.

[88] Osborne, *True Tragicomedy*, p. 114.

[89] Martha C. Nussbaum, "The Comic Soul; Or, This Phallus That Is Not One," in *The Soul of Tragedy*, ed. Victoria Pedrick and Steven M. Oberhelman, Chicago, 2005, pp. 155-180.

[90] Vittorio Lingiardi, *Men in Love: Male Homosexualities from Ganymede to Batman*, translated by Robert H. Hopcke and Paul A. Schwartz, Chicago and LaSalle, 2002, p. 179.

[91] Vendler, *Art of Shakespeare's Sonnets*, p. 47.

[92] Symonds, *Renaissance in Italy*, vol. 1, p. 651.

[93] Ibid., p. 653.

[94] J. B. Leishman, *Themes and Variations in Shakespeare's Sonnets*, London, 1961, p. 115-6.

[95] *The Poetry of Michelangelo*, translated by James M. Saslow, New Haven, 1991, p. 236.

[96] *The Poems of Shakespeare*, ed. George Wyndham, London, 1898, pp. 260-268.

[97] Kerrigan, *Sonnets*, p. 14.

[98] MacD. P. Jackson, "Shakespeare's Sonnets: Rhyme and Reason in the Dark Lady Series," *Notes and Queries*, vol. 244 (1999), p. 222.

[99] See the list of sonnet sequences in *Sonnets and Poems*, ed. Burrow, pp. 168-169.

[100] *Shakespeare's Sonnets*, ed. Stephen Booth, New Haven, 1977, p. 526. Kerrigan, *Sonnets*, p. 383. In *Henry V* (3.4.47-53) French *con* is pronounced like English *coun*. See Partridge, *Shakespeare's Bawdy*, New York, 1948, p. 95.

[101] Vendler, *Art of Shakespeare's Sonnets* , p. 640.

[102] Anonymous, "New Views of Shakespeare's Sonnets," *Blackwood's Edinburgh Magazine*, vol. 135, 1884, pp. 753-4.

[103] Auden, *Forewords and Afterwords*, New York, 1990, p. 102.

[104] Bradley, *Oxford Lectures*, p. 350.

[105] George Santayana, *Interpretations of Poetry and Religion*, New York, 1900, pp. 152, 163.

[106] John M. Robertson, *Montaigne and Shakspere* [sic], London, 1897, p. 162.

[107] Michel Lord of Montaigne, *Essays*, translated by John Florio (Everyman's Library), London and New York, n.d., vol. 1, p. 87.

[108] For conflicting views on sonnet 146, see B. C. Southam, "Shakespeare's Christian Sonnet? Number 146," *Shakespeare Quarterly*, vol. 11, 1960, 67-71; Charles A. Huttar, "The Christian Basis of Shakespeare's Sonnet 146," *Shakespeare Quarterly*, vol. 19, 1968, 355-65; Michael West, "The Internal Dialogue of Shakespeare's Sonnet 146," *Shakespeare Quarterly*, vol. 25, 1974, 109-22; and Joseph Pequigney, *Such Is My Love*, pp. 168-173. None of these take Montaigne's essay into account.

[109] See especially Vendler, *Art of Shakespeare's Sonnets*, pp. 445-447.

[110] Brandes, *William Shakespeare* in *Samlede Skrifter*, vol. 8, Copenhagen, 1901, pp. 340-50.

[111] Richard Simpson, *An Introduction to the Philosophy of Shakespeare's Sonnets*, London, 1868, p. 6.

[112] William Minto, *Characteristics of English Poets from Chaucer to Shirley*, 2d ed., London and Edinburgh, 1885, p. 216.

[113] Vendler, *Art of Shakespeare's Sonnets*, p. 16.

[114] Bradley, *Oxford Lectures*, p. 335.

[115] John Sutherland and Cedric Watts, *Henry V, War Criminal? And Other Shakespeare Puzzles*, Oxford, 2000, p. 161.

[116] Minto, *Characteristics of English Poets*, pp. 21-31.

[117] Havelock Ellis, *Chapman*, Bloomsbury, 1934, p. 2.

[118] E.K. Chambers, *The Elizabethan Stage*, 4 vols., Oxford, 1923 (rev. ed. 1967), vol. 3, p. 250. Lucy Munro (*Children of the Queen's Revels*, p. 34) says that Chapman's appointment as sewer "is almost certainly untrue," but offers no explanation.

[119] *Chapman's Homer: The Iliad*, ed. Allardyce Nicoll, Princeton, paperback ed., 1998, p. xiii.

[120] Ibid., p. 23.

[121] There is evidence that Shakespeare read the *Aeneid* in the original Latin. See Shakespeare, *The Poems* (Arden Edition) 1960, ed. F. T. Prince, p. 134.

[122] J. A. K. Thomson, *Shakespeare and the Classics*, London, 1952, pp. 168-173.

[123] *The Poems of George Chapman*, ed. Phyllis Brooks Bartlett, New York, 1941, pp. 174-5.

[124] Ibid., pp. 83, 49.

[125] Arthur Acheson, *Shakespeare's Lost Years in London, 1586-1592*, first printed 1922, reprint New York, 1971, pp. 93, 186.

[126] Noted by Thomson, *Shakespeare and the Classics*, p. 175.

[127] See Arthur Acheson, *Shakespeare's Sonnet Story 1592-1598*, London, 1922, pp. 298-338.

[128] *Poems of Chapman*, p. 27.

[129] Ibid., p. 41.

[130] Taylor, Introduction, *Henry V* (Oxford Shakespeare), Oxford, 1982, p. 54.

[131] Arthur Acheson, *Shakespeare and the Rival Poet*, London and New York, 1903, p. 175. Neglected by recent commentators, Acheson is on pretty solid ground in his dating of *Henry V*.

[132] *Transactions of the New Shakspere Society*, 1880-86, p. 84*.

[133] On *Troilus and Cressida* as a reply to Chapman, see Thomas Tyler, "Shakspere Idolatry," *Transactions of the New Shakspere Society* 1887-92, pp. 208-9; Thomson, *Shakespeare and the Classics*, pp. 210-215; Geoffrey Bullough in his introduction to *Narrative and Dramatic Sources of Shakespeare*, vol. 6, London and New York, 1966, pp. 87-89..

[134] See Adolphus William Ward, *A History of English Dramatic Literature to the Death of Queen Anne*, rev. ed., London, 1899, vol. 2, p. 146. Most editors date Shakespeare's *Troilus* to 1601. The evidence they cite is circumstantial. Much weight is given to the "armed prologue" that appears in Jonson's *Poetaster*, which was written in 1601. This is supposed to have influenced Shakespeare when he wrote the prologue to *Troilus*. But the assumption begs the question of which came first. The similarities between the two prologues are very superficial. More striking is the similarity between the prologue to *Troilus* and the prologue to *Henry V*, which was written in 1599. James P. Bednarz (*Shakespeare & the Poets' War*, 2001) examines the evidence for the 1601 date. He ignores, however, the possible evidential value of the *Troilus* allusion in *Histriomastix* (1599).

[135] Duncan-Jones, *Sonnets*, p. xv.

[136] Paul Edmondson and Stanley Wells, *Shakespeare's Sonnets* (Oxford Shakespeare Topics) Oxford, 2004, p. 38.

[137] Duncan-Jones, *Sonnets*, p. 2.

[138] *The Poems of Sir Philip Sidney* , ed. William A. Ringler, Jr., Oxford, 1962, pp. 439, 471.

[139] J. G. R., *Notes and Queries*, 2d series, vol. 7 (1859) p. 125.

[140] Laurence Michel, "Shakespeare's Sonnet CVII," *Journal of English and Germanic Philology*, vol. 54, 1955, pp. 301-305.

[141] E. K. Chambers, *Shakespearean Gleanings*, Oxford, 1944, pp. 139-143.

[142] Leslie Hotson, *Mr. W. H.*, London, 1964, pp. 75-76 .

[143] Walter B. Stone, "Shakespeare and the Sad Augurs," *Journal of English and Germanic Philology*, vol. 52, 1953, pp. 457-77.

[144] G. B. Harrison, *A Second Jacobean Journal*, London, 1958, pp. 132-3. That sonnet 107 alluded to the 1609 treaty was first suggested by F. T. Palgrave in his edition of the sonnets, 1865.

[145] Gervase Markham, *Honour in His Perfection*, quoted in Shakespeare, *The Sonnets*, ed. G. Blakemore Evans, Cambridge, 1996, p. 218.

[146] *Poems of Chapman*, p. 173,

[147] John Kerrigan would make "drops of this most balmy time" refer to the balm used in the ceremony in which James was crowned King of England. This is a very

strained reading. Balm is an unguent that does not form drops, a fact that Kerrigan virtually admits (Kerrigan, *Sonnets*, pp. 318, 422.)

[148] *Poems of Chapman*, pp. 173, 192, 181, 178, 200.

[149] Auden, *Forewords*, p. 88.

[150] Ibid., p. 104.

[151] *Coleridge's Shakespearean Criticism*, ed. T. M. Raysor, Cambridge, MA, 1930, vol. 2, pp. 355-6.

[152] Peter Stallybrass, "Editing as Cultural Formation: The Sexing of Shakespeare's Sonnets," in *Shakespeare's Sonnets*, ed. James Schiffer, New York and London, 1999, p. 83.

[153] *Sonnets*, ed. Alden, p. 382.

[154] Byrne Fone, *Homophobia*, New York, 2000, p. 335.

[155] Crompton, *Homosexuality and Civilization*, p. 533.

[156] Lewis, *English Literature in the Sixteenth Century*, Oxford, 1954. p. 503.

[157] *Sonnets*, ed. Alden, p. 465; *Complete Sonnets and Poems*, ed. Burrow, p. 100.

[158] See the portrait of Herbert in *Ben Jonson*, vol. 8, frontispiece and commentary, p. x.

[159] Simpson, *An Introduction to the Philosophy of Shakespeare's Sonnets*, p. 6.

[160] Ibid., p. 6.

[161] Ibid., p. 18.

[162] Symonds, *Renaissance in Italy*, vol. 1, p. 785.

[163] Ibid., p. 187.

[164] *The Complete Letters of Oscar Wilde*, ed. Merlin Holland and Rupert Hart-Davis, New York, 2000, pp. 407-408.

[165] *Complete Works of Oscar Wilde*, ed. J.B. Foreman, new ed., London and Glasgow, 1966, p. 1194.

[166] Ibid., p. 1154.

[167] J. Dover Wilson in his edition of the sonnets (Cambridge, 1966) was among the first of the scholarly commentators not to shirk the word "boy" in describing the Fair Youth.

[168] According to T. Wright, *A Succinct Philosophicall declaration of the Clymactericall Yeeres*, published in 1604, adolescence covered the years fourteen to twenty. See *Transactions of the New Shakespere Society*, 1887-92, p. 35.

[169] Hotson, *Mr. W. H.*, p. 40.

[170] Bergeron, *Royal Family, Royal Lovers*, p. 76.

[171] *The Works of Michael Drayton*, ed. J. W. Hebel, Oxford, vol. 1, 1931, p. 481.

[172] J. Dover Wilson came within a whisker of identifying Prince Henry as the Fair Youth (*Sonnets*, Cambridge, 1966, pp.lxix-lxxi) on the basis of Chapman's poems. He failed to see the connection because he assumed the sonnets were written before 1603.

[173] Palk, "The Puzzle of 'the Sonnets' – A Solution?" *Times Literary Supplement*, April 20, 1916, p. 189.

[174] *A Jacobean Journal, Being a Record of Those Things Most Talked of During the Years 1603-1606*, by G. B. Harrison, New York, 1941, p. 43.

[175] *The Poetical Works of Sir William Alexander, Earl of Stirling*, ed. L. E. Kastner and H. B. Charlton, vol. 2, Edinburgh and London, 1929, p. 402.

[176] Harington, *Nugae Antiquae*, 2 vols., 1804, vol. 2, p. 3.

[177] Joshua Sylvester, "Lacrymæ Lacrymarum: or The Spirit of Teares, distilled for the Untimely Death of the Incomparable Prince Henrie (late) Prince of Wales" in *The Complete Works of Joshua Sylvester*, ed. Alexander B. Grosart, 2 vols., reprint, New York, 1967, vol. 2, p. 277. This is a revised version of *Lachrimæ Lachrimarum*, which Sylvester published in 1612.

[178] Quoted in *James I By His Contemporaries*, ed. Robert Ashton, London, 1969, p. 98n.

[179] Bergeron, *Royal Family, Royal Lovers*, p. 104.

[180] Nicolo Molin, *Relazione* of 1607, quoted in Strong, *Henry, Prince of Wales*, pp. 14-15.

[181] *The Autobiography of Phineas Pett*, ed. W. G. Perrin (Publications of the Navy Records Society, vol. 51 [London]) 1918, pp. 20-23; Strong, *Henry, Prince of Wales*, p. 57.

[182] W. H., *The True Picture and Relation of Prince Henry*, quoted in Strong, *Henry, Prince of Wales*, p. 12.

[183] *Ben Jonson*, vol. 7, pp. 343-4.

[184] Mary Bradford Whiting, "Henry, Prince of Wales: 'A Scarce Blown Rose,'" *Contemporary Review*, vol. 137, 1930, p. 492.

[185] "Elegie on the untimely Death of the Incomparable Prince Henry" in Joshua Sylvester, *Lachrymae Lachrymarum*, 3rd ed., London, 1613, sig. D2.

[186] Gorges, *The Olympian Catastrophe*, Kensington, 1925, p. 59.

[187] "An Epicede or Funeral Song," *Poems of Chapman*, p. 261.

[188] John Hayward, *The Lives of the III. Normans, Kings of England* (1613), quoted in J. W. Williamson, *The Myth of the Conqueror: Prince Henry Stuart: A Study of 17th Century Personation*, New York, 1978, p.70.

[189] On this subject see Williamson, *Myth of the Conqueror*.

[190] Sir Charles Cornwallis, *The Life and Character of Henry-Frederic, Prince of Wales*, London, 1738, p. 21.

[191] H. Montgomery Hyde, *Oscar Wilde*. New York, 1975, p. 219.

[192] This interpretation of "passion" was first noted by Edward Dowden in his 1881 edition of the *Sonnets*. It derives from Thomas Watson's *Hekatompathia or A Passionate Century of Love*, 1582.

[193] Thomas Marc Parrott, *The Plays and Poems of George Chapman*, New York, 1910, p. 537.

[194] See E.K. Chambers, *Elizabethan Stage*, vol. 3, p. 253; Lucy Monro, *Children of the Queen's Revels*, p. 156.

[195] Chambers (*Elizabethan Stage*, vol. 3, p. 258) says that the play was produced either at Whitefriars in 1609-1612 or at Blackfriars in 1608-1609. He adds that the play was probably written to accompany *Bussy*. If so, it seems likely that Chapman would take advantage of the 1607-1608 revival and not wait until later.

[196] *Blackwood's Magazine*, vol. 139, 1886, pp. 340-41.

[197] *The Poetry of Michelangelo*, pp. 226, 440, 195. Oscar Wilde in his "The Portrait of Mr. W.H.," published in 1889, was among the first to consider the poet and the Italian sculptor as soul mates in many respects. Georg Brandes in his *Shakespeare*, 1895-6, was perhaps the first to devote considerable space to an examination of the kinship between the two geniuses. See above, p. 99.

[198] Simpson, *Philosophy of Shakespeare's Sonnets*, p. 47.

[199] Auden, *Forewords*, p. 103.

[200] G. B. Harrison, *Second Jacobean Journal*, p. 118, drawing on *Calendar of State Papers and Manuscripts, relating to English Affairs . . . in the Archives of Venice and other Libraries of Northern Italy*, ed. Horatio F. Brown, vol. 2, 1905, p. 393.

[201] Francis Osborne, quoted in Stewart, *Cradle King*, p. 248.

[202] Rowse, *Shakespeare's Southampton*, pp. 180-181.

[203] Strong, *Henry, Prince of Wales*, p. 229.

[204] David Riggs, *Ben Jonson*, Cambridge and London, 1989, p. 200, quoting Sir Simonds D'Ewes.

[205] G. B. Harrison, *Second Jacobean Journal*, p. 216; David Lindley, *The Trials of Frances Howard*, New York and London, 1993, p. 65.

[206] Lindley, *Trials of Frances Howard*, p. 65.

[207] Francis Osborne, *True Tragicomedy*, pp. 55-57, 62.

[208] Sir A[nthony] W[eldon], *The Court and Character of King James*, London, 1817, p. 27.

[209] G. B. Harrison, *Second Jacobean Journal*, pp. 130-31.

[210] *The Autobiography of Phineas Pett*, pp. lxxviii, 52, 60, 62, 66.

[211] John Southworth, *Shakespeare the Player: A Life in the Theatre*, Gloucestershire, 2000, p. 232.

[212] Cornwallis, *Henry-Frederic*, p. 14.

[213] William McElwee, *The Wisest Fool in Christendom*, New York, 1958, p. 171.

[214] Arthur Wilson, quoted in Bergeron, *Royal Family, Royal Lovers*, p. 105.

[215] Cornwallis, *Henry-Frederic*, p. 26.

[216] Roger Coke, quoted in Bergeron, p. 92.

[217] Chambers, *Shakespeare*, vol. 2, p. 213.

[218] Williamson, *Myth of the Conqueror*, p. 32.

[219] William Haydon, quoted in Bergeron, *Royal Family*, p. 105.

[220] Lewis, *English Literature in the Sixteenth Century*, p. 503.

[221] Havelock Ellis, *Chapman*, p. 71.

[222] *Poems of Chapman*, p. 41.

[223] *Chapman's Homer*, p. 5.

[224] Ibid., p. 4.

[225] Ibid., p. 6 (lines 144-5; cf. line 47).

[226] Chambers, *Elizabethan Stage*, vol. 3, p. 250.

[227] Akrigg, *Jacobean Pageant*, p. 128.

[228] Chapman had an extensive knowledge of ancient Greek. See Ellis, *Chapman*, p. 42, citing Lohff, *George Chapman's Ilias-Überstezung*, 1903.

[229] J.A.K. Thomson says, "When we look into the matter we find that he made out the sense of the Greek by the aid of the Latin translators, of Spondanus and Scapula's lexicon (*Shakespeare and the Classics*, p.167.)

[230] See John Channing Briggs, "Chapman's Seaven Bookes of the Iliades: Mirror for Essex," in *Homer*, ed. Katherine Callen King, New York and London, 1994, pp. 30-47.

[231] Kestrel was another name for the windfucker. See *Ben Jonson*, vol. 10, p. 12.

[232] *Chapman's Homer*, p. 16. Wyndham in his 1898 edition of Shakespeare's poems saw that Hews might be Chapman's Hews, but could make nothing of the possibility.

[233] *Chapman's Homer*, pp. 14–15, 17–18.

[234] Alfred Harbage, *Shakespeare and the Rival Traditions*, New York, 1952, p. 116.

[235] On *Troilus* as a mock of Chapman's Homer, see Acheson, *Shakespeare and the Rival*, pp. 167-206; Acheson, *Shakespeare's Sonnet Story* , pp. 491-503; and Thomson, *Shakespeare and the Classics*, pp. 210-15.

[236] Stylometric studies suggest that sonnets 126-154 were composed before the Fair Youth sonnets. See A. Kent Heiatt, Charles W. Heiatt, and Anne Lake Prescott, "When Did Shakespeare Write *Sonnets* 1609," *Studies in Philology*, vol. 88 (1991), pp. 69-109.

[237] *Poems of Chapman*, pp. 173, 177.

[238] *Chapman's Homer*, p. 3.

[239] "Tears of Peace," in *Poems of Chapman*, p. 195.

[240] George Chapman, *The Conspiracy and Tragedy of Charles Duke of Byron*, ed. John Margeson, Manchester and New York, 1988, p. 2.

[241] Chambers, *Shakespeare*, vol. 2, pp. 213-4.

[242] See *Ben Jonson*, vol. 4, p. 193.

[243] Not so strange, says Kerrigan, *Sonnets*, pp. 12-15, citing Daniel's *Delia* of 1592, which includes fifty sonnets and a poem in rhyme royal, *The Complaint of Rosamond*.

[244] See John Kerrigan's survey of the evidence in his edition of *Sonnets*, pp. 389-90.

[245] Duncan-Jones, *Sonnets*, p. 92.

[246] Duncan-Jones in her edition of the *Sonnets* comments, pages 92-94, on the similarity of the young courtier of the "Complaint" to the Fair Youth.

[247] Shakespeare may have been somewhat effeminate in manner. Acheson in his study of the sonnets (*Shakespeare's Sonnet Story*, p. 574) says, "It has been argued that Shakespeare is caricatured in the character of Androgyne in [Jonson's] *Volpone*, but the reasons advanced are unconvincing, considering that it was presented in 1605 by Shakespeare's company." That Jonson described him as "gentle" Shakespeare may conceivably have some bearing on this point. As far as is known, Shakespeare the actor never played robust young men. Acheson's source may have been either Henry Brown, *The Sonnets of Shakespeare Solved*, London, 1876, p. 16; or Jacob Feis, *Shakespere and Montaigne*, London, 1884, p. 183. Feis deduces that Shakespeare was androgynous by pointing out that the poet had a wife but also "cultivated an intimate friendship" with William Herbert. Androgynous apparently meant bisexual, physically attracted to both sexes.

[248] *Shakespeare and Chapman*, London, 1917, pp. 7-95.

[249] Ibid., p. 95.

[250] Brian Vickers, an expert in Shakespeare attribution studies, proposed John Davies of Hereford, a minor but prolific poet, as the author of the "Complaint," first in an essay in *TLS*, 5 December 2003. Subsequently in *Shakespeare, A Lover's Complaint, and John Davies of Hereford* (Cambridge, 2007), Vickers devoted 300 pages to an examination of stylistic similarities. But Vickers' diligence could not conceal some basic flaws in his argument. First of all, the skeptical reader must wonder whether there might not be as many similarities between other poems of the period and "A Complaint." Vickers says virtually nothing, for instance, about the case that can be made for Chapman, and where Chapman is mentioned, it is the dramatic work that is referred to, not the poetry, where the language is most affected and recondite and most like "A Complaint." (Compare Robertson's analysis of Chapman's style, *Shakespeare and Chapman*, pp. 21-31.) Secondly, Vickers fails to explain how Davies could have composed, before the sonnets were published, a poem that interlocks with them at so many points. And, finally, why would Davies consent to having his work passed off as Shakespeare's?

[251] See Foster, *Elegy by W.S.*, pp. 226-231; and Duncan-Jones, *Sonnets*, 1997, pp. 36-41.

[252] Edmondson and Wells, *Shakespeare's Sonnets*, p. 10. See the discussion in *Sonnets*, ed. G. Blakemore Evans, pp. 280-282.

[253] See Donald W. Foster, "Master W. H., R.I.P." *PMLA*, vol. 102, 1987, pp. 43-4; and Cuming Walters, *The Mystery of Shakespeare's Sonnets*, New York, 1972 reprint, p. 43.

[254] Gerald Massey, *The Secret Drama of Shakspeare's Sonnets Unfolded with the Characters Identified*, 2d ed., London, 1872, pp. 421-3.

[255] Drake quoted in *Sonnets*, ed. Alden, p. 5.

[256] See J. A. Fort, "The Story Contained in the Second Series of Shakespeare's Sonnets,," *Review of English Studies*, vol. 3, 1927, pp. 406-14.

[257] Strong, *Henry, Prince of Wales*, pp. 11, 227.

[258] Thomas Birch, *The Life of Henry, Prince of Wales*, London, 1760, p. 348.

[259] Bernard Shaw, *Three Plays for Puritans*, Standard Edition, 1931, pp. xxix.

[260] "All too Short a Date: Internal Evidence in Shakespeare's Sonnets," *Essays in Criticism*, vol. 2 (1952), p. 316.

[261] *The Tragedie of Anthonie and Cleopatra*, ed. Horace Howard Furness (New Variorum Edition), Philadelphia, 1907, p. 382.

[262] Ibid., p. 383.

[263] See Kenneth Muir, *Shakespeare the Professional and Related Studies*, Totowa, NJ., 1973, pp. 210-211.

[264] Lukas Erne, *Shakespeare as Literary Dramatist*, Cambridge, 2003, p. 113.

[265] *Shakespeare's Plutarch*, ed. T.J.B. Spencer, Penguin Books, 1964, p. 297.

[266] Cornwallis, *The Short Life and Much Lamented Death of That Most Magnanimous Prince, Henry, Prince of Wales* (1644), quoted in Akrigg, *Jacobean Pageant*, p. 129.

[267] *Shakespeare's Plutarch*, p. 297.

[268] Ibid., pp. 297, 300.

[269] Robert Shephard, "Sexual Rumours in English Politics: The Cases of Elizabeth I and James I," in *Desire and Discipline*, eds. Murray and Eisenblicher, p. 109.

[270] Young, *King James and the History of Homosexuality*, pp. 81-2.

[271] *The Autobiography of Phineas Pett*, p. lxv; and Williamson, *The Myth of the Conqueror*, pp. 54-5.

[272] Cornwallis, *Henry-Frederic*, p.27.

[273] Francis Osborne, quoted in Stewart, *Cradle King*, p. 248.

[274] Akrigg, *Jacobean Pageant*, p. 134.

[275] Cornwallis, *Henry-Frederic*, pp. 25, 27, 38.

[276] *The Secret History of the Reign of King James I* in *The Autobiography and Correspondence of Sir Simonds D'Ewes, Bart.*, ed. J. O. Halliwell, 2 vols., London, 1845, vol. 1, p. 47.

[277] *Autobiography. . . . of Sir Simonds D'Ewes*, vol. 1, p. 46.

[278] Rowse, *Shakespeare's Southampton*, pp. 214-5.

[279] *Works of Cyril Tourneur*, ed. Allardyce Nicoll, New York, 1963, p. 271.

[280] Chambers, *Elizabethan Stage*, vol. 3, p. 250.

[281] *The Complete Works of John Webster*, ed. F.L. Lucas, London, 1927, vol. 3, p. 281.

[282] Chambers, *Shakespeare*, vol. 2, p. 249.

SHAKE-SPEARES

SONNETS.

Neuer before Imprinted.

AT LONDON
By *G. Eld* for *T. T.* and are
to be folde by *Iohn Wright*, dwelling
at Chrift Church gate.
1609,

TO.THE.ONLIE.BEGETTER.OF.
THESE.INSVING.SONNETS.
M^r.W.H. ALL.HAPPINESSE.
AND.THAT.ETERNITIE.
PROMISED.

BY.

OVR.EVER-LIVING.POET.

WISHETH.

THE.WELL-WISHING.
ADVENTVRER.IN.
SETTING.
FORTH.

T. T.

SHAKE-SPEARES,
SONNETS.

FRom faireſt creatures we deſire increaſe,
That thereby beauties *Roſe* might neuer die,
But as the riper ſhould by time deceaſe,
His tender heire might beare his memory:
But thou contracted to thine owne bright eyes,
Feed'ſt thy lights flame with ſelfe ſubſtantiall fewell,
Making a famine where aboundance lies,
Thy ſelfe thy foe,to thy ſweet ſelfe too cruell:
Thou that art now the worlds freſh ornament,
And only herauld to the gaudy ſpring,
Within thine owne bud burieſt thy content,
And tender chorle makſt waſt in niggarding:
    Pitty the world,or elſe this glutton be,
    To eate the worlds due,by the graue and thee.

2

VVHen fortie Winters ſhall beſeige thy brow,
And digge deep trenches in thy beauties field,
Thy youthes proud liuery ſo gaz'd on now,
Wil be a totter'd weed of ſmal worth held:
Then being askt,where all thy beautie lies,
Where all the treaſure of thy luſty daies;
To ſay within thine owne deepe ſunken eyes,
Were an all-eating ſhame,and thriftleſſe praiſe.
How much more praiſe deſeru'd thy beauties vſe,
If thou couldſt anſwere this faire child of mine
Shall ſum my count,and make my old excuſe
Proouing his beautie by ſucceſſion thine.

B   This

This were to be new made when thou art ould,
And see thy blood warme when thou feel'st it could,

3

LOoke in thy glasse and tell the face thou vewest,
Now is the time that face should forme an other,
Whose fresh repaire if now thou not renewest,
Thou doo'st beguile the world,vnblesse some mother.
For where is she so faire whose vn-eard wombe
Disdaines the tillage of thy husbandry?
Or who is he so fond will be the tombe,
Of his selfe loue to stop posterity?
Thou art thy mothers glasse and she in thee
Calls backe the louely Aprill of her prime,
So thou through windowes of thine age shalt see,
Dispight of wrinkles this thy goulden time.
    But if thou liue remembred not to be,
    Die single and thine Image dies with thee.

4

VNthrifty louelinesse why dost thou spend,
Vpon thy selfe thy beauties legacy?
Natures bequest giues nothing but doth lend,
And being franck she lends to those are free:
Then beautious nigard why doost thou abuse,
The bountious largesse giuen thee to giue?
Profitles vserer why doost thou vse
So great a summe of summes yet can'st not liue?
For hauing traffike with thy selfe alone,
Thou of thy selfe thy sweet selfe dost deceaue,
Then how when nature calls thee to be gone,
What acceptable *Audit* can'st thou leaue?
    Thy vnus'd beauty must be tomb'd with thee,
    Which vsed liues th'executor to be.

5

THose howers that with gentle worke did frame,
The louely gaze where euery eye doth dwell
Will play the tirants to the very same,

And that vnfaire which fairely doth excell:
For neuer resting time leads Summer on,
To hidious winter and confounds him there,
Sap checkt with frost and lustie leau's quite gon,
Beauty ore-snow'd and barenes euery where,
Then were not summers distillation left
A liquid prisoner pent in walls of glasse,
Beauties effect with beauty were bereft,
Nor it nor noe remembrance what it was.
  But flowers distil'd though they with winter meete,
  Leese but their show, their substance still liues sweet.

6

THen let not winters wragged hand deface,
  In thee thy summer ere thou be distil'd:
Make sweet some viall; treasure thou some place,
With beautits treasure ere it be selfe kil'd:
That vse is not forbidden vsery,
Which happies those that pay the willing lone;
That's for thy selfe to breed an other thee,
Or ten times happier be it ten for one,
Ten times thy selfe were happier then thou art,
If ten of thine ten times refigur'd thee,
Then what could death doe if thou should'st depart,
Leauing thee liuing in posterity?
  Be not selfe-wild for thou art much too faire,
  To be deaths conquest and make wormes thine heire.

7

LOe in the Orient when the gracious light,
  Lifts vp his burning head, each vnder eye
Doth homage to his new appearing sight,
Seruing with lookes his sacred maiesty,
And hauing climb'd the steepe vp heauenly hill,
Resembling strong youth in his middle age,
Yet mortall lookes adore his beauty still,
Attending on his goulden pilgrimage:
But when from high-most pich with wery car,

B 2   Like

Like feeble age he reeleth from the day,
The eyes(fore dutious)now conuerted are
From his low tract and looke an other way:
    So thou,thy selfe out-going in thy noon:
    Vnlok'd on dieſt vnleſſe thou get a ſonne.

8

MVſick to heare,why hear'ſt thou muſick ſadly,
   Sweets with ſweets warre not , ioy delights in ioy:
Why lou'ſt thou that which thou receauſt not gladly,
Or elſe receau'ſt with pleaſure thine annoy ?
If the true concord of well tuned ſounds,
By vnions married do offend thine eare,
They do but ſweetly chide thee , who confounds
In ſingleneſſe the parts that thou ſhould'ſt beare:
Marke how one ſtring ſweet husband to an other,
Strikes each in each by mutuall ordering;
Reſembling ſier,and child, and happy mother,
Who all in one,one pleaſing note do ſing:
    Whoſe ſpeechleſſe ſong being many,ſeeming one,
    Sings this to thee thou ſingle wilt proue none.

9.

IS it for feare to wet a widdowes eye,
   That thou conſum'ſt thy ſelfe in ſingle life?
Ah;if thou iſſuleſſe ſhalt hap to die,
The world will waile thee like a makeleſſe wife,
The world wilbe thy widdow and ſtill weepe,
That thou no forme of thee haſt left behind,
When euery priuat widdow well may keepe,
By childrens eyes,her husbands ſhape in minde:
Looke what an vnthrift in the world doth ſpend
Shifts but his place,for ſtill the world inioyes it,
But beauties waſte hath in the world an end,
And kept vnvſde the vſer ſo deſtroyes it:
    No loue toward others in that boſome ſits
    That on himſelfe ſuch murdrous ſhame commits.

10

FOr shame deny that thou bear'st loue to any
Who for thy selfe art so vnprouident
Graunt if thou wilt,thou art belou'd of many,
But that thou none lou'st is most euident:
For thou art so possest with murdrous hate,
That gainst thy selfe thou stickst not to conspire,
Seeking that beautious roose to ruinate
Which to repaire should be thy chiefe desire :
O change thy thought,that I may change my minde,
Shall hate be fairer log'd then gentle loue?
Be as thy presence is gracious and kind,
Or to thy selfe at least kind harted proue,
　　Make thee an other selfe for loue of me,
　　That beauty still may liue in thine or thee.

11

AS fast as thou shalt wane so fast thou grow'st,
In one of thine,from that which thou departest,
And that fresh bloud which yongly thou bestow'st,
Thou maist call thine,when thou from youth conuertest,
Herein liues wisdome,beauty,and increase,
Without this follie,age,and could decay,
If all were minded so,the times should cease,
And threescoore yeare would make the world away:
Let those whom nature hath not made for store,
Harsh,featurelesse,and rude , barrenly perrish,
Looke whom she best indow'd,she gaue the more;
Which bountious guift thou shouldst in bounty cherrish,
　　She caru'd thee for her seale,and ment therby,
　　Thou shouldst print more,not let that coppy die.

12

VVHen I doe count the clock that tels the time,
　　And see the braue day sunck in hidious night,
When I behold the violet past prime,
And sable curls or siluer'd ore with white :
When lofty trees I see barren of leaues,
Which erst from heat did canopie the herd

B 3　　　　　　　　　　　　　　　And

And Sommers greene all girded vp in sheaues
Borne on the beare with white and bristly beard:
Then of thy beauty do I question make
That thou among the wastes of time must goe,
Since sweets and beauties do them-selues forsake,
  And die as fast as they see others grow,
    And nothing gainst Times sieth can make defence
    Saue breed to braue him,when he takes thee hence.

13

O That you were your selfe,but loue you are
  No longer yours,then you your selfe here liue,
Against this cumming end you should prepare,
And your sweet semblance to some other giue.
So should that beauty which you hold in lease
Find no determination,then you were
You selfe again after your selfes decease,
When your sweet issue your sweet forme should beare.
Who lets so faire a house fall to decay,
Which husbandry in honour might vphold,
Against the stormy gusts of winters day
And barren rage of deaths eternall cold?
  O none but vnthrifts,deare my loue you know,
  You had a Father,let your Son say so.

14

NOt from the stars do I my iudgement plucke,
  And yet me thinkes I haue Astronomy,
But not to tell of good,or euil lucke,
Of plagues,of dearths,or seasons quallity,
Nor can I fortune to breefe mynuits tell;
Pointing to each his thunder,raine and winde,
Or say with Princes if it shal go wel
By oft predict that I in heauen finde,
But from thine eies my knowledge I deriue,
And constant stars in them I read such art
As truth and beautie shal together thriue
If from thy selfe,to store thou wouldst conuert:

Or else of thee this I prognosticate,
Thy end is Truthes and Beauties doome and date.

WHen I consider euery thing that growes
Holds in perfection but a little moment.
That this huge stage presenteth nought but showes
Whereon the Stars in secret influence comment.
When I perceiue that men as plants increase,
Cheared and checkt euen by the selfe-same skie:
Vaunt in their youthfull sap, at height decrease,
And were their braue state out of memory.
Then the conceit of this inconstant stay,
Sets you most rich in youth before my sight,
Where wastfull time debateth with decay
To change your day of youth to sullied night,
    And all in war with Time for loue of you
    As he takes from you, I ingraft you new.

BVt wherefore do not you a mightier waie
Make warre vppon this bloudie tirant time?
And fortifie your selfe in your decay
With meanes more blessed then my barren rime?
Now stand you on the top of happie houres,
And many maiden gardens yet vnset,
With vertuous wish would beare your liuing flowers,
Much liker then your painted counterfeit:
So should the lines of life that life repaire
Which this (Times pensel or my pupill pen)
Neither in inward worth nor outward faire
Can make you liue your selfe in eies of men,
    To giue away your selfe, keeps your selfe still,
    And you must liue drawne by your owne sweet skill,

VVHo will beleeue my verse in time to come
If it were fild with your most high deserts?
Though

Though yet heauen knowes it is but as a tombe
Which hides your life, and shewes not halfe your parts:
If I could write the beauty of your eyes,
And in fresh numbers number all your graces,
The age to come would say this Poet lies,
Such heauenly touches nere toucht earthly faces.
So should my papers (yellowed with their age)
Be scorn'd, like old men of lesse truth then tongue,
And your true rights be termd a Poets rage,
And stretched miter of an Antique song.
　　But were some childe of yours aliue that time,
　　You should liue twise in it, and in my rime.

SHall I compare thee to a Summers day?
Thou art more louely and more temperate:
Rough windes do shake the darling buds of Maie,
And Sommers lease hath all too short a date:
Sometime too hot the eye of heauen shines,
And often is his gold complexion dimm'd,
And euery faire from faire some-time declines,
By chance, or natures changing course vntrim'd:
But thy eternall Sommer shall not fade,
Nor loose possession of that faire thou ow'st,
Nor shall death brag thou wandr'st in his shade,
When in eternall lines to time thou grow'st,
　　So long as men can breath or eyes can see,
　　So long liues this, and this giues life to thee,

DEuouring time blunt thou the Lyons pawes,
And make the earth deuoure her owne sweet brood,
Plucke the keene teeth from the fierce Tygers yawes,
And burne the long liu'd Phœnix in her blood,
Make glad and sorry seasons as thou fleet'st,
And do what ere thou wilt swift-footed time
To the wide world and all her fading sweets:
But I forbid thee one most hainous crime,

O carue not with thy howers my loues faire brow,
Nor draw noe lines there with thine antique pen,
Him in thy course vntainted doe allow,
For beauties patterne to succeding men.
  Yet doe thy worst ould Time dispight thy wrong,
  My loue shall in my verse euer liue young.

20

A Womans face with natures owne hand painted,
  Haste thou the Master Mistris of my passion,
A womans gentle hart but not acquainted
With shifting change as is false womens fashion,
An eye more bright then theirs, lesse false in rowling:
Gilding the obiect where-vpon it gazeth,
A man in hew all *Hews* in his controwling,
Which steales mens eyes and womens soules amaseth,
And for a woman wert thou first created,
Till nature as she wrought thee fell a dotinge,
And by addition me of thee defeated,
By adding one thing to my purpose nothing.
  But since she prickt thee out for womens pleasure,
  Mine be thy loue and thy loues vse their treasure.

21

SO is it not with me as with that Muse,
  Stird by a painted beauty to his verse,
Who heauen it selfe for ornament doth vse,
And euery faire with his faire doth reherse,
Making a coopelment of proud compare
With Sunne and Moone, with earth and seas rich gems:
With Aprills first borne flowers and all things rare,
That heauens ayre in this huge rondure hems,
O let me true in loue but truly write,
And then beleeue me, my loue is as faire,
As any mothers childe, though not so bright
As those gould candells fixt in heauens ayer:
  Let them say more that like of heare-say well,
  I will not prayse that purpose not to sell.

C   22

22

MY glaſſe ſhall not perſwade me I am ould,
So long as youth and thou are of one date,
But when in thee times ſorrwes I behould,
Then look I death my daies ſhould expiate.
For all that beauty that doth couer thee,
Is but the ſeemely rayment of my heart,
Which in thy breſt doth liue, as thine in me,
How can I then be elder then thou art?
O therefore loue be of thy ſelfe ſo wary,
As I not for my ſelfe, but for thee will,
Bearing thy heart which I will keepe ſo chary
As tender nurſe her babe from faring ill,
    Preſume not on thy heart when mine is ſlaine,
    Thou gau'ſt me thine not to giue backe againe.

23

AS an vnperfect actor on the ſtage,
Who with his feare is put beſides his part,
Or ſome fierce thing repleat with too much rage,
Whoſe ſtrengths abondance weakens his owne heart;
So I for feare of truſt, forget to ſay,
The perfect ceremony of loues right,
And in mine owne loues ſtrength ſeeme to decay,
Ore-charg'd with burthen of mine owne loues might:
O let my books be then the eloquence,
And domb preſagers of my ſpeaking breſt,
Who pleade for loue, and look for recompence,
More then that tonge that more hath more expreſt.
    O learne to read what ſilent loue hath writ,
    To heare wit eies belongs to loues fine wiht.

24

MIne eye hath play'd the painter and hath ſteeld,
Thy beauties forme in table of my heart,
My body is the frame wherein ti's held,
And perſpectiue it is beſt Painters art.
For through the Painter muſt you ſee his skill,

To finde where your true Image pictur'd lies,
Which in my bosomes shop is hanging stil,
That hath his windowes glazed with thine eyes:
Now see what good-turnes eyes for eies haue done,
Mine eyes haue drawne thy shape,and thine for me
Are windowes to my brest, where-through the Sun
Delights to peepe,to gaze therein on thee
   Yet eyes this cunning want to grace their art
   They draw but what they see,know not the hart.

25

Et those who are in fauor with their stars,
Of publike honour and proud titles bost,
Whilst I whome fortune of such tryumph bars
Vnlookt for ioy in that I honour most;
Great Princes fauorites their faire leaues spread,
But as the Marygold at the suns eye,
And in them-selues their pride lies buried,
For at a frowne they in their glory die.
The painefull warrier famosed for worth,
After a thousand victories once foild,
Is from the booke of honour rased quite,
And all the rest forgot for which he toild:
   Then happy I that loue and am beloued
   Where I may not remoue,nor be remoued.

26

Ord of my loue,to whome in vassalage
Thy merrit hath my dutie strongly knit;
To thee I send this written ambassage
To witnesse duty, not to shew my wit.
Duty so great,which wit so poore as mine
May make seeme bare,in wanting words to shew it;
But that I hope some good conceipt of thine
In thy soules thought(all naked) will bestow it:
Til whatsoeuer star that guides my mouing,
Points on me gratiously with faire aspect,
And puts apparrell on my tottered louing,

To show me worthy of their sweet respect,
Then may I dare to boast how I doe loue thee,
Til then,not show my head where thou maist proue me.

27

WEary with toyle,I hast me to my bed,
   The deare repose for lims with trauaill tired,
But then begins a iourny in my head
To worke my mind,when boddies work's expired.
For then my thoughts(from far where I abide)
Intend a zelous pilgrimage to thee,
And keepe my drooping eye-lids open wide,
Looking on darknes which the blind doe see.
Saue that my soules imaginary sight
Presents their shaddoe to my sightles view,
Which like a iewell(hunge in gastly night)
Makes blacke night beautious,and her old face new.
   Loe thus by day my lims,by night my mind,
   For thee,and for my selfe,noe quiet finde.

28

HOw can I then returne in happy plight
   That am debard the benifit of rest?
When daies oppression is not eazd by night,
But day by night and night by day oprest.
And each(though enimes to ethers raigne)
Doe in consent shake hands to torture me,
The one by toyle,the other to complaine
How far I toyle,still farther off from thee.
I tell the Day to please him thou art bright,
And do'st him grace when clouds doe blot the heauen:
So flatter I the swart complexiond night,
When sparkling stars twire not thou guil'st th' eauen.
   But day doth daily draw my sorrowes longer,(stronger
   And night doth nightly make greefes length seeme

29

VVHen in disgrace with Fortune and mens eyes,
   I all alone beweepe my out-cast state,

And

And trouble deafe heauen with my bootleſſe cries,
And looke vpon my ſelfe and curſe my fate.
Wiſhing me like to one more rich in hope,
Featur'd like him, like him with friends poſſeſt,
Deſiring this mans art, and that mans skope,
With what I moſt inioy contented leaſt,
Yet in theſe thoughts my ſelfe almoſt deſpiſing,
Haplye I thinke on thee, and then my ſtate,
(Like to the Larke at breake of daye ariſing)
From ſullen earth ſings himns at Heauens gate,
 For thy ſweet loue remembred ſuch welth brings,
 That then I skorne to change my ſtate with Kings.

30

VVHen to the Seſſions of ſweet ſilent thought,
 I ſommon vp remembrance of things paſt,
I ſigh the lacke of many a thing I ſought,
And with old woes new waile my deare times waſte:
Then can I drowne an eye (vn-vſ'd to flow)
For precious friends hid in deaths dateles night,
And weepe a freſh loues long ſince canceld woe,
And mone th'expence of many a vanniſht ſight.
Then can I greeue at greeuances fore-gon,
And heauily from woe to woe tell ore
The ſad account of fore-bemoned mone,
Which I new pay as if not payd before.
 But if the while I thinke on thee (deare friend)
 All loſſes are reſtord, and ſorrowes end.

31

Thy boſome is indeared with all hearts,
 Which I by lacking haue ſuppoſed dead,
And there raignes Loue and all Loues louing parts,
And all thoſe friends which I thought buried.
How many a holy and obſequious teare
Hath deare religious loue ſtolne from mine eye,
As intereſt of the dead, which now appeare,
But things remou'd that hidden in there lie.

    To

Thou art the graue where buried loue doth liue,
Hung with the tropheis of my louers gon,
Who all their parts of me to thee did giue,
That due of many, now is thine alone.
  Their images I lou'd, I view in thee,
  And thou (all they) haſt all the all of me.

32

IF thou ſuruiue my well contented daie,
When that churle death my bones with duſt ſhall couer
And ſhalt by fortune once more re-ſuruay:
Theſe poore rude lines of thy deceaſed Louer:
Compare them with the bett'ring of the time,
And though they be out-ſtript by euery pen,
Reſerue them for my loue, not for their rime,
Exceeded by the hight of happier men.
Oh then voutſafe me but this louing thought,
Had my friends Muſe growne with this growing age,
A dearer birth then this his loue had brought:
To march in ranckes of better equipage:
  But ſince he died and Poets better proue,
  Theirs for their ſtile ile read, his for his loue.

33

FVll many a glorious morning haue I ſeene,
Flatter the mountaine tops with ſoueraine eie,
Kiſſing with golden face the meddowes greene;
Guilding pale ſtreames with heauenly alcumy:
Anon permit the baſeſt cloudes to ride,
With ougly rack on his celeſtiall face,
And from the forlorne world his viſage hide
Stealing vnſeene to weſt with this diſgrace:
Euen ſo my Sunne one early morne did ſhine,
With all triumphant ſplendor on my brow,
But out alack, he was but one houre mine,
The region cloude hath mask'd him from me now.
  Yet him for this, my loue no whit diſdaineth,
  Suns of the world may ſtaine, whē heauens ſun ſtainteh.

34

WHy didſt thou promiſe ſuch a beautious day,
   And make me trauaile forth without my cloake,
To let bace cloudes ore-take me in my way,
Hiding thy brau'ry in their rotten ſmoke.
Tis not enough that through the cloude thou breake,
To dry the raine on my ſtorme-beaten face,
For no man well of ſuch a ſa'ue can ſpeake,
That heales the wound, and cures not the diſgrace:
Nor can thy ſhame giue phiſicke to my griefe,
Though thou repent, yet I haue ſtill the loſſe,
Th'offenders ſorrow lends but weake reliefe
To him that beares the ſtrong offenſes loſſe.
   Ah but thoſe teares are pearle which thy loue ſheeds,
   And they are ritch, and ranſome all ill deeds.

35

NO more bee greeu'd at that which thou haſt done,
   Roſes haue thornes; and ſiluer fountaines mud,
Cloudes and eclipſes ſtaine both Moone and Sunne,
And loathſome canker liues in ſweeteſt bud.
All men make faults, and euen I in this,
Authorizing thy treſpas with compare,
My ſelfe corrupting ſaluing thy amiſſe,
Excuſing their ſins more then their ſins are:
For to thy ſenſuall fault I bring in ſence,
Thy aduerſe party is thy Aduocate,
And gainſt my ſelfe a lawfull plea commence,
Such ciuill war is in my loue and hate,
   That I an acceſſary needs muſt be,
   To that ſweet theefe which ſourely robs from me,

36

LEt me confeſſe that we two muſt be twaine,
   Although our vndeuided loues are one:
So ſhall thoſe blots that do with me remaine,
Without thy helpe, by me be borne alone.
In our two loues there is but one reſpect,

                   Though

Though in our liues a seperable spight,
Which though it alter not loues sole effect,
Yet doth it steale sweet houres from loues delight,
I may not euer-more acknowledge thee,
Least my bewailed guilt should do thee shame,
Nor thou with publike kindnesse honour me,
Vnlesse thou take that honour from thy name:
    But doe not so, I loue thee in such sort,
    As thou being mine, mine is thy good report.

37

AS a decrepit father takes delight,
    To see his actiue childe do deeds of youth,
So I, made lame by Fortunes dearest spight
Take all my comfort of thy worth and truth.
For whether beauty, birth, or wealth, or wit,
Or any of these all, or all, or more
Intitled in their parts, do crowned sit,
I make my loue ingrafted to this store:
So then I am not lame, poore, nor dispis'd,
Whilst that this shadow doth such substance giue,
That I in thy abundance am suffic'd,
And by a part of all thy glory liue:
    Looke what is best, that best I wish in thee,
    This wish I haue, then ten times happy me.

38

HOw can my Muse want subiect to inuent
    While thou dost breath that poor'st into my verse,
Thine owne sweet argument, to excellent,
For euery vulgar paper to rehearse:
Oh giue thy selfe the thankes if ought in me,
Worthy perusal stand against thy sight,
For who's so dumbe that cannot write to thee,
When thou thy selfe dost giue inuention light?
Be thou the tenth Muse, ten times more in worth
Then those old nine which rimers inuocate,
And he that calls on thee, let him bring forth

                                        Eternall

Eternal numbers to out-liue long date.
  If my flight Mufe doe pleafe thefe curious daies,
  The paine be mine,but thine fhal be the praife.

39

OH how thy worth with manners may I finge,
  When thou art all the better part of me?
What can mine owne praife to mine owne felfe bring:
And what is't but mine owne when I praife thee,
Euen for this,let vs deuided liue,
And our deare loue loofe name of fingle one,
That by this feperation I may giue:
That due to thee which thou deferu'ft alone:
Oh abfence what a torment wouldft thou proue,
Were it not thy foure leifure gaue fweet leaue,
To entertaine the time with thoughts of loue,
VVhich time and thoughts fo fweetly doft deceiue.
  And that thou teacheft how to make one twaine,
  By praifing him here who doth hence remaine.

40

TAke all my loues,my loue,yea take them all,
  What haft thou then more then thou hadft before?
No loue,my loue,that thou maift true loue call,
All mine was thine,before thou hadft this more:
Then iffor my loue,thou my loue recciueft,
I cannot blame thee,for my loue thou vfeft,
But yet be blam'd,if thou this felfe deceaueft
By wilfull tafte of what thy felfe refufeft.
I doe forgiue thy robb'rie gentle theefe
Although thou fteale thee all my pouerty:
And yet loue knowes it is a greater griefe
To beare loues wrong,then hates knowne iniury.
  Lafciuious grace,in whom all il wel fhowes,
  Kill me with fpights yet we muft not be foes.

41

THofe pretty wrongs that liberty commits,
  When I am fome-time abfent from thy heart,

D   Thy.

Thy beautie,and thy yeares full well befits,
For still temptation followes where thou art.
Gentle thou art,and therefore to be wonne,
Beautious thou art,therefore to be assailed.
And when a woman woes,what womans sonne,
Will sourely leaue her till he haue preuailed.
Aye me,but yet thou mighst my seate forbeare,
And chide thy beauty,and thy straying youth,
Who lead thee in their ryot euen there
Where thou art forst to breake a two-fold truth:
　　Hers by thy beauty tempting her to thee,
　　Thine by thy beautie beeing false to me.

42

THat thou hast her it is not all my griefe,
　　And yet it may be said I lou'd her deerely,
That she hath thee is of my wayling cheefe,
A losse in loue that touches me more neerely.
Louing offendors thus I will excuse yee,
Thou doost loue her,because thou knowst I loue her,
And for my sake euen so doth she abuse me,
Suffring my friend for my sake to approoue her,
If I loose thee,my losse is my loues gaine,
And loosing her,my friend hath found that losse,
Both finde each other,and I loose both twaine,
And both for my sake lay on me this crosse,
　　But here's the ioy,my friend and I are one,
　　Sweete flattery,then she loues but me alone.

43

WHen most I winke then doe mine eyes best see,
　　For all the day they view things vnrespected,
But when I sleepe,in dreames they looke on thee,
And darkely bright,are bright in darke directed.
Then thou whose shaddow shaddowes doth make bright,
How would thy shadowes forme,forme happy show,
To the cleere day with thy much cleerer light,
When to vn-seeing eyes thy shade shines so?

How

How would (I say)mine eyes be bleſſed made,
By looking on thee in the liuing day?
When in dead night their faire imperfect ſhade,
Through heauy ſleepe on ſightleſſe eyes doth ſtay?
   All dayes are nights to ſee till I ſee thee,
   And nights bright daies when dreams do ſhew thee me,

44

IF the dull ſubſtance of my fleſh were thought,
Iniurious diſtance ſhould not ſtop my way,
For then diſpight of ſpace I would be brought,
From limits farre remote,where thou dóoſt ſtay,
No matter then although my foote did ſtand
Vpon the fartheſt earth remoou'd from thee,
For nimble thought can iumpe both ſea and land,
As ſoone as thinke the place where he would be.
But ah,thought kills me that I am not thought
To leape large lengths of miles when thou art gone,
But that ſo much of earth and water wrought,
I muſt attend,times leaſure with my mone.
   Receiuing naughts by elements ſo ſloe,
   But heauie teares,badges of eithers woe.

45

THe other two,ſlight ayre,and purging fire,
Are both with thee,where euer I abide,
The firſt my thought,the other my deſire,
Theſe preſent abſent with ſwift motion ſlide.
For when theſe quicker Elements are gone
In tender Embaſſie of loue to thee,
My life being made of foure,with two alone,
Sinkes downe to death,oppreſt with melancholie.
Vntill liues compoſition be recured,
By thoſe ſwift meſſengers return'd from thee,
Who euen but now come back againe aſſured,
Of their faire health,recounting it to me.
   This told,I ioy,but then no longer glad,
   I ſend them back againe and ſtraight grow ſad.

        Mine

46

MIne eye and heart are at a mortall warre,
How to deuide the conqueſt of thy ſight,
Mine eye,my heart their pictures ſight would barre,
My heart,mine eye the freeedome of that right,
My heart doth plead that thou in him dooſt lye,
(A cloſet neuer pearſt with chriſtall eyes)
But the defendant doth that plea deny,
And ſayes in him their faire appearance lyes.
To ſide this title is impannelled
A queſt of thoughts,all tennants to the heart,
And by their verdict is determined
The cleere eyes moyitie,and the deare hearts part.
  As thus,mine eyes due is their outward part,
  And my hearts right,their inward loue of heart.

47

BEtwixt mine eye and heart a league is tooke,
And each doth good turnes now vnto the other,
When that mine eye is famiſht for a looke,
Or heart in loue with ſighes himſelfe doth ſmother;
With my loues picture then my eye doth feaſt,
And to the painted banquet bids my heart:
An other time mine eye is my hearts gueſt,
And in his thoughts of loue doth ſhare a part.
So either by thy picture or my loue,
Thy ſeiſe away,are preſent ſtill with me,
For thou nor farther then my thoughts canſt moue,
And I am ſtill with them,and they with thee.
  Or if they ſleepe, thy picture in my ſight
  Awakes my heart,to hearts and eyes delight.

48

HOw carefull was I when I tooke my way,
Each trifle vnder trueſt barres to thruſt,
That to my vſe it might vn-vſed ſtay
From hands of falſehood,in ſure wards of truſt?
But thou,to whom my iewels trifles are,

Moſt

Moſt worthy comfort,now my greateſt griefe,
Thou beſt of deereſt,and mine onely care,
Art left the prey of euery vulgar theefe.
Thee haue I not lockt vp in any cheſt,
Saue where thou art not,though I feele thou art,
Within the gentle cloſure of my breſt,
From whence at pleaſure thou maiſt come and part,
   And euen thence thou wilt be ſtolne I feare,
   For truth prooues theeuiſh for a prize ſo deare.

49

AGainſt that time (if euer that time come)
   When I ſhall ſee thee frowne on my defeĉts,
When as thy loue hath caſt his vtmoſt ſumme,
Cauld to that audite by aduiſ'd reſpeĉts,
Againſt that time when thou ſhalt ſtrangely paſſe,
And ſcarcely greete me with that ſunne thine eye,
When loue conuerted from the thing it was
Shall reaſons finde of ſetled grauitie.
Againſt that time do I inſconce me here
Within the knowledge of mine owne deſart,
And this my hand,againſt my ſelfe vpreare,
To guard the lawfull reaſons on thy part,
   To leaue poore me,thou haſt the ſtrength of lawes,
   Since why to loue,I can alledge no cauſe.

50

HOw heauie doe I iourney on the way,
   When what I ſeeke (my wearie trauels end)
Doth teach that eaſe and that repoſe to ſay
Thus farre the miles are meaſurde from thy friend.
The beaſt that beares me,tired with my woe,
Plods duly on,to beare that waight in me,
As if by ſome inſtinĉt the wretch did know
His rider lou'd not ſpeed being made from thee:
The bloody ſpurre cannot prouoke him on,
That ſome-times anger thruſts into his hide,
Which heauily he anſwers with a grone,

More

More sharpe to me then spurring to his side,
For that same grone doth put this in my mind,
My greefe lies onward and my ioy behind.

51

THus can my loue excuse the slow offence,
Of my dull bearer,when from thee I speed,
From where thou art,why shoulld I hast me thence,
Till I returne of posting is noe need.
O what excuse will my poore beast then find,
When swift extremity can seeme but slow,
Then should I spurre though mounted on the wind,
In winged speed no motion shall I know,
Then can no horse with my desire keepe pace,
Therefore desire(of perfects loue being made)
Shall naigh noe dull flesh in his fiery race,
But loue,for loue,thus shall excuse my iade,
  Since from thee going,he went wilfull slow,
  Towards thee ile run,and giue him leaue to goe.

52

SO am I as the rich whose blessed key,
Can bring him to his sweet vp-locked treasure,
The which he will not eu'ry hower suruay,
For blunting the fine point of seldome pleasure.
Therefore are feasts so sollemne and so rare,
Since sildom comming in the long yeare set,
Like stones of worth they thinly placed are,
Or captaine Iewells in the carconet.
So is the time that keepes you as my chest,
Or as the ward-robe which the robe doth hide,
To make some speciall instant speciall blest,
By new vnfoulding his imprison'd pride.
  Blessed are you whose worthinesse giues skope,
  Being had to tryumph,being lackt to hope.

53

VVHat is your substance,whereof are you made,
That millions of strange shaddowes on you tend?
                                        Since

Since euery one, hath euery one, one shade,
And you but one, can euery shaddow lend:
Describe *Adonis* and the counterfet,
Is poorely immitated after you,
On *Hellens* cheeke all art of beautie set,
And you in *Grecian* tires are painted new:
Speake of the spring, and foyzon of the yeare,
The one doth shaddow of your beautie show,
The other as your bountie doth appeare,
And you in euery blessed shape we know.
  In all externall grace you haue some part,
  But you like none, none you for constant heart.

54

OH how much more doth beautie beautious seeme,
  By that sweet ornament which truth doth giue,
The Rose lookes faire, but fairer we it deeme
For that sweet odor, which doth in it liue:
The Canker bloomes haue full as deepe a die,
As the perfumed tincture of the Roses,
Hang on such thornes, and play as wantonly,
When sommers breath their masked buds disclofes:
But for their virtue only is their show,
They liue vnwoo'd, and vnrefpected fade,
Die to themselues . Sweet Roses doe not so,
Of their sweet deathes, are sweetest odors made:
  And so of you, beautious and louely youth,
  When that shall vade, by verse distils your truth.

55

NOt marble, nor the guilded monument,
  Of Princes shall out-liue this powrefull rime,
But you shall shine more bright in these contents
Then vnswept stone, besmeer'd with sluttish time.
When wastefull warre shall *Statues* ouer-turne,
And broiles roote out the worke of masonry,
Nor *Mars* his sword, nor warres quick fire shall burne
The liuing record of your memory.

                              Gainst

Gainſt death,and all obliuious emnity
Shall you pace forth, your praiſe ſhall ſtil finde roome,
Euen in the eyes of all poſterity
That weare this world out to the ending doome.
  So til the iudgement that your ſelfe ariſe,
  You liue in this,and dwell in louers eies.

56

Sweet loue renew thy force , be it not ſaid
Thy edge ſhould blunter be then apetite,
Which,but too daie by feeding is alaied,
To morrow ſharpned in his former might.
So loue be thou,although too daie thou fill
Thy hungrie eies,euen till they winck with fulneſſe,
Too morrow ſee againe,and doe not kill
The ſpirit of Loue,with a perpetual dulneſſe:
Let this ſad *Intrim* like the Ocean be
Which parts the ſhore,where two contracted new,
Come daily to the banckes,that when they ſee,
Returne of loue,more bleſt may be the view.
  As cal it Winter,which being ful of care,
  Makes Sōmers welcome,thrice more wiſh'd,more rare.

57

BEing your ſlaue what ſhould I doe but tend,
Vpon the houres,and times of your deſire?
I haue no precious time at al to ſpend;
Nor ſeruices to doe til you require.
Nor dare I chide the world without end houre,
Whilſt I(my ſoueraine)watch the clock for you,
Nor thinke the bitterneſſe of abſence ſowre,
VVhen you haue bid your ſeruant once adieue.
Nor dare I queſtion with my iealious thought,
VVhere you may be,or your affaires ſuppoſe,
But like a ſad ſlaue ſtay and thinke of nought
Saue where you are , how happy you make thoſe.
  So true a foole is loue,that in your Will,
  (Though you doe any thing)he thinkes no ill.

58

THat God forbid, that made me firſt your ſlaue,
  I ſhould in thought controule your times of pleaſure,
Or at your hand th' account of houres to craue,
Being your vaſſail bound to ſtaie your leiſure.
Oh let me ſuffer(being at your beck)
Th' impriſon'd abſence of your libertie,
And patience tame, to ſufferance bide each check,
Without accuſing you of iniury.
Be where you liſt, your charter is ſo ſtrong,
That you your ſelfe may priuiledge your time
To what you will, to you it doth belong,
Your ſelfe to pardon of ſelfe-doing crime.
  I am to waite, though waiting ſo be hell,
  Not blame your pleaſure be it ill or well.

59

IF their bee nothing new, but that which is,
  Hath beene before, how are our braines beguild,
Which laboring for inuention beare amiſſe
The ſecond burthen of a former child ?
Oh that record could with a back-ward looke,
Euen of fiue hundreth courſes of the Sunne,
Show me your image in ſome antique booke,
Since minde at firſt in carrecter was done.
That I might ſee what the old world could ſay,
To this compoſed wonder of your frame,
Whether we are mended, or where better they,
Or whether reuolution be the ſame.
  Oh ſure I am the wits of former daies,
  To ſubiects worſe haue giuen admiring praiſe.

60

LIke as the waues make towards the pibled ſhore,
  So do our minuites haſten to their end,
Each changing place with that which goes before,
In ſequent toile all forwards do contend.
Natiuity once in the maine of light.

E   Crawle

Crawles to maturity, wherewith being crown'd,
Crooked eclipfes gainft his glory fight,
And time that gaue, doth now his gift confound.
Time doth transfixe the florifh fet on youth,
And delues the paralels in beauties brow,
Feedes on the rarities of natures truth,
And nothing ftands but for his fieth to mow.
　　And yet to times in hope, my verfe fhall ftand
　　Praifing thy worth, difpight his cruell hand.

61

I S it thy wil, thy Image fhould keepe open
　My heauy eie-ids to the weary night?
Doft thou defire my flumbers fhould be broken,
While fhadowes like to thee do mocke my fight?
Is it thy fpirit that thou fend'ft from thee
So farre from home into my deeds to prye,
To find out fhames and idle houres in me,
The skope and tenure of thy Ieloufie?
O no, thy loue though much, is not fo great,
It is my loue that keepes mine eie awake,
Mine owne true loue that doth my reft defeat,
To plaie the watch-man euer for thy fake.
　　For thee watch I, whilft thou doft wake elfewhere,
　　From me farre of, with others all to neere.

62

S Inne of felfe-loue poffeffeth al mine eie,
　And all my foule, and al my euery part;
And for this finne there is no remedie,
It is fo grounded inward in my heart.
Me thinkes no face fo gratious is as mine,
No fhape fo true, no truth of fuch account,
And for my felfe mine owne worth do define,
As I all other in all worths furmount.
But when my glaffe fhewes me my felfe indeed
Beated and chopt with tand antiquitie,
Mine owne felfe loue quite contrary I read

Selfe

Selfe,ſo ſelfe louing were iniquity,
  T'is thee(my ſelfe)that for my ſelfe I praiſe,
  Painting my age with beauty of thy daies,

63

AGainſt my loue ſhall be as I am now
  With times iniurious hand chruſht and ore-worne,
When houres haue dreind his blood and fild his brow
With lines and wrincles,when his youthfull morne
Hath trauaild on to Ages ſteepie night,
And all thoſe beauties whereof now he's King
Are vaniſhing,or vaniſht out of ſight,
Stealing away the treaſure of his Spring.
For ſuch a time do I now fortifie
Againſt confounding Ages cruell knife,
That he ſhall neuer cut from memory
My ſweet loues beauty,though my louers life.
  His beautie ſhall in theſe blacke lines be ſeene,
  And they ſhall liue, and he in them ſtill greene.

64

VVHen I haue ſeene by times fell hand defaced
  The rich proud coſt of outworne buried age,
When ſometime loftie towers I ſee downe raſed,
And braſſe eternall ſlaue to mortall rage.
When I haue ſeene the hungry Ocean gaine
Aduantage on the Kingdome of the ſhoare,
And the firme ſoile win of the watry maine,
Increaſing ſtore with loſſe,and loſſe with ſtore.
When I haue ſeene ſuch interchange of ſtate,
Or ſtate it ſelfe confounded, to decay,
Ruine hath taught me thus to ruminate
That Time will come and take my loue away.
  This thought is as a death which cannot chooſe
  But weepe to haue,that which it feares to looſe,

65

SInce braſſe,nor ſtone,nor earth,nor boundleſſe ſea,
  But ſad mortallity ore-ſwaies their power,

How

How with this rage shall beautie hold a plea,
Whose action is no stronger then a flower?
O how shall summers hunny breath hold out,
Against the wrackfull siedge of battring dayes,
When rocks impregnable are not so stoute,
Nor gates of steele so strong but time decayes?
O fearefull meditation, where alack,
Shall times best Iewell from times chest lie hid?
Or what strong hand can hold his swift foote back,
Or who his spoile or beautie can forbid?
   O none, vnlesse this miracle haue might,
   That in black inck my loue may still shine bright.

66

TYr'd with all these for restfull death I cry,
As to behold desert a begger borne,
And needie Nothing trimd in iollitie,
And purest faith vnhappily forsworne,
And gilded honor shamefully misplast,
And maiden vertue rudely strumpeted,
And right perfection wrongfully disgrac'd,
And strength by limping sway disabled,
And arte made tung-tide by authoritie,
And Folly (Doctor-like) controuling skill,
And simple-Truth miscalde Simplicitie,
And captiue-good attending Captaine ill.
   Tyr'd with all these, from these would I be gone,
   Saue that to dye, I leaue my loue alone.

67

AH wherefore with infection should he liue,
And with his presence grace impietie,
That sinne by him aduantage should atchiue,
And lace it selfe with his societie?
Why should false painting immitate his cheeke,
And steale dead seeing of his liuing hew?
Why should poore beautie indirectly seeke,
Roses of shaddow, since his Rose is true?

Why

Why should he liue,now nature banckrout is,
Beggerd of blood to blush through liuely vaines,
For she hath no exchecker now but his,
And proud of many,liues vpon his gaines?
   O him she stores,to show what welth she had,
   In daies long since,before these last so bad.

68

THus is his cheeke the map of daies out-worne,
  When beauty liu'd and dy'ed as flowers do now,
Before these bastard signes of faire were borne,
Or durst inhabit on a liuing brow:
Before the goulden tresses of the dead,
The right of sepulchers,were shorne away,
To liue a scond life on second head,
Ere beauties dead fleece made another gay:
In him those holy antique howers are seene,
Without all ornament,it selfe and true,
Making no summer of an others greene,
Robbing no ould to dresse his beauty new,
   And him as for a map doth Nature store,
   To shew faulse Art what beauty was of yore.

69

THose parts of thee that the worlds eye doth view,
  Want nothing that the thought of hearts can mende
All toungs(the voice of soules)giue thee that end,
Vttring bare truth,euen so as foes Commend.
Their outward thus with outward praise is crownd,
But those same toungs that giue thee so thine owne,
In other accents doe this praise confound
By seeing farther then the eye hath showne.
They looke into the beauty of thy mind,
And that in guesse they measure by thy deeds,
Then churls their thoughts(although their eies were kind)
To thy faire flower ad the rancke smell of weeds,
   But why thy odor matcheth not thy show,
   The solye is this,that thou doest common grow.

          Thas

70

THat thou are blam'd shall not be thy defect,
For slanders marke was euer yet the faire,
The ornament of beauty is suspect,
A Crow that flies in heauens sweeteft ayre.
So thou be good, slander doth but approue,
Their worth the greater beeing woo'd of time,
For Canker vice the sweetest buds doth loue,
And thou present'st a pure vnstayined prime.
Thou haft paft by the ambush of young daies,
Either not assayld, or victor beeing charg'd,
Yet this thy praise cannot be soe thy praise,
To tye vp enuy, euermore inlarged,
    If some suspect of ill maskt not thy show,
    Then thou alone kingdomes of hearts shouldst owe.

71

NOe Longer mourne for me when I am dead,
Then you shall heare the surly sullen bell
Giue warning to the world that I am fled
From this vile world with vildest wormes to dwell:
Nay if you read this line, remember not,
The hand that writ it, for I loue you so,
That I in your sweet thoughts would be forgot,
If thinking on me then should make you woe.
O if (I say) you looke vpon this verse,
When I (perhaps) compounded am with clay,
Do not so much as my poore name reherse;
But let your loue euen with my life decay.
    Leaft the wise world should looke into your mone,
    And mocke you with me after I am gon.

72

O Leaft the world should taske you to recite,
What merit liu'd in me that you should loue
After my death (deare loue) for get me quite,
For you in me can nothing worthy proue.
Vnlesse you would deuise some vertuous lye,

To doe more for me then mine owne defert,
And hang more praife vpon deceafed I,
Then nigard truth would willingly impart:
O leaft your true loue may feeme falce in this,
That you for loue fpeake well of me vntrue,
My name be buried where my body is,
And liue no more to fhame nor me,nor you.
  For I am fham'd by that which I bring forth,
  And fo fhould you,to loue things nothing worth.

73

THat time of yeeare thou maift in me behold,
  When yellow leaues,or none,or few doe hange
Vpon thofe boughes which fhake againft the could,
Bare rn'wd quiers,where late the fweet birds fang.
In me thou feeft the twi-light of fuch day,
As after Sun-fet fadeth in the Weft,
Which by and by blacke night doth take away,
Deaths fecond felfe that feals vp all in reft.
In me thou feeft the glowing of fuch fire,
That on the afhes of his youth doth lye,
As the death bed,whereon it muft expire,
Confum'd with that which it was nurrifht by.
  This thou perceu'ft,which makes thy loue more ftrong,
  To loue that well,which thou muft leaue ere long.

74

BVt be contented when that fell areft,
  With out all bayle fhall carry me away,
My life hath in this line fome intereft,
Which for memoriall ftill with thee fhall ftay.
When thou reueweft this,thou doeft reuew,
The very part was confecrate to thee,
The earth can haue but earth,which is his due,
My fpirit is thine the better part of me,
So then thou haft but loft the dregs of life,
The pray of wormes,my body being dead,
The coward conqueft of a wretches knife,

To base of thee to be remembred,
  The worth of that,is that which it containes,
  And that is this, and this with thee remaines.

75

SO are you to my thoughts as food to life,
  Or as sweet seaſon'd ſhewers are to the ground;
And for the peace of you I hold ſuch ſtrife,
As twixt a miſer and his wealth is found,
Now proud as an inioyer,and anon
Doubting the filching age will ſteale his treaſure,
Now counting beſt to be with you alone,
Then betterd that the world may ſee my pleaſure,
Some-time all ful with feaſting on your ſight,
And by and by cleane ſtarued for a looke,
Poſſeſſing or purſuing no delight
Saue what is had,or muſt from you be tooke.
  Thus do I pine and ſurfet day by day,
  Or gluttoning on all,or all away,

76

VVHy is my verſe ſo barren of new pride?
  So far from variation or quicke change?
Why with the time do I not glance aſide
To new found methods,and to compounds ſtrange?
Why write I ſtill all one,euer the ſame,
And keepe inuention in a noted weed,
That euery word doth almoſt fel my name,
Shewing their birth,and where they did proceed?
O know ſweet loue I alwaies write of you,
And you and loue are ſtill my argument:
So all my beſt is dreſſing old words new,
Spending againe what is already ſpent:
  For as the Sun is daily new and old,
  So is my loue ſtill telling what is told,

77

THy glaſſe will ſhew thee how thy beauties were,
  Thy dyall how thy pretious mynuits waſte,

The

The vacant leaues thy mindes imprint will beare,
And of this booke,this learning maiſt thou taſte.
The wrinckles which thy glaſſe will truly ſhow,
Of mouthed graues will giue thee memorie,
Thou by thy dyals ſhady ſtealth maiſt know,
Times theeuiſh progreſſe to eternitie.
Looke what thy memorie cannot containe,
Commit to theſe waſte blacks,and thou ſhalt finde
Thoſe children nurſt,deliuerd from thy braine,
To take a new acquaintance of thy minde.
 Theſe offices,ſo oft as thou wilt looke,
 Shall profit thee,and much inrich thy booke.

78

SO oft haue I inuok'd thee for my Muſe,
 And found ſuch faire aſſiſtance in my verſe,
As euery *Alien* pen hath got my vſe,
And vnder thee their poëſie diſperſe.
Thine eyes,that taught the dumbe on high to ſing,
And heauie ignorance aloft to flie,
Haue added fethers to the learneds wing,
And giuen grace a double Maieſtie.
Yet be moſt proud of that which I compile,
Whoſe influence is thine,and borne of thee,
In others workes thou dooſt but mend the ſtile,
And Arts with thy ſweete graces graced be.
 But thou art all my art,and dooſt aduance
 As high as learning,my rude ignorance.

79

WHilſt I alone did call vpon thy ayde,
 My verſe alone had all thy gentle grace,
But now my gracious numbers are decayde,
And my ſick Muſe doth giue an other place.
I grant (ſweet loue)thy louely argument
Deſerues the trauaile of a worthier pen,
Yet what of thee thy Poet doth inuent,
He robs thee of,and payes it thee againe,
     F

           He

He lends thee vertue, and he ſtole that word,
From thy behauiour, beautie doth he giue
And found it in thy cheeke: he can affoord
No praiſe to thee, but what in thee doth liue.
   Then thanke him not for that which he doth ſay,
   Since what he owes thee, thou thy ſelfe dooſt pay.

80

O How I faint when I of you do write,
  Knowing a better ſpirit doth vſe your name,
And in the praiſe thereof ſpends all his might,
To make me toung-tide ſpeaking of your fame,
But ſince your worth (wide as the Ocean is)
The humble as the proudeſt ſaile doth beare,
My ſawſie barke (inferior farre to his)
On your broad maine doth wilfully appeare.
Your ſhalloweſt helpe will hold me vp a floate,
Whilſt he vpon your ſoundleſſe deepe doth ride,
Or (being-wrackt) I am a worthleſſe bote,
He of tall building, and of goodly pride.
   Then If he thriue and I be caſt away,
   The worſt was this, my loue was my decay.

81

O R I ſhall liue your Epitaph to make,
  Or you ſuruiue when I in earth am rotten,
From hence your memory death cannot take,
Although in me each part will be forgotten.
Your name from hence immortall life ſhall haue,
Though I (once gone) to all the world muſt dye,
The earth can yeeld me but a common graue,
When you intombed in mens eyes ſhall lye,
Your monument ſhall be my gentle verſe,
Which eyes not yet created ſhall ore-read,
And toungs to be, your beeing ſhall rehearſe,
When all the breathers of this world are dead,
   You ſtill ſhall liue (ſuch vertue hath my Pen)
   Where breath moſt breaths, euen in the mouths of men.

I grant

82

I Grant thou wert not married to my Muse,
And therefore maiest without attaint ore-looke
The dedicated words which writers vse
Of their faire subiect,blessing euery booke.
Thou art as faire in knowledge as in hew,
Finding thy worth a limmit past my praise,
And therefore art inforc'd to seeke anew,
Some fresher stampe of the time bettering dayes.
And do so loue,yet when they haue deuisde,
What strained touches Rhethorick can lend,
Thou truly faire,wert truly simpathizde,
In true plaine words,by thy true telling friend.
  And their grosse painting might be better vs'd,
  Where cheekes need blood,in thee it is abus'd.

83

I Neuer saw that you did painting need,
And therefore to your faire no painting set,
I found (or thought I found) you did exceed,
The barren tender of a Poets debt :
And therefore haue I slept in your report,
That you your selfe being extant well might show,
How farre a moderne quill doth come to short,
Speaking of worth,what worth in you doth grow,
This silence for my sinne you did impute,
Which shall be most my glory being dombe,
For I impaire not beautie being mute,
When others would giue life,and bring a tombe.
  There liues more life in one of your faire eyes,
  Then both your Poets can in praise deuise.

84

WHo is it that sayes most,which can say more,
  Then this rich praise,that you alone,are you,
In whose confine immured is the store,
Which should example where your equall grew,
Leane penurie within that Pen doth dwell,

F 2   That

That to his subiect lends not some small glory,
But he that writes of you,if he can tell,
That you are you,so dignifies his story.
Let him but coppy what in you is writ,
Not making worse what nature made so cleere,
And such a counter-part shail fame his wit,
Making his stile admired euery where.
　　You to your beautious blessings adde a curse,
　　Being fond on praise,which makes your praises worse.

85

MY toung-tide Muse in manners holds her still,
　While comments of your praise richly compil'd,
Reserue their Character with goulden quill,
And precious phrase by all the Muses fil'd.
I thinke good thoughts,whilst other write good wordes,
And like vnlettered clarke still crie Amen,
To euery Himne that able spirit affords,
In polisht forme of well refined pen.
Hearing you prais'd,I say 'tis so, 'tis true,
And to the most of praise adde some-thing more,
But that is in my thought,whose loue to you
(Though words come hind-most)holds his ranke before,
　　Then others,for the breath of words respect,
　　Me for my dombe thoughts,speaking in effect.

86

WAs it the proud full saile of his great verse,
　Bound for the prize of (all to precious) you,
That did my ripe thoughts in my braine inhearce,
Making their tombe the wombe wherein they grew?
Was it his spirit,by spirits taught to write,
Aboue a mortall pitch,that struck me dead?
No,neither he,nor his compiers by night
Giuing him ayde,my verse astonished.
He nor that affable familiar ghost
Which nightly gulls him with intelligence,
As victors of my silence cannot boast,

　　　　　　　　　　　　　　　　　I was

I was not sick of any feare from thence,
But when your countinance fild vp his line,
Then lackt I matter, that infeebled mine.

87

FArewell thou art too deare for my poffeffing,
And like enough thou knowft thy eftimate,
The Cha ter of thy worth giues thee releafing:
My bonds in thee are all determinate.
For how do I hold thee but by thy granting,
And for that ritches where is my deferuing?
The caufe of this faire guift in me is wanting,
And fo my pattent back againe is fweruing.
Thy felfe thou gau'ft, thy owne worth then not knowing,
Or mee to whom thou gau'ft it, elfe miftaking,
So thy great guift vpon mifprifion growing,
Comes home againe, on better iudgement making.
  Thus haue I had thee as a dreame doth flatter,
  In fleepe a King, but waking no fuch matter.

88

VVHen thou fhalt be difpode to fet me light,
And place my merrit in the eie of skorne,
Vpon thy fide, againft my felfe ile fight,
And proue thee virtuous, though thou art forfworne:
With mine owne weakeneffe being beft acquainted,
Vpon thy part I can fet downe a ftory
Of faults conceald, wherein I am attainted :
That thou in loofing me, fhall win much glory:
And I by this wil be a gainer too,
For bending all my louing thoughts on thee,
The iniuries that to my felfe I doe,
Doing thee vantage, duble vantage me.
  Such is my loue, to thee I fo belong,
  That for thy right, my felfe will beare all wrong.

89

SAy that thou didft forfake mee for fome falt,
And I will comment vpon that offence,

The

Speake of my lamenesse, and I straight will halt:
Against thy reasons making no defence.
Thou canst not(loue)disgrace me halfe so ill,
To set a forme vpon desired change,
As ile my selfe disgrace,knowing thy wil,
I will acquaintance strangle and looke strange:
Be absent from thy walkes and in my tongue,
Thy sweet beloued name no more shall dwell,
Least I(too much proface)should do it wronge:
And haplie of our old acquaintance tell.
   For thee,against my selfe ile vow debate,
   For I must nere loue him whom thou dost hate.

90

THen hate me when thou wilt, if euer,now,
  Now while the world is bent my deeds to crosse,
Ioyne with the spight of fortune,make me bow,
And doe not drop in for an after losse:
Ah doe not,when my heart hath scapte this sorrow,
Come in the rereward of a conquerd woe,
Giue not a windy night a rainie morrow,
To linger out a purposd ouer-throw.
If thou wilt leaue me, do not leaue me last,
When other pettie griefes haue done their spight,
But in the onset come,so stall I taste
At first the very worst of fortunes might,
   And other straines of woe, which now seeme woe,
   Compar'd with losse of thee,will not seeme so.

91

SOme glory in their birth,some in their skill,
  Some in their wealth, some in their bodies force,
Some in their garments though new-fangled ill:
Some in their Hawkes and Hounds,some in their Horse,
And euery humor hath his adiunct pleasure,
Wherein it findes a ioy aboue the rest,
But these perticulers are not my measure,
All these I better in one generall best.

                          Thy

Thy loue is bitter then high birth to me,
Richer then wealth,prouder then garments cost,
Of more delight then Hawkes or Horses bee:
And hauing thee,of all mens pride I boast,
    Wretched in this alone,that thou maist take,
    All this away,and me most wretched make.

92

BVt doe thy worst to steale thy selfe away,
For tearme of life thou art assured mine,
And life no longer then thy loue will stay,
For it depends vpon that loue of thine.
Then need I not to feare the worst of wrongs,
When in the least of them my life hath end,
I see,a better state to me belongs
Then that,which on thy humor doth depend.
Thou canst not vex me with inconstant minde,
Since that my life on thy reuolt doth lie,
Oh what a happy title do I finde ,
Happy to haue thy loue, happy to die!
    But whats so blessed faire that feares no blot,
    Thou maist be false, and yet I know it not.

93

SO shall I liue,supposing thou art true,
Like a deceiued husband ,so loues face,
May still seeme loue to me,though alter'd new:
Thy lookes with me,thy heart in other place.
For their can liue no hatred in thine eye,
Therefore in that I cannot know thy change,
In manies lookes,the false hearts history
Is writ in moods and frounes and wrinckles strange.
But heauen in thy creation did decree,
That in thy face sweet loue should euer dwell,
What ere thy thoughts, or thy hearts workings be,
Thy lookes should nothing thence, but sweetnesse tell.
    How like *Eaues* apple doth thy beauty grow,
    If thy sweet vertue answere not thy show.

94

THey that haue powre to hurt,and will doe none,
That doe not do the thing,they moſt do ſhowe,
Who mouing others,are themſelues as ſtone,
Vnmooued,could,and to temptation ſlow:
They rightly do inherrit heauens graces,
And husband natures ritches from expence,
They are the Lords and owners of their faces,
Others,but ſtewards of their excellence:
The ſommers flowre is to the ſommer ſweet,
Though to it ſelfe,it onely liue and die,
But if that flowre with baſe infection meete,
The baſeſt weed out-braues his dignity:
　　For ſweeteſt things turne ſowreſt by their deedes,
　　Lillies that feſter,ſmell far worſe then weeds.

95

HOw ſweet and louely doſt thou make the ſhame,
Which like a canker in the fragrant Roſe,
Doth ſpot the beautie of thy budding name?
Oh in what ſweets doeſt thou thy ſinnes incloſe!
That tongue that tells the ſtory of thy daies,
(Making laſciuious comments on thy ſport)
Cannot diſpraiſe,but in a kinde of praiſe,
Naming thy name,bleſſes an ill report.
Oh what a manſion haue thoſe vices got,
Which for their habitation choſe out thee,
Where beauties vaile doth couer euery blot,
And all things turnes to faire,that eies can ſee!
　　Take heed(deare heart)of this large priuiledge,
　　The hardeſt kniſe ill vſ'd doth looſe his edge.

96

SOme ſay thy fault is youth,ſome wantoneſſe,
Some ſay thy grace is youth and gentle ſport,
Both grace and faults are lou'd of more and leſſe:
Thou makſt faults graces,that to thee reſort:
As on the finger of a throned Queene,

　　　　　　　　　　　　　　　　The

The bafeft Iewell wil be well efteem'd:
So are thofe errors that in thee are feene,
To truths tranflated, and for true things deem'd.
How many Lambs might the fterne Wolfe betray,
If like a Lambe he could his lookes tranflate,
How many gazers mighft thou lead away,
If thou wouldft vfe the ftrength of all thy ftate?
　But doe not fo, I loue thee in fuch fort,
　As thou being mine, mine is thy good report.

97

How like a Winter hath my abfence beene
From thee, the pleafure of the fleeting yeare?
　What freezings haue I felt, what darke daies feene?
What old Decembers barenefle euery where?
And yet this time remou'd was fommers time,
The teeming Autumne big with ritch increafe,
Bearing the wanton burthen of the prime,
Like widdowed wombes after their Lords deceafe:
Yet this aboundant iffue feem'd to me,
But hope of Orphans, and vn-fathered fruite,
For Sommer and his pleafures waite on thee,
And thou away, the very birds are mute.
　Or if they fing, tis with fo dull a cheere,
　That leaues looke pale, dreading the Winters neere.

98

From you haue I beene abfent in the fpring,
When proud pide Aprill (dreft in all his trim)
Hath put a fpirit of youth in euery thing:
That heauie *Saturne* laught and leapt with him.
Yet nor the laies of birds, nor the fweet fmell
Of different flowers in odor and in hew,
Could make me any fummers ftory tell:
Or from their proud lap pluck them where they grew:
Nor did I wonder at the Lillies white,
Nor praife the deepe vermillion in the Rofe,
They weare but fweet, but figures of delight:
　　　　G　　　　　　　　　Drawne

Drawne after you, you patterne of all those.
   Yet seem'd it Winter still, and you away,
   As with your shaddow I with these did play.

99

THe forward violet thus did I chide,
   Sweet theefe whence didst thou steale thy sweet that
If not from my loues breath, the purple pride,   (smels
Which on thy soft cheeke for complexion dwells?
In my loues veines thou hast too grosely died,
The Lillie I condemned for thy hand,
And buds of marierom had stolne thy haire,
The Roses fearefully on thornes did stand,
Our blushing shame, an other white dispaire:
A third nor red, nor white, had stolne of both,
And to his robbry had annext thy breath,
But for his theft in pride of all his growth
A vengfull canker eate him vp to death.
   More flowers I noted, yet I none could see,
   But sweet, or culler it had stolne from thee.

100

VVHere art thou Muse that thou forgetst so long,
   To speake of that which giues thee all thy might?
Spendst thou thy furie on some worthlesse songe,
Darkning thy powre to lend base subiects light.
Returne forgetfull Muse, and straight redeeme,
In gentle numbers time so idely spent,
Sing to the eare that doth thy laies esteeme,
And giues thy pen both skill and argument.
Rise resty Muse, my loues sweet face suruay,
If time haue any wrincle grauen there,
If any, be a *Satire* to decay,
And make times spoiles dispised euery where.
   Giue my loue fame faster then time wasts life,
   So thou preuenst his sieth, and crooked knife.

101

OH truant Muse what shalbe thy amends,

For thy neglect of truth in beauty di'd?
Both truth and beauty on my loue depends:
So doſt thou too, and therein dignifi'd:
Make anſwere Muſe, wilt thou not haply ſaie,
Truth needs no collour with his collour fixt,
Beautie no penſell, beauties truth to lay:
But beſt is beſt, if neuer intermixt.
Becauſe he needs no praiſe, wilt thou be dumb?
Excuſe not ſilence ſo, for't lies in thee,
To make him much out-liue a gilded tombe:
And to be praiſd of ages yet to be.
    Then do thy office Muſe, I teach thee how,
    To make him ſeeme long hence, as he ſhowes now.

102

MY loue is ſtrengthned though more weake in ſee-
I loue not leſſe, thogh leſſe the ſhow appeare, (ming
That loue is marchandiz'd, whoſe ritch eſteeming,
The owners tongue doth publiſh euery where.
Our loue was new, and then but in the ſpring,
When I was wont to greet it with my laies,
As *Philomell* in ſummers front doth ſinge,
And ſtops his pipe in growth of riper daies:
Not that the ſummer is leſſe pleaſant now
Then when her mournefull himns did huſh the night,
But that wild muſick burthens euery bow,
And ſweets growne common looſe their deare delight.
    Therefore like her, I ſome-time hold my tongue:
    Becauſe I would not dull you with my ſonge.

103

ALack what pouerty my Muſe brings forth,
That hauing ſuch a skope to ſhow her pride,
The argument all bare is of more worth
Then when it hath my added praiſe beſide.
Oh blame me not if I no more can write!
Looke in your glaſſe and there appeares a face,
That ouer-goes my blunt inuention quite,
Dulling my lines, and doing me diſgrace.

Were

Were it not sinfull then striuing to mend,
To marre the subiect that before was well,
For to no other passe my verses tend,
Then of your graces and your gifts to tell.
  And more,much more then in my verse can sit,
  Your owne glasse showes you,when you looke in it.

104

TO me faire friend you neuer can be old,
  For as you were when first your eye I eyde,
Such seemes your beautie still:Three Winters colde,
Haue from the forrests shooke three summers pride,
Three beautious springs to yellow *Autumne* turn'd,
In processe of the seasons haue I seene,
Three Aprill perfumes in three hot Iunes burn'd,
Since first I saw you fresh which yet are greene.
Ah yet doth beauty like a Dyall hand,
Steale from his figure,and no pace perceiu'd,
So your sweete hew,which me thinkes still doth stand
Hath motion,and mine eye may be deceaued.
  For feare of which,heare this thou age vnbred,
  Ere you were borne was beauties summer dead.

105

LEt not my loue be cal'd Idolatrie,
  Nor my beloued as an Idoll show,
Since all alike my songs and praises be
To one,of one,still such,and euer so.
Kinde is my loue to day,to morrow kinde,
Still constant in a wondrous excellence,
Therefore my verse to constancie confin'de,
One thing expressing,leaues out difference.
Faire,kinde,and true,is all my argument,
Faire,kinde and true,varrying to other words,
And in this change is my inuencion spent,
Three theams in one,which wondrous scope affords.
  Faire,kinde,and true,haue often liu'd alone.
  Which three till now,neuer kept seate in one.

                        When

106

WHen in the Chronicle of wasted time,
    I see discriptions of the fairest wights,
And beautie making beautifull old rime,
In praise of Ladies dead, and louely Knights,
Then in the blazon of sweet beauties best,
Of hand, of foote, of lip, of eye, of brow,
I see their antique Pen would haue exprest,
Euen such a beauty as you maister now.
So all their praises are but prophesies
Of this our time, all you prefiguring,
And for they look'd but with deuining eyes,
They had not still enough your worth to sing:
    For we which now behold these present dayes,
    Haue eyes to wonder, but lack toungs to praise.

107

NOt mine owne feares, nor the prophetick soule,
    Of the wide world, dreaming on things to come,
Can yet the lease of my true loue controule,
Supposde as forfeit to a confin'd doome.
The mortall Moone hath her eclipse indur'de,
And the sad Augurs mock their owne presage,
Incertenties now crowne them-selues assur'de,
And peace proclaimes Oliues of endlesse age,
Now with the drops of this most balmie time,
My loue lookes fresh, and death to me subscribes,
Since spight of him Ile liue in this poore rime,
While he insults ore dull and speachlesse tribes.
    And thou in this shalt finde thy monument,
    When tyrants crests and tombs of brasse are spent.

108

WHat's in the braine that Inck may character,
    Which hath not figur'd to thee my true spirit,
What's new to speake, what now to register,
That may expresse my loue, or thy deare merit?
Nothing sweet boy, but yet like prayers diuine,

G 3   I must

I muſt each day ſay ore the very ſame,
Counting no old thing old,thou mine,I thine,
Euen as when firſt I hallowed thy faire name.
So that eternall loue in loues freſh caſe,
Waighes not the duſt and iniuty of age,
Nor giues to neceſſary wrinckles place,
But makes antiquitie for aye his page,
 Finding the firſt conceit of loue there bred,
 Where time and outward forme would ſhew it dead,

109

O Neuer ſay that I was falſe of heart,
 Though abſence ſeem'd my flame to quallifie,
As eaſie might I from my ſelfe depart,
As from my ſoule which in thy breſt doth lye :
That is my home of loue, if I haue rang'd,
Like him that trauels I returne againe,
Iuſt to the time,not with the time exchang'd,
So that my ſelfe bring water for my ſtaine,
Neuer beleeue though in my nature raign'd,
All frailties that beſiege all kindes of blood,
That it could ſo prepoſterouſlie be ſtain'd,
To leaue for nothing all thy ſumme of good :
 For nothing this wide Vniuerſe I call,
 Saue thou my Roſe,in it thou art my all.

110

A Las 'tis true,I haue gone here and there,
 And made my ſelfe a motley to the view,
Gor'd mine own thoughts, ſold cheap what is moſt deare,
Made old offences of affections new.
Moſt true it is,that I haue lookt on truth
Aſconce and ſtrangely: But by all aboue,
Theſe blenches gaue my heart an other youth,
And worſe eſſaies prou'd thee my beſt of loue,
Now all is done,haue what ſhall haue no end,
Mine appetite I neuer more will grin'de
On newer proofe,to trie an older friend,
A God in loue,to whom I am confin'd.

          Then

Then giue me welcome,next my heauen the beſt,
Euen to thy pure and moſt moſt louing breſt.

111

O For my ſake doe you wiſh fortune chide,
　The guiltie goddeſſe of my harmfull deeds,
That did not better for my life prouide,
Then publick meanes which publick manners breeds.
Thence comes it that my name receiues a brand,
And almoſt thence my nature is ſubdu'd
To what it workes in,like the Dyers hand,
Pitty me then,and wiſh I were renu'de,
Whilſt like a willing pacient I will drinke,
Potions of Eyſell gainſt my ſtrong infection,
No bitterneſſe that I will bitter thinke,
Nor double pennance to correct correction.
　Pittie me then deare friend,and I aſſure yee,
　Euen that your pittie is enough to cure mee.

112

YOur loue and pittie doth th'impreſſion fill,
　Which vulgar ſcandall ſtampt vpon my brow,
For what care I who calles me well or ill,
So you ore-greene my bad,my good alow?
You are my All the world,and I muſt ſtriue,
To know my ſhames and praiſes from your tounge,
None elſe to me,nor I to none aliue,
That my ſteel'd ſence or changes right or wrong,
In ſo profound *Abiſme* I throw all care
Of others voyces,that my Adders ſence,
To cryttick and to flatterer ſtopped are:
Marke how with my neglect I doe diſpence.
　You are ſo ſtrongly in my purpoſe bred,
　That all the world beſides me thinkes y'are dead.

113

SInce I left you,mine eye is in my minde,
　And that which gouernes me to goe about,
Doth part his function,and is partly blind,

Seemes

Seemes seeing, but effectually is out:
For it no forme deliuers to the heart
Of bird, of flowre, or shape which it doth lack,
Of his quick obiects hath the minde no part,
Nor his owne vision houlds what it doth catch:
For if it see the rud'st or gentlest sight,
The most sweet-fauor or deformedst creature,
The mountaine, or the sea, the day, or night:
The Croe, or Doue, it shapes them to your feature.
  Incapable of more repleat, with you,
  My most true minde thus maketh mine vntrue.

114

OR whether doth my minde being crown'd with you
Drinke vp the monarks plague this flattery?
Or whether shall I say mine eie saith true,
And that your loue taught it this *Alcumie?*
To make of monsters, and things indigest,
Such cherubines as your sweet selfe resemble,
Creating euery bad a perfect best
As fast as obiects to his beames assemble:
Oh tis the first, tis flatry in my seeing,
And my great minde most kingly drinkes it vp,
Mine eie well knowes what with his gust is greeing,
And to his pallat doth prepare the cup.
  If it be poison'd, tis the lesser sinne,
  That mine eye loues it and doth first beginne.

115

THose lines that I before haue writ doe lie,
Euen those that said I could not loue you deerer,
Yet then my iudgement knew no reason why,
My most full flame should afterwards burne cleerer.
But reckening time, whose milliond accidents
Creepe in twixt vowes, and change decrees of Kings,
Tan sacred beautie, blunt the sharp'st intents,
Diuert strong mindes to th' course of altring things:
Alas why fearing of times tiranie,

                                        Might

Might I not then say now I loue you best,
When I was certaine ore in-certainty,
Crowning the present,doubting of the rest:
 Loue is a Babe, then might I not say so
 To giue full growth to that which still doth grow.

119

LEt me not to the marriage of true mindes
 Admit impediments,loue is not loue
Which alters when it alteration findes,
Or bends with the remouer to remoue.
O no,it is an euer fixed marke
That lookes on tempests and is neuer shaken;
It is the star to euery wandring barke,
Whose worths vnknowne,although his higth be taken.
Lou's not Times foole,though rosie lips and cheeks
Within his bending sickles compasse come,
Loue alters not with his breefe houres and weekes,
But beares it out euen to the edge of doome:
 If this be error and vpon me proued,
 I neuer writ,nor no man euer loued.

117

ACcuse me thus,that I haue scanted all,
 Wherein I should your great deserts repay,
Forgot vpon your dearest loue to call,
Whereto al bonds do tie me day by day,
That I haue frequent binne with vnknown mindes,
And giuen to time your owne deare purchas'd right,
That I haue hoysted saile to al the windes
Which should transport me farthest from your sight.
Booke both my wilfulnesse and errors downe,
And on iust proofe surmise,accumilate,
Bring me within the leuel of your frowne,
But shoote not at me in your wakened hate:
 Since my appeale saies I did striue to prooue
 The constancy and virtue of your loue

H

118

Like as to make our appetites more keene
With eager compounds we our pallat vrge,
As to preuent our malladies vnseene,
We sicken to shun sicknesse when we purge.
Euen so being full of your nere cloying sweetnesse,
To bitter sawces did I frame my feeding;
And sicke of wel-fare found a kind of meetnesse,
To be diseas'd ere that there was true needing.
Thus pollicie in loue t'anticipate
The ills that were, not grew to faults assured,
And brought to medicine a healthfull state
Which rancke of goodnesse would by ill be cured.
　But thence I learne and find the lesson true,
　Drugs poyson him that so fell sicke of you.

119

WHat potions haue I drunke of *Syren* teares
Distil'd from Lymbecks foule as hell within,
Applying feares to hopes, and hopes to feares,
Still loosing when I saw my selfe to win?
What wretched errors hath my heart committed,
Whilst it hath thought it selfe so blessed neuer?
How haue mine eies out of their Spheares bene fitted
In the distraction of this madding feuer?
O benefit of ill, now I find true
That better is, by euil still made better.
And ruin'd loue when it is built anew
Growes fairer then at first, more strong, far greater.
　So I returne rebukt to my content,
　And gaine by ills thrise more then I haue spent.

120

THat you were once vnkind be-friends mee now,
And for that sorrow, which I then didde feele,
Needes must I vnder my transgression bow,
Vnlesse my Nerues were brasse or hammered steele.
For if you were by my vnkindnesse shaken

As I by yours , y'haue paſt a hell of Time,
And I a tyrant haue no leaſure taken
To waigh how once I ſuffered in your crime.
O that our night of wo might haue remembred
My deepeſt ſence,how hard true ſorrow hits,
And ſoone to you,as you to me then tendred
The humble ſalue,which wounded boſomes fits!
    But that your treſpaſſe now becomes a fee,
    Mine ranſoms yours,and yours muſt ranſome mee.

121

TIS better to be vile then vile eſteemed,
  When not to be,receiues reproach of being,
And the iuſt pleaſure loſt,which is ſo deemed,
Not by our feeling,but by others ſeeing.
For why ſhould others falſe adulterat eyes
Giue ſalutation to my ſportiue blood?
Or on my frailties why are frailer ſpies;
Which in their wils count bad what I think good?
Noe,I am that I am,and they that leuell
At my abuſes,reckon vp their owne,
I may be ſtraight though they them-ſelues be beuel
By their rancke thoughtes,my deedes muſt not be ſhown,
    Vnleſſe this generall euill they maintaine,
    All men are bad and in their badneſſe raigne.

122.

THy guiſt,,thy tables,are within my braine
  Full charaċterd with laſting memory,
Which ſhall aboue that idle rancke remaine
Beyond all date,euen to eternity.
Or at the leaſt,ſo long as braine and heart
Haue facultie by nature to ſubſiſt,
Til each to raz'd obliuion yeeld his part,
Of thee,thy record neuer can be miſt:
That poore retention could not ſo much hold,
Nor need I tallies thy deare loue to skore,
Therefore to giue them from me was I bold,

To truſt thoſe tables that receaue thee more,
To keepe an adiunckt to remember thee,
Were to import forgetfulneſſe in mee.

123

NO! Time, thou ſhalt not boſt that I doe change,
Thy pyramyds buylt vp with newer might
To me are nothing nouell, nothing ſtrange,
They are but dreſſings of a former ſight:
Our dates are breefe, and therefor we admire,
What thou doſt foyſt vpon vs that is ould,
And rather make them borne to our deſire,
Then thinke that we before haue heard them tould:
Thy regiſters and thee I both defie,
Not wondring at the preſent, nor the paſt,
For thy records, and what we ſee doth lye,
Made more or les by thy continuall haſt:
  This I doe vow and this ſhall euer be,
  I will be true diſpight thy ſyeth and thee.

124

YF my deare loue were but the childe of ſtate,
It might for fortunes baſterd be vnfathered,
As ſubiect to times loue, or to times hate,
Weeds among weeds, or flowers with flowers gatherd.
No it was buylded far from accident,
It ſuffers not in ſmilinge pomp, nor falls
Vnder the blow of thralled diſcontent,
Whereto th'inuiting time our faſhion calls:
It feares not policy that _Heriticke_,
Which workes on leaſes of ſhort numbred howers,
But all alone ſtands hugely pollitick,
That it nor growes with heat, nor drownes with ſhowres.
  To this I witnes call the foles of time,
  Which die for goodnes, who haue liu'd for crime.

125

VVEr't ought to me I bore the canopy,
With my extern the outward honoring,

Or

Or layd great bases for eternity,
Which proues more short then wast or ruining?
Haue I not seene dwellers on forme and fauor
Lose all, and more by paying too much rent
For compound sweet; Forgoing simple sauor,
Pittifull thriuors in their gazing spent.
Noe, let me be obsequious in thy heart,
And take thou my oblacion, poore but free,
Which is not mixt with seconds, knows no art,
But mutuall render, onely me for thee.
    Hence, thou subbornd *Informer*, a trew soule
    When most impeacht, stands least in thy controule.

126

O Thou my louely Boy who in thy power,
    Doest hould times sickle glasse, his sickle, hower:
Who hast by wayning growne, and therein shou'st,
Thy louers withering, as thy sweet selfe grow'st.
If Nature (soueraine misteres ouer wrack)
As thou goest onwards still will plucke thee backe,
She keepes thee to this purpose, that her skill.
May time disgrace, and wretched mynuit kill.
Yet feare her O thou minnion of her pleasure,
She may detaine, but not still keepe her tresure!
Her *Audite* (though delayd) answer'd must be,
And her *Quietus* is to render thee.
          (   )
          (   )

127

I N the ould age blacke was not counted faire,
  Or if it weare it bore not beauties name:
But now is blacke beauties successiue heire,
And Beautie slanderd with a bastard shame,
For since each hand hath put on Natures power,
Fairing the foule with Arts faulse borrow'd face,
Sweet beauty hath no name no holy boure,
But is prophan'd, if not liues in disgrace.

Therefore

Therefore my Mifterffe eyes are Rauen blacke,
Her eyes fo futed, and they mourners feeme,
At fuch who not borne faire no beauty lack,
Slandring Creation with a falfe efteeme,
   Yet fo they mourne becomming of their woe,
   That euery toung faies beauty fhould looke fo.

128

How oft when thou my mufike mufike playft,
  Vpon that bleffed wood whofe motion founds
With thy fweet fingers when thou gently fwayft,
The wiry concord that mine eare confounds,
Do I enuie thofe Iackes that nimble leape,
To kiffe the tender inward of thy hand,
Whilft my poore lips which fhould that harueft reape,
At the woods bouldnes by thee blufhing ftand.
To be fo tikled they would change their ftate,
And fituation with thofe dancing chips,
Ore whome their fingers walke with gentle gate,
Making dead wood more bleft then liuing lips,
   Since faufie Iackes fo happy are in this,
   Giue them their fingers, me thy lips to kiffe.

129

TH'expence of Spirit in a wafte of fhame
  Is luft in action, and till action, luft
Is periurd, murdrous, blouddy full of blame,
Sauage, extreame, rude, cruell, not to truft,
Inioyd no fooner but difpifed ftraight,
Paft reafon hunted, and no fooner had
Paft reafon hated as a fwollowed bayt,
On purpofe layd to make the taker mad.
Made In purfut and in poffeffion fo,
Had, hauing, and in queft, to haue extreame,
A bliffe in proofe and proud and very wo,
Before a ioy propofd behind a dreame,
   All this the world well knowes yet none knowes welt,
   To fhun the heauen that leads men to this hell.

My

130

MY Miſtres eyes are nothing like the Sunne,
Currall is farre more red,then her lips red,
If ſnow be white,why then her breſts are dun:
If haires be wiers,black wiers grow on her head:
I haue ſeene Roſes damaskt,red and white,
But no ſuch Roſes ſee I in her cheekes,
And in ſome perfumes is there more delight,
Then in the breath that from my Miſtres reekes.
I loue to heare her ſpeake,yet well I know,
That Muſicke hath a farre more pleaſing ſound:
I graunt I neuer ſaw a goddeſſe goe,
My Miſtres when ſhee walkes treads on the ground.
    And yet by heauen I thinke my loue as rare,
    As any ſhe beli'd with falſe compare.

131

THou art as tiranous,ſo as thou art,
As thoſe whoſe beauties proudly make them cruell:
For well thou know'ſt to my deare doting hart
Thou art the faireſt and moſt precious Iewell.
Yet in good faith ſome ſay that thee behold,
Thy face hath not the power to make loue grone;
To ſay they erre,I dare not be ſo bold,
Although I ſweare it to my ſelfe alone.
And to be ſure that is not falſe I ſweare
A thouſand grones but thinking on thy face,
One on anothers necke do witneſſe beare
Thy blacke is faireſt in my iudgements place.
    In nothing art thou blacke ſaue in thy deeds,
    And thence this ſlaunder as I thinke proceeds.

132

THine eies I loue,and they as pittying me,
Knowing thy heart torment me with diſdaine,
Haue put on black,and louing mourners bee,
Looking with pretty ruth vpon my paine.

And

And truly not the morning Sun of Heauen
Better becomes the gray cheeks of th' East,
Nor that full Starre that vshers in the Eauen
Doth halfe that glory to the sober West
As those two morning eyes become thy face:
O let it then as well beseeme thy heart
To mourne for me since mourning doth thee grace,
And sute thy pitty like in euery part.
    Then will I sweare beauty her selfe is blacke,
    And all they foule that thy complexion lacke.

133

BEshrew that heart that makes my heart to groane
For that deepe wound it giues my friend and me;
I'st not ynough to torture me alone,
But slaue to slauery my sweet'st friend must be.
Me from my selfe thy cruell eye hath taken,
And my next selfe thou harder hast ingrossed,
Of him, my selfe, and thee I am forsaken,
A torment thrice three-fold thus to be crossed:
Prison my heart in thy steele bosomes warde,
But then my friends heart let my poore heart bale,
Who ere keepes me, let my heart be his garde,
Thou canst not then vse rigor in my Iaile.
    And yet thou wilt, for I being pent in thee,
    Perforce am thine and all that is in me.

134

SO now I haue confest that he is thine,
And I my selfe am morgag'd to thy will,
My selfe Ile forfeit, so that other mine,
Thou wilt restore to be my comfort still:
But thou wilt not, nor he will not be free,
For thou art couetous, and he is kinde,
He learnd but suretie-like to write for me,
Vnder that bond that him as fast doth binde.
The statute of thy beauty thou wilt take,
Thou vsurer that put'st forth all to vse,

And

And sue a friend, came debter for my sake,
So him I loose through my vnkinde abuse.
　Him haue I lost, thou hast both him and me,
　He paies the whole, and yet am I not free.

135

WHo euer hath her wish, thou hast thy *Will*,
　And *Will* too boote, and *Will* in ouer-plus,
More then enough am I that vexe thee still,
To thy sweet will making addition thus.
Wilt thou whose will is large and spatious,
Not once vouchsafe to hide my will in thine,
Shall will in others seeme right gracious,
And in my will no faire acceptance shine:
The sea all water, yet receiues raine still,
And in aboundance addeth to his store,
So thou beeing rich in *Will* adde to thy *Will*,
One will of mine to make thy large *Will* more.
　Let no vnkinde, no faire beseechers kill,
　Thinke all but one, and me in that one *Will*.

136

IF thy soule check thee that I come so neere,
Sweare to thy blind soule that I was thy *Will*,
And will thy soule knowes is admitted there,
Thus farre for loue, my loue-sute sweet fullfill.
Will, will fulfill the treasure of thy loue,
I fill it full with wils, and my will one,
In things of great receit with ease we prooue,
Among a number one is reckon'd none.
Then in the number let me passe vntold,
Though in thy stores account I one must be,
For nothing hold me, so it please thee hold,
That nothing me, a some-thing sweet to thee.
　Make but my name thy loue, and loue that still,
　And then thou louest me for my name is *Will*.

137

THou blinde foole loue, what doost thou to mine eyes,

I　　　　　That

That they behold and fee not what they fee :
They know what beautie is,fee where it lyes,
Yet what the beft is,take the worft to be.
If eyes corrupt by ouer-partiall lookes,
Be anchord in the baye where all men ride,
Why of eyes falfehood haft thou forged hookes,
Whereto the iudgement of my heart is tide ?
Why fhould my heart thinke that a feuerall plot,
Which my heart knowes the wide worlds common place?
Or mine eyes feeing this,fay this is not
To put faire truth vpon fo foule a face,
　　In things right true my heart and eyes haue erred,
　　And to this falfe plague are they now transferred.

138

WHen my loue fweares that fhe is made of truth,
　　I do beleeue her though I know fhe lyes,
That fhe might thinke me fome vntuterd youth,
Vnlearned in the worlds falfe fubtilties.
Thus vainely thinking that fhe thinkes me young,
Although fhe knowes my dayes are paft the beft,
Simply I credit her falfe fpeaking tongue,
On both fides thus is fimple truth fuppreft :
But wherefore fayes fhe not fhe is vniuft ?
And wherefore fay not I that I am old ?
O loues beft habit is in feeming truft,
And age in loue,loues not t'haue yeares told.
　　Therefore I lye with her,and fhe with me,
　　And in our faults by lyes we flattered be.

139

OCall not me to iuftifie the wrong,
　　That thy vnkindneffe layes vpon my heart,
Wound me not with thine eye but with thy toung,
Vfe power with power,and flay me not by Art,
Tell me thou lou'ft elfe-where;but in my fight,
Deare heart forbeare to glance thine eye afide,
What needft thou wound with cunning when thy might

Is more then my ore-prest defence can bide?
Let me excuse thee, ah my loue well knowes,
Her prettie lookes haue beene mine enemies,
And therefore from my face she turnes my foes,
That they else-where might dart their iniuries:
    Yet do not so, but since I am neere slaine,
    Kill me out-right with lookes, and rid my paine.

140

BE wise as thou art cruell, do not presse
My toung-tide patience with too much disdaine:
Least sorrow lend me words and words expresse,
The manner of my pittie wanting paine.
If I might teach thee witte better it weare,
Though not to loue, yet loue to tell me so,
As testie sick-men when their deaths be neere,
No newes but health from their Phisitions know.
For if I should dispaire I should grow madde,
And in my madnesse might speake ill of thee,
Now this ill wresting world is growne so bad,
Madde slanderers by madde eares beleeued be.
    That I may not be so, nor thou be lyde,   (wide.
    Beare thine eyes straight, though thy proud heart goe

141

IN faith I doe not loue thee with mine eyes,
For they in thee a thousand errors note,
But 'tis my heart that loues what they dispise,
Who in dispight of view is pleasd to dote.
Nor are mine eares with thy toungs tune delighted,
Nor tender feeling to base touches prone,
Nor taste, nor smell, desire to be inuited
To any sensuall feast with thee alone:
But my fiue wits, nor my fiue sences can
Diswade one foolish heart from seruing thee,
Who leaues vnswai'd the likenesse of a man,
Thy proud hearts slaue and vassall wretch to be:
    Onely my plague thus farre I count my gaine,
    That she that makes me sinne, awards me paine.

I 2   Loue

142

Loue is my sinne,and thy deare vertue hate,
Hate of my sinne,grounded on sinfull louing,
O but with mine,compare thou thine owne state,
And thou shalt finde it merrits not reproouing,
Or if it do,not from those lips of thine,
That haue prophan'd their scarlet ornaments,
And seald false bonds of loue as oft as mine,
Robd others beds reuenues of their rents.
Be it lawfull I loue thee as thou lou'st those,
Whome thine eyes wooe as mine importune thee,
Roote pittie in thy heart that when it growes,
Thy pitty may deserue to pittied bee.
      If thou doost seeke to haue what thou doost hide,
      By selfe example mai'st thou be denide.

143

Loe as a carefull huswife runnes to catch,
One of her fethered creatures broake away,
Sets downe her babe and makes all swift dispatch
In pursuit of the thing she would haue stay:
Whilst her neglected child holds her in chace,
Cries to catch her whose busie care is bent,
To follow that which flies before her face:
Not prizing her poore infants discontent;
So runst thou after that which flies from thee,
Whilst I thy babe chace thee a farre behind,
But if thou catch thy hope turne back to me:
And play the mothers part kisse me,be kind.
      So will I pray that thou maist haue thy *Will*,
      If thou turne back and my loude crying still.

144

Two loues I haue of comfort and dispaire,
Which like two spirits do sugiest me still,
The better angell is a man right faire:
The worser spirit a woman collour'd il.
To win me soone to hell my femall euill,

Tempteth

Tempteth my better angel from my sight,
And would corrupt my saint to be a diuel:
Wooing his purity with her sowle pride,
And whether that my angel be turn'd finde,
Suspect I may, yet not directly tell,
But being both from me both to each friend,
I gesse one angel in an others hel.
  Yet this shal I nere know but liue in doubt,
  Till my bad angel fire my good one out.

145

THose lips that Loues owne hand did make,
  Breath'd forth the sound that said I hate,
To me that languisht for her sake:
But when she saw my wofull state,
Straight in her heart did mercie come,
Chiding that tongue that euer sweet,
Was vsde in giuing gentle dome:
And tought it thus a new to greete:
I hate she alterd with an end,
That follow'd it as gentle day,
Doth follow night who like a fiend
From heauen to hell is flowne away.
  I hate, from hate away she threw,
  And sau'd my life saying not you.

146

POore soule the center of my sinfull earth,
  My sinfull earth these rebbell powres that thee array,
Why dost thou pine within and suffer dearth,
Painting thy outward walls so costlie gay?
Why so large cost hauing so short a lease,
Dost thou vpon thy fading manfion spend?
Shall wormes inheritors of this excesse,
Eate vp thy charge? is this thy bodies end?
Then soule liue thou vpon thy seruants losse,
And let that pine to aggrauat thy store;
Buy tearmes diuine in selling houres of drosse:

Within

Within be fed, without be rich no more,
  So shalt thou feed on death, that feeds on men,
  And death once dead, ther's no more dying then.

147

MY loue is as a feauer longing still,
  For that which longer nurseth the disease,
Feeding on that which doth preserue the ill,
Th'vncertaine sicklie appetite to please:
My reason the Phisition to my loue,
Angry that his prescriptions are not kept
Hath left me, and I desperate now approoue,
Desire is death, which Phisick did except.
Past cure I am, now Reason is past care,
And frantick madde with euer-more vnrest,
My thoughts and my discourse as mad mens are,
At randon from the truth vainely exprest.
  For I haue sworne thee faire, and thought thee bright,
  Who art as black as hell, as darke as night.

148

O Me! what eyes hath loue put in my head,
  Which haue no correspondence with true sight,
Or if they haue, where is my iudgment fled,
That censures falsely what they see aright?
If that be faire whereon my false eyes dote,
What meanes the world to say it is not so?
If it be not, then loue doth well denote,
Loues eye is not so true as all mens:no,
How can it? O how can loues eye be true,
That is so vext with watching and with teares?
No maruaile then though I mistake my view,
The sunne it selfe sees not, till heauen cleeres.
  O cunning loue, with teares thou keepst me blinde,
  Least eyes well seeing thy soule faults should finde.

149

CAnst thou O cruell, say I loue thee not,
  When I against my selfe with thee pertake:

Doe

Doe I not thinke on thee when I forgot
Am of my selfe, all tirant for thy sake?
Who hateth thee that I doe call my friend,
On whom froun'st thou that I doe faune vpon,
Nay if thou lowrst on me doe I not spend
Reuenge vpon my selfe with present mone?
What merrit do I in my selfe respect,
That is so proude thy seruice to dispise,
When all my best doth worship thy defect,
Commanded by the motion of thine eyes.
　But loue hate on for now I know thy minde,
　Those that can see thou lou'st, and I am blind.

150

OH from what powre hast thou this powrefull might,
　With insufficiency my heart to sway,
To make me giue the lie to my true sight,
And swere that brightnesse doth not grace the day?
Whence hast thou this becomming of things il,
That in the very refuse of thy deeds,
There is such strength and warranti'e of skill,
That in my minde thy worst all best exceeds?
Who taught thee how to make me loue thee more,
The more I heare and see iust cause of hate,
Oh though I loue what others doe abhor,
With others thou shouldst not abhor my state.
　If thy vnworthinesse raisd loue in me,
　More worthy I to be belou'd of thee.

151

LOue is too young to know what conscience is,
　Yet who knowes not conscience is borne of loue,
Then gentle cheater vrge not my amisse,
Least guilty of my faults thy sweet selfe proue.
For thou betraying me, I doe betray
My nobler part to my grose bodies treason,
My soule doth tell my body that he may,
Triumph in loue, flesh staies no farther reason,

But

But ryfing at thy name doth point out thee,
As his triumphant prize, proud of this pride,
He is contented thy poore drudge to be
To ftand in thy affaires, fall by thy fide.

No want of confcience hold it that I call,
Her loue, for whofe deare loue I rife and fall.

152

IN louing thee thou know'ft I am forfworne,
But thou art twice forfworne to me loue fwearing,
In act thy bed-vow broake and new faith torne,
In vowing new hate after new loue bearing:
But why of two othes breach doe I accufe thee,
When I breake twenty: I am periur'd moft,
For all my vowes are othes but to mifufe thee:
And all my honeft faith in thee is loft.
For I haue fworne deepe othes of thy deepe kindneffe:
Othes of thy loue, thy truth, thy conftancie,
And to inlighten thee gaue eyes to blindneffe,
Or made them fwere againft the thing they fee.

For I haue fworne thee faire: more periurde eye,
To fwere againft the truth fo foule a lie.

153

CVpid laid by his brand and fell a fleepe,
A maide of Dyans this aduantage found,
And his loue-kindling fire did quickly fteepe
In a could vallie-fountaine of that ground:
Which borrowd from this holie fire of loue,
A dateleffe liuely heat ftill to indure,
And grew a feething bath which yet men proue,
Againft ftrang mailadies a foueraigne cure:
But at my miftres eie loues brand new fired,
The boy for triall needes would touch my breft,
I fick withall the helpe of bath defired,
And thether hied a fad diftemperd gueft.

But found no cure, the bath for my helpe lies,
Where Cupid got new fire; my miftres eye.

THe little Loue-God lying once a sleepe,
Laid by his side his heart inflaming brand,
Whilst many Nymphes that vou'd chast life to keep,
Came tripping by,but in her maiden hand,
The fayrest votary tooke vp that fire,
Which many Legions of true hearts had warm'd,
And so the Generall of hot desire,
Was sleeping by a Virgin hand disarm'd.
This brand she quenched in a coole Well by,
Which from loues fire tooke heat perpetuall,
Growing a bath and healthfull remedy,
For men diseasd,but I my Mistrisse thrall,
   Came there for cure and this by that I proue,
   Loues fire heates water,water cooles not loue.

FINIS.

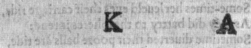

K   A

A Louers complaint.

BY

WILLIAM SHAKE-SPEARE.

FRom off a hill whose concaue wombe reworded,
A plaintfull story from a sistring vale
My spirrits t'attend this doble voyce accorded,
And downe I laid to list the sad tun'd tale,
Ere long espied a fickle maid full pale
Tearing of papers breaking rings a twaine,
Storming her world with sorrowes, wind and raine.

Vpon her head a plattid hiue of straw,
Which fortified her visage from the Sunne,
Whereon the thought might thinke sometime it saw
The carkas of a beauty spent and donne,
Time had not sithed all that youth begun,
Nor youth all quit, but spight of heauens fell rage,
Some beauty peept, through lettice of sear'd age.

Oft did she heaue her Napkin to her eyne,
Which on it had conceited characters:
Laundring the silken figures in the brine,
That seasoned woe had pelleted in teares,
And often reading what contents it beares:
As often shriking vndistinguisht wo,
In clamours of all size both high and low.

Some-times her leueld eyes their carriage ride,
As they did battry to the spheres intend:
Sometime diuerted their poore balls are tide,
To th'orbed earth; sometimes they do extend,
Their view right on, anon their gases lend,

To euery place at once and no where fixt,
The mind and fight diſtractedly commxit.

Her haire nor looſe nor ti'd in formall plat,
Proclaimd in her a careleſſe hand of pride;
For ſome vntuck'd deſcended her ſheu'd hat,
Hanging her pale and pined cheeke beſide,
Some in her threeden fillet ſtill did bide,
And trew to bondage would not breake from thence,
Though ſlackly braided in looſe negligence.

A thouſand fauours from a maund ſhe drew,
Of amber chriſtall and of bedded Iet,
Which one by one ſhe in a riuer threw,
Vpon whoſe weeping margent ſhe was ſet,
Like vſery applying wet to wet,
Or Monarches hands that lets not bounty fall,
Where want cries ſome;but where exceſſe begs all.

Of folded ſchedulls had ſhe many a one,
Which ſhe peruſ d,ſighd,tore and gaue the flud,
Crackt many a ring of Poſied gold and bone,
Bidding them find their Sepulchers in mud,
Found yet mo letters ſadly pend in blood,
With ſleided ſilke,feate and affectedly
Enſwath'd and ſeald to curious ſecrecy.

Theſe often bath'd ſhe in her fluxiue eies,
And often kiſt,and often gaue to teare,
Cried O falſe blood thou regiſter of lies,
What vnapproued witnes dooſt thou beare!
Inke would haue ſeem'd more blacke and damned heare!
This ſaid in top of rage the lines ſhe rents,
Big diſcontent,ſo breaking their contents.

A reuerend man that graz'd his cattell ny,

K 2   Some

Sometime a blusterer that the ruffle knew
Of Court of Cittie, and had let go by
The swiftest houres obserued as they flew,
Towards this afflicted fancy fastly drew:
And priuiledg'd by age desires to know
In breese the grounds and motiues of her wo,

So slides he downe vppon his greyned bat;
And comely distant sits he by her side,
When hee againe desires her, being satte,
Her greeuance with his hearing to deuide:
If that from him there may be ought applied
Which may her suffering extasie asswage
Tis promist in the charitie of age.

Father she saies, though in mee you behold
The iniury of many a blasting houre;
Let it not tell your Iudgement I am old,
Not age, but sorrow, ouer me hath power;
I might as yet haue bene a spreading flower
Fresh to my selfe, if I had selfe applyed
Loue to my selfe, and to no Loue beside.

But wo is mee, too early I atttended
A youthfull suit it was to gaine my grace;
O one by natures outwards so commended,
That maidens eyes stucke ouer all his face,
Loue lackt a dwelling and made him her place,
And when in his faire parts shee didde abide,
Shee was new lodg'd and newly Deified.

His browny locks did hang in crooked curles,
And euery light occasion of the wind
Vpon his lippes their silken parcels hurles,
Whats sweet to do, to do wil aptly find,
Each eye that saw him did inchaunt the minde:

For on his vifage was in little drawne,
What largeneffe thinkes in parradife was fawne.

Smal fhew of man was yet vpon his chinne,
His phenix downe began but to appeare
Like vnfhorne veluet, on that termleffe skin
Whofe bare out-brag'd the web it feem'd to were,
Yet fhewed his vifage by that coft more deare,
And nice affections wauering ftood in doubt
If beft were as it was, or beft without.

His qualities were beautious as his forme,
For maiden tongu'd he was and thereof free;
Yet if men mou'd him, was he fuch a ftorme
As oft twixt May and Aprill is to fee,
When windes breath fweet, vnruly though they bee.
His rudeneffe fo with his authoriz'd youth,
Did liuery falfeneffe in a pride of truth.

Wel could hee ride, and often men would fay
That horfe his mettell from his rider takes
Proud of fubiection, noble by the fwaie,   (makes
What rounds, what bounds, what courfe what ftop he
And controuerfie hence a queftion takes,
Whether the horfe by him became his deed,
Or he his mannad'g, by'th wel doing Steed.

But quickly on this fide the verdict went,
His reall habitude gaue life and grace
To appertainings and to ornament,
Accomplifht in him-felfe not in his cafe:
All ayds them-felues made fairer by their place,
Can for addicions, yet their purpof'd trimme
Peec'd not his grace but were al grac'd by him.

So on the tip of his fubduing tongue

All kinde of arguments and question deepe,
Al replication prompt,and reason strong
For his aduantage still did wake and sleep,
To make the weeper laugh,the laugher weepe:
He hadthe dialect and different skil,
Catching al passions in his craft of will.

That hee didde in the general bosome raigne
Of young, of old,and sexes both inchanted,
To dwel with him in thoughts,or to remaine
In personal duty,following where he haunted,
Consent's bewitcht, ere he desire haue granted,
And dialogu'd for him what he would say,
Askt their own wils and made their wils obey.

Many there were that did his picture gette
To serue their eies,and in it put their mind,
Like fooles that in th' imagination set
The goodly obiects which abroad they find
Oflands and mansions,theirs in thought assign'd,
And labouring in moe pleasures to bestow them,
Then the true gouty Land-lord which doth owe them.

So many haue that neuer toucht his hand
Sweetly suppos'd them mistresse of his hearte
My wofull selfe that did in freedome stand,
And was my owne fee simple(not in part)
What with his art in youth and youth in art
Threw my affections in his charmed power,
Reseru'd the stalke and gaue him al my flower.

Yet did I not as some my equals did
Demaund of him,nor being desired yeelded,
Finding my selfe in honour so forbidde,
With safest distance I mine honour sheelded,
Experience for me many bulwarkes builded

Of proofs new bleeding which remaind the foile
Of this false Iewell, and his amorous spoile.

But ah who euer shun'd by precedent,
The destin'd ill she must her selfe assay,
Or forc'd examples gainst her owne content
To put the by-past perrils in her way?
Counsaile may stop a while what will not stay:
For when we rage, aduise is often seene
By blunting vs to make our wits more keene.

Nor giues it satisfaction to our blood,
That wee must curbe it vppon others proose,
To be forbod the sweets that seemes so good,
For feare of harmes that preach in our behoose;
O appetite from iudgement stand aloofe!
The one a pallate hath that needs will taste,
Though reason weepe and cry it is thy last.

For further I could say this mans vntrue,
And knew the patternes of his foule beguiling,
Heard where his plants in others Orchards grew,
Saw how deceits were guilded in his smiling,
Knew vowes, were euer brokers to defiling,
Thought Characters and words meerly but art,
And bastards of his foule adulterat heart.

And long vpon these termes I held my Citty,
Till thus hee gan besiege me : Gentle maid
Haue of my suffering youth some feeling pitty
And be not of my holy vowes affraid,
Thats to ye sworne to none was euer said,
For feasts of loue I haue bene call'd vnto
Till now did nere inuite nor neuer vovv.

All my offences that abroad you see
K 4   Are

Are errors of the blood none of the mind:
Loue made them not, with acture they may be,
Where neither Party is nor trew nor kind,
They sought their shame that so their shame did find,
And so much lesse of shame in me remaines,
By how much of me their reproch containes,

Among the many that mine eyes haue seene,
Not one whose flame my hart so much as warmed,
Or my affection put to th, smallest teene.
Or any of my leisures euer Charmed,
Harme haue I done to them but nere was harmed,
Kept hearts in liueries, but mine owne was free,
And raignd commaunding in his monarchy.

Looke heare what tributes wounded fancies sent me,
Of palyd pearles and rubies red as blood:
Figuring that they their passions likewise lent me
Of greefe and blushes, aptly vnderstood
In bloodlesse white, and the encrimson'd mood,
Effects of terror and deare modesty,
Encampt in hearts but fighting outwardly.

And Lo behold these tallents of their heir,
With twisted mettle amorously empleacht
I haue receau'd from many a seueral faire,
Their kind acceptance, wepingly beseecht,
With th'annexions of faire gems inricht,
And deepe brain'd sonnets that did amplifie
Each stones deare Nature, worth and quallity.

The Diamond? why twas beautifull and hard,
Whereto his inuis'd properties did tend,
The deepe greene Emrald in whose fresh regard,
Weake sights their sickly radience do amend.
The heauen hewd Saphir and the Opall blend

With

With obiects manyfold; each feuerall ftone,
With wit well blazond fmil'd or made fome mone.

Lo all thefe trophies of affections hot,
Of penfiu'd and fubdew'd defires the tender,
Nature hath chargd me that I hoord them not,
But yeeld them vp where I my felfe muft render:
That is to you my origin and ender :
For thefe of force muft your oblations be,
Since I their Aulter, you enpatrone me.

Oh then aduance(of yours)that phrafeles hand,
Whofe white weighes downe the airy fcale of praife,
Take all thefe fimilies to your owne command,
Hollowed with fighes that burning lunges did raife:
What me your minifter for you obaies
Workes vnder you,and to your audit comes
Their diftract parcells,in combined fummes.

Lo this deuice was fent me from a Nun,
Or Sifter fanctified of holieft note,
Which late her noble fuit in court did fhun,
Whofe rareft hauings made the bloffoms dote,
For fhe was fought by fpirits of ritcheft cote,
But kept cold diftance,and did thence remoue,
To fpend her liuing in eternall loue.

But oh my fweet what labour ift to leaue,
The thing we haue not,maftring what not ftriues,
Playing the Place which did no forme receiue,
Playing patient fports in vnconftraind giues,
She that her fame fo to her felfe contriues,
The fcarres of bartaile fcapeth by the flight,
And makes her abfence valiant,not her might.

Oh pardon me in that my boaft is true,

L   The

The accident which brought me to her eie,
Vpon the moment did her force subdewe,
And now she would the caged cloister flie:
Religious loue put out religions eye:
Not to be tempted would she be enur'd,
And now to tempt all liberty procure.

How mightie then you are, Oh heare me tell,
The broken bosoms that to me belong,
Haue emptied all their fountaines in my well:
And mine I powre your Ocean all amonge:
I strong ore them and you ore me being strong,
Must for your victorie vs all congest,
As compound loue to phisick your cold brest.

My parts had powre to charme a sacred Sunne,
Who disciplin'd I dieted in grace,
Beleeu'd her eies, when they t' assaile begun,
All vowes and consecrations giuing place:
O most potentiall loue, vowe, bond, nor space
In thee hath neither sting, knot, nor confine
For thou art all and all things els are thine.

When thou impressest what are precepts worth
Of stale example? when thou wilt inflame,
How coldly those impediments stand forth
Of wealth of filliall feare, lawe, kindred fame,   ſhame
Loues armes are peace, gainst rule, gainst sence, gainst
And sweetens in the suffring pangues it beares,
The *Alloes* of all forces, shockes and feares.

Now all these hearts that doe on mine depend,
Feeling it breake, with bleeding groanes they pine,
And supplicant their sighes to you extend
To leaue the battrie that you make gainst mine,
Lending soft audience, to my sweet desigue,

And

And credent foule,to that ftrong bonded oth,
That fhall preferre and vndertake my troth.

This faid,his watrie eies he did difmount,
Whofe fightes till then were leaueld on my face,
Each cheeke a riuer running from a fount,
With brynifh currant downe-ward flowed a pace:
Oh how the channell to the ftreame gaue grace!
Who glaz'd with Chriftail gate the glowing Rofes,
That flame through water which their hew inclofes,

Oh father,what a hell of witch-craft lies,
In the fmall orb of one perticular teare?
But with the invndation of the eies:
What rocky heart to water will not weare?
What breft fo cold that is not warmed heare,
Or cleft effect,cold modefly hot wrath:
Both fire from hence,and chill extincture hath.

For loe his paffion but an art of craft,
Euen there refolu'd my reafon into teares,
There my white ftole of chaftity I daft,
Shooke off my fober gardes,and ciuill feares,
Appeare to him as he to me appeares:
All melting,though our drops this diffrence bore,
His poifon'd me, and mine did him reftore.

In him a plenitude of fubtle matter,
Applied to Cautills,all ftraing formes receiues,
Of burning blufhes,or of weeping water,
Or founding palenefe : and he takes and leaues,
In eithers aptnefe as it beft deceiues:
To blufh at fpeeches ranck ,to weepe at woes
Or to turne white and found at tragick fhowes.

That not a heart which in his leuell came,

L a   Could

Could scape the haile of his all hurting ayme,
Shewing faire Nature is both kinde and tame:
And vaild in them did winne whom he would maime,
Against the thing he sought,he would exclaime,
When he most burnt in hart-wisht luxurie,
He preacht pure maide,and praisd cold chastitie.

Thus meerely with the garment of a grace,
The naked and concealed feind he couerd,
That th'vnexperient gaue the tempter place,
Which like a Cherubin aboue them houerd,
Who young and simple would not be so louerd.
Aye me I fell,and yet do question make,
What I should doe againe for such a sake.

O that infected moysture of his eye,
O that false fire which in his cheeke so glowd:
O that forc'd thunder from his heart did flye,
O that sad breath his spungie lungs bestowed,
O all that borrowed motion seeming owed,
Would yet againe betray the fore-betrayed,
And new peruert a reconciled Maide.

FINIS.

500 COPIES PRINTED
SET IN VAN DIJCK TYPES
PRINTED ON MOHAWK PAPER
DESIGNED BY JERRY KELLY